22/3
BE

P

Bo

The Daily Telegraph
DICTIONARY OF TOMMIES'
SONGS AND SLANG, 1914–18

This edition is dedicated
to the memory of
JOHN BROPHY (1899–1965)
and ERIC PARTRIDGE (1894–1979)
soldiers of the Great War
and creators of this seminal work

The Daily Telegraph

DICTIONARY OF TOMMIES' SONGS AND SLANG, 1914–18

JOHN BROPHY & ERIC PARTRIDGE

Introduction by MALCOLM BROWN

FRONTLINE BOOKS, LONDON

The Daily Telegraph Dictionary of Tommies' Songs and Slang, 1914–18

This edition published in 2008 by Frontline Books,
an imprint of Pen and Sword Books Ltd,
47 Church Street, Barnsley, S. Yorkshire, S70 2AS

www.frontline-books.com

New Introduction © Pen & Sword Books Limited, 2008

This edition © Pen & Sword Books Limited, 2008

ISBN: 978-1-84115-710-5

For more information on our books, please visit
www.frontline-books.com, email info@frontline-books.com
or write to us at the above address.

Prelims typeset by MATS www.typesetter.biz
Printed and bound in Great Britain by Biddles Ltd, King's Lynn

Contents

Illustrations

AFTER NINETY YEARS

MALCOLM BROWN

This book is a jewel. It's a tribute to the indestructibility of the human spirit under the most demanding and challenging conditions. It's also possibly the greatest work by that most distinguished if elusive of writers, Anonymous, to be published in modern times.

The Great War of 1914–18 is now seen as a supreme example of a literary war. Never was the poetry more searing, never was the prose more trenchant. The names of its most famous writers resound in the mind like members of a great brotherhood: Charles Hamilton Sorley, Edmund Blunden, Siegfried Sassoon, Robert Graves, Wilfred Owen, Edward Thomas. These all fought as officers, but there is also place in the pantheon for certain exceptional 'other ranks', such as Isaac Rosenberg or Ivor Gurney. Due to the acknowledged excellence of their joint testimony, there's almost a tendency to state: that's it, close the circle, lock the gates. War has been found out and defined for good; no others writers need apply. Even the best of the Second World War poets, or poets of later wars, such as they were, or are, can stay out in the cold.

However, there is another voice demanding to be heard and it is to be found in the following pages. It's the voice of the underclass, of those thought of as occupying the lowest rungs of a nation in conflict, and therefore, almost by definition, without a name. These are the true forgotten voices of the First World War; forgotten, and, as individuals, beyond recall.

This book was first published in 1930, just as the great names listed above, with their revisionist doctrine of disenchantment and disillusion, were beginning to dominate the Great War agenda. When it was republished in 1965, that doctrine – though not without protest from numerous eloquent opponents – was well established as expressing the accepted view. In that edition one of the original co-editors, John Brophy, contributed a special Introduction which seems to me to be one of the most incisive and memorable essays I have ever read about the 1914–1918 war. In no way did he denigrate, or even discuss, the war's by then standard interpretation. He had an alternative agenda. He wanted to raise the profile of the unsung, the uncelebrated, the hitherto ignored, who had made their own contribution to the literature of that conflict which he felt deserved appropriate, even perhaps equal, attention. He wrote the following about the provenance of the songs given their place in the sun in the book:

> They come from the ranks, especially from the private soldiers without ambition to bear office or special responsibility. The very roughness of the metre, the assonances, the faulty rhyming and the occasional omission of rhyme indicate their illiterate or semi-literate origin. They are the songs of homeless men, evoked by exceptional and distressing circumstances; the songs of an itinerant community, continually altering within itself under the incidence of death and mutilation.

As for their authorship, he stated:

> Like mediaeval songs, these songs are anonymous, and even the method of their composition is a mystery . . . The only author to whom they can be attributed is 'Warrior, or Warriors Unknown'.

I like that. We're so used to the concept of the 'Unknown Warrior' as a symbol of grief and mourning that there's something refreshing and positive about the thought that he can be seen here in a different context, as the creator of the songs and snatches that took the edge off the horrors of that war and even found rich humour in it.

Because *that* is the point of this book. It is not one long paean of misery and complaint. Oh yes, there's anger, and cynicism, and a world-weary longing for the whole damned thing to be over, and couldn't we all go back to dear old Blighty? But there's also a strong sense that by slagging off the war, and finding ways of laughing, even jeering, at it, the men deputed to fight it could find a courage that gave them the determination to win through. Joke at the unjokeable and you're more likely to survive than if you allow yourself to be overwhelmed by the circumstances in which you find yourselves. As Brophy put it in his Introduction in a telling and powerful passage:

> When the victims can mock Juggernaut even as they writhe under the wheels, then by so much do they subtract from his victory. That a man should be familiar with *Hush! Here comes a Whizz-Bang* or the second stanza of *If the Sergeant Steals Your Rum* did not, during a bombardment, alter or diminish the incidence of shells that burst around him, but knowledge of such songs may well have reduced the emotional distress caused by fear, and aided him, after the experience, to pick his uncertain way back to sanity again. Similarly, when the romantic conception of war proved false, out of date, useless, the man in the line was helped in his daily endurances if he could ridicule all heroics and sing, with apparent shamelessness *I Don't Want to be a Soldier* or *Far Far from Ypres I Want to Be.* These songs satirized more than war: they poked fun at the soldier's own desire for peace and rest and so prevented it from overwhelming his will to go on doing his duty. They were not symptoms of defeatism, but strong bulwarks against it.

Brophy's essay is, of course, published in full in this edition. Writing this new Introduction over forty years later, I find his observations of such vividness and insight that I cannot resist quoting from him here, while also recommending the reader to go through his essay paragraph by paragraph and line by line. It deserves the most careful attention. In addition to its virtues so far discussed, it includes an incisive statement about the role and status of the ordinary soldier in the 1914–18 war. This was how he defined the lot of the vast majority of the men who had rushed to enlist in response to the nation's call to arms in the war's first months – and the same would apply to countless others who volunteered or were conscripted later:

They had engaged to serve, twenty-four hours a day, seven days a week, fifty-two weeks a year, for an undetermined number of years, as private soldiers in a complex organisation incidentally designed to enforce the will of each and every superior on those in the lowest ranks of all, to make them jerk into action at the word of command, stand still at the word of command, go anywhere and do anything at the word of command. In order to carry out what they had conceived, for the most part romantically and generously, as a patriotic duty, the young civilians were compelled to a preliminary process not unlike what would now be called conditioning. It involved an almost total surrender of personal liberty and an immediate, unconsidered obedience to orders . . .

As soon as a private soldier realised the power of the organisation to which, body and soul, he now belonged, he realised also that, while he might learn certain ways of outwitting it, outwardly he had no choice but to submit. Any form of direct defiance was worst than useless.

The songs printed in these pages *do* represent a form of defiance, though obviously an indirect one. But for the necessarily earthy terms of expression to be found in them, they might almost be seen as – on of course a far more modest scale – the equivalent of those more famous products of another society where there was a distinctive kept-down underclass: the Negro Spirituals.

But what of the editors, John Brophy and Eric Partridge? What was their competence in this matter? They were both well able to deal with this astonishing literary phenomenon because they themselves had served in the war as private soldiers. They were not doing top-down research when they pulled this anthology together. They came at it from the bottom up. They'd sung the songs themselves.

And what songs they were. John Brophy's earlier references to four of them (see previous page) point up a quartet of special quality and significance, but for my own part I find a particular edge in such songs as the one to be sung to the tune of the well-known evangelical hymn 'Take it to the Lord in Prayer' (see page 57), which begins:

When this blasted war is over,
Oh, how happy I shall be!,
When I get my civvy clothes on,
No more soldiering for me.

Or the song which to my mind comments brilliantly on the
constant need for more and more troops to be despatched to the
fighting front, *Send Out the Army and the Navy* (page 58), ending
with the lines:

Send out my mother,
Send out my sister and my brother,
But for Gawd's sake don't send me!

Side by side with that there's the song *The Bells of Hell* (page
48) which makes it crystal clear that the thought of dying
splendidly to save one's comrades was not high on the ordinary
soldier's list of priorities, stating unequivocally

The bells of hell go ting-a-ling-a-ling
For you but not for me.

And while turning the book's later pages don't miss either the
fact that you will also find here the song whose title, slightly
adapted, engaged, indeed angered, a whole generation through
that most caustic of shows and films *Oh What a Lovely War!*

Sex of course was also bound to rear its head, ugly or
otherwise, in this context. Here you'll find the song suggesting
that given the choice the Tommies would much prefer to stay
at home rather than fight, and spend the rest of their lives in
unbridled lascivious activity. Or, to quote the exact text as
printed on page 67:

I'd rather stay in England,
In merry, merry England,
And ——— my bloody life away.'

Clearly the omitted word has to be 'fornicate'. The editors were
prepared to concede the adjective 'bloody', but even this blander
'f' word, they felt, went too far; sexual excess still needed a

certain amount of discretion. As for the standard, now much used 'f' word, search as you might you won't discover any use of it here. In their preface to the 1930 version the editors stated that 'propriety has suppressed one or two of the songs and amended a few others'. Clearly they felt no need to include every last syllable and yet they still managed to produce a work with a vivid, indeed a gripping sense of reality, which in its way can be hailed almost as a kind of Golden Treasury of the songs of war, and all within the scope of one small slim volume.

As with the songs, so with the slang. The editors knew it because they'd used it. In France it had been, as it were, their *lingua franca*. This book shows that a whole new vocabulary sprang up with the Western Front war, almost a new language. And here too the war could be poked fun at, even the briefest of definitions showing a capacity to raise two fingers to the authorities:

> LEG: Show a leg = begin to get up, waken. Bawled by the responsible N.C.O.'s in huts, tents or billets at reveille.

Or what about their marvellous explanation of a certain popular concept of the time?

> LATRINE RUMOUR: Wild and insubstantial stories and prophecies . . . Some battalions were always about to be removed to India, Egypt or even Samoa; others were to be employed sweeping the paths in the grounds of G.H.Q. chateaux. Such rumours became associated with latrines because these shanties were practically the only places in which a private soldier could be comparatively secure from the eye and voice of authority. Consequently men sat there for long periods, reading newspapers, gossiping and exercising their imagination and credulity . . .

For me, however, my favourite entry is the one referring to a very special First World War institution, the name of which can still be seen spelled out on the walls of certain ancient establishments, especially, to my observation, in the region of the Franco-Belgian border:

ESTAMINET: There is no equivalent in Great Britain. On the Western Front an *estaminet* was not a pub. Neither was it a café or a restaurant. It had some of the qualities of all three. It was never large and was found only in villages and very minor towns. It had low ceilings, an open iron stove; it was warm and fuggy; it had wooden benches and table. It sold wine, cognac and thin beer, as well as coffee, soup, eggs and chips and omelettes. The proprietress (a proprietor was unthinkable) had a daughter or two, or nieces, or younger sisters who served at table and made no objection to tobacco smoke and ribald choruses in English and pidgin French. No doubt some estaminets overcharged but in general they provided for the soldier off duty behind the line many and many a happy hour. The name had a magical quality in 1914–18 – and still has for those who survive.

I quoted this passage in my 1996 volume *The Imperial War Museum Book of the Somme* to point the difference between the means of relief from the rigours of fighting on that most challenging of battle fronts available to officers and those available to the men. For the former there was the prospect of a relaxing aside in the cathedral city of Amiens, depicted, in the diary of one artillery officer, as 'full of colour and movement, with crowds thronging the pavements and the shops, and military and civilian cars jostling each other in the crowded streets.' In his *Memoirs of an Infantry Officer*, Siegfried Sassoon described an occasion when he and a friend, briefly in Amiens, 'lunched like dukes in a green-shuttered private room in the well-known Godbert Restaurant [on] langoustes, roast duck, and two bottles of their best "bubbly". Heaven knows,' he added, 'what else the meal contained.'

By contrast the men had their estaminets, offering distinctly less exotic fare, but with the supreme virtue that they were by definition officer-free zones. No need to jerk to attention, to stand and salute, to assume the routine attitudes of military servility. These cheerful, noisy, smoke-filled rooms were as open to off-message comments as the afore-mentioned latrines, with the extra advantage that the men would be off duty when they visited them, would be out of the range of shot and shell, and, with luck, might even detect a tingling hint of femininity in the air. Small wonder that such places were stored lovingly in the memory of the countless ordinary Tommies. Indeed, the estaminets offer proof that men could look back on the war and not find it a cause for anger. There were good things about that conflict that deserved to be celebrated, and this book is, among many other things, a notable memorial to them.

§

But who were they, ex-Private Brophy and ex-Private Partridge, these soldier/authors to whom we owe so great a debt?

Eric Partridge, or, to give him his full name, Eric Honeywood Partridge, was the older man and came to the war by the longer journey. He was born in 1894 in New Zealand, moved in 1907 with his family to Brisbane, Australia, where he was educated at Toowoomba Grammar School and subsequently at the University of Queensland, where he studied first Classics, and then French and English. Afterwards he worked as a school teacher for three years before his life was changed totally by the onset of war, though he was not among the first to volunteer, finally enlisting in April 1915. He joined the Australian infantry, serving first in Egypt, then at Gallipoli, and finally on the Western Front. In a contribution to a book published in 1929 entitled *Three Personal Records of the War*, of which the other authors were R.H. Mottram and John Easton, he detailed, writing in the third person, the adventures of one Frank Honywood (sic), who must be presumed to be his own alter ego. By May 1916, after the withdrawal from Gallipoli, Honywood is fighting in the Armentières sector and from July inwards he is engaged in the Somme battle. Wounded by shrapnel, he is sent to England to recover, returning to France in March 1917, to find himself, in the year of the notorious Passchendaele campaign, serving in the vicinity of Ypres and the Menin Road, but tonsillitis and trench fever combine to end his active involvement in the field. He returns to Australia and he is back in Brisbane when the war comes to an end.

John Brophy was born in December 1899 in Liverpool. This meant that he was only fourteen when war broke out, but nevertheless, although well under the legal age, he contrived to enlist on 6 September in the King's Liverpool Regiment, running away from school to do so. He served on the Western Front as a private throughout the war, managing to come through without being wounded, though clearly his experience left its mark. In the words of the *Oxford Dictionary of National Biography*: 'It was while on infantry service in France and Belgium that he accumulated the information that was to be the basis of much of his writing.'

Both men subsequently enjoyed remarkably rich literary careers Partridge, having taken his BA degree in Australia in 1921, became a Queensland Travelling Fellow and then went to Oxford, where he studied for two higher degrees before teaching at a Grammar School in Lancashire and later at the Universities of Manchester and London. Never a comfortable public speaker he abandoned teaching in 1927 and pronounced himself 'a man of letters'. He founded his own publishing house, the Scholartis Press (the name springing from a conjunction of the words 'scholarly' and 'artistic'), even contributing three novels to the imprint, written under the pseudonym of Corrie Denison. The press foundered in 1931 during the depression, leaving him bankrupt, but not before it had given to the world the original of the present work, published, as already stated, in 1930. Thereafter he produced a spate of books for other publishing houses, most of them in the field of etymology and lexicology, making himself famous over fifty years as the almost daily occupier of desk K1 at the British Museum Library: as it were, the Karl Marx of his day. During the Second World War he interrupted his literary labours to serve with the Army Education Corps and subsequently with the correspondence department of the Royal Air Force. Thereafter he returned to his second home in the British Museum and to his favourite obsessions. His addiction to his chosen subject was such that he once described himself as 'cheerfully and incorrigibly serving a life sentence.' He continued publishing until his eighties, his last work, *A Dictionary of Catch Phrases* appearing in 1977, two years before his death.

John Brophy returned to Liverpool after the war, taking a degree at Liverpool University, and subsequently spent a year at Durham University. Marrying, in 1924, the daughter of a clergyman from Chicago, he took a teaching job in Egypt, but the couple returned to England after two years on account of a problem with his wife's health. He then embarked on a brief career in advertising, first on behalf of a large store in Liverpool and then taking a post in London as head copywriter for a leading London firm. Thanks to a growing interest in literature he became the chief reviewer of fiction for the *Daily Telegraph*, and he wrote also for *Time and Tide* and the BBC.

The success of his first novel, published in 1928, established him as a writer and also as a notable commentator on the recent conflict. Entitled *The Bitter End*, the book featured a semi-autobiographical hero, Donald Foster, who gave voice to the sense of loss and disappointment in England a decade after the end of the war which had begun with so much hope and had left so huge a shadow. (Indeed, you will find in it passages which carry the distinctive hallmarks of the incisive analytical style of writing as revealed in his *After Fifty Years* essay printed here.) In 1929, as well as publishing two further novels, he again mined the military seam by producing a prose-anthology entitled *The Soldiers' War* and then in 1930, explored it even further by his collaboration with Eric Partridge in the editing of the present work.

It is notable that in their Preface to this first edition the editors expressed their special thanks to a number of friends who had given helpful comments on, and suggestions for, the glossary, among whom the most distinguished was a Mr T.E. Shaw, the then alias of the famous war-hero known world-wide as Lawrence of Arabia, at that time serving as a lowly service-man in the ranks of the Royal Air Force. This was the product of a friendship with John Brophy, which had begun through Brophy's admiration for Lawrence's *Seven Pillars of Wisdom* but had developed through his fellow-feeling with the aircraftman whose ambition was to be an artist in letters and who was never sure he had the right equipment. Brophy was especially proud when, as he put it, 'our friendship ripened to the point when we could address each other by our initials and abuse each others' opinions without restraint.' This is a quotation from Brophy's contribution to that remarkable volume, containing the tributes of a vast cast of comrades and admirers, published in 1937, following the war hero's premature death, under the title of *T.E. Lawrence by His Friends*.

Happily, his essay includes a memorable reference to the present work. Wrote Brophy: 'When I was editing, with Eric Partridge, *Songs and Slang of the British Soldier, 1914–1918*, I sent galley proofs to T.E. for his comments. They came back with the margins filled with emendations in the familiar "Indian ink", erudite, witty and often ribald.' I think that says much about both men, educated, intelligent, and with the highest of literary standards, yet aware that the language of the common man had its own vocabulary and its own vulgar, yet honourable, modes of expression.

Brophy continued to publish almost a volume per year for the rest of his life. It was his source of income, it was his *raison d'être*. He made his own modest but notable contribution to the Second World War by joining the Home Guard, using his writing skills to produce handbooks and manuals and even writing 'a character study' of the organisation called *Britain's Home Guard*, which was published in 1945. Strangely enough, his work on the 1965 edition of the present work proved to be his last. He died at the Royal Waterloo Hospital, Lambeth, London, of heart failure, on 12 November of that year, shortly after the publication of his minor masterpiece of First World War reminiscence as reprinted in this book. He was survived by his wife and daughter, Brigid Brophy, herself a writer of considerable distinction.

Ninety years after the end of the war in which he and his distinguished collaborator fought, and which they did so much to commemorate through their knowledge, wisdom, wit and style, we honour their achievements and salute their memory.

Malcolm Brown, 2008

AFTER FIFTY YEARS

JOHN BROPHY

1

To those who have survived so long, things which happened half a century ago can be vivid in memory and yet dreamlike, unreal. The paradox may be a result of the vast accumulation of later experiences, for in the twentieth century the pace of history has, notoriously, quickened. It is not only the amount and the detail of later memories which tend to make the five years 1914–18 a little hard for those who, as the French say, assisted at the event to believe, in retrospect: the fact is, we who have survived are not, in many ways, the same people that we were. In August 1914 we were young, perhaps very young, and now we are so old that every cell in our bodies has been renewed over and over again and, with many of us, both the content and the processes of our minds have been modified drastically. The youngsters of 1914–18 sometimes look to us more like ancestral figures than earlier versions of our present selves.

While it was in bewildered progress, the 1914–18 war was generally called 'the war' and large numbers who took part in it earnestly believed that it was 'the war to end wars'. Only when, after two decades of untranquil peace, Hitler made political-military seizures of territory from Austria, Czechoslovakia and Poland, did the 1914–18 conflict slide into historical perspective as World War One. Now there is a generation of men and women, well on in their thirties, to whom even Hitler's war, World War Two, is something which happened before they grew up, something belonging to the historical past. All this, plus international communism, space travel and stockpiles of cataclysmic bombs, has been crammed into the past fifty years. Some of the younger historians consider a half-century a convenient measurement for marking off the way in which the recent becomes the historical, and are now making re-assessments of various aspects of the 1914–18 war. They are right to do so, for while they can consult an immense stock of 'documents', much of it contemporary with the events, much put down, as reminiscences, fiction and commentary, during the 1920s and 1930s, they have the further advantage, which historians almost always lack, that there are living survivors of the period who can check, and if necessary correct, the factual records from which history proceeds or ought to proceed.

This book, of which the original version was published in 1930, has a dual nature: it is a document of social and military history and yet has the informal, personal and highly detailed quality of oral reminiscence. It was also closely examined, criticised and amended, through two subsequent and enlarged editions, by readers whose wartime memories were then comparatively fresh and unconfused. It began as a casual suggestion made when I offered Eric Partridge (at that time a small but enterprising, almost one-man publishing firm in Museum Street) a collection of essays, which he duly published the same year as *Fanfare*. One of these essays was called 'Ribaldry in Soldiers' Songs': it quoted, in snippets, eleven of the songs here set out. I cannot be sure, for I have never been one to keep records of such things, but I believe the essay had been turned down by several periodicals – some professing to be shocked – and the collection as a whole politely declined by another book publisher. I had already, the previous year, added an eleven-page glossary, which included a number of slang terms, to an anthology, *The Soldier's War*, which I edited for Dent's. It may therefore seem inevitable that the idea of a book recording what soldiers sang and what words and phrases they used among themselves should spring up in conversation between Eric Partridge and myself, but it was by no means inevitable that the book should get into print, be published and in time become quite famous. That was due to the enterprise and publishing courage of Eric Partridge, who, I am pretty sure, had no idea, at the start, that the venture was to entice him into a distinguished career as lexicographer.

2

That was in 1929 and 1930, the years of The Recession in the United States which a little later hit this country as The Slump.

Hitler was almost ready to achieve absolute power in a Germany we still thought of as defeated and down and out. If it is difficult to remember the atmosphere, the feel of things, in that brief period when the post-War 1920s were yielding place to the indubitably pre-War 1930s, it seems downright impossible to recall and convey the air, the feel, the mental climate of early 1914. From the here and now of 1964 it looks almost like another country and another age. Or so it seems to one who was then a schoolboy, still two years short of 'Matric' and highly excited by glimpses of what was apparently about to happen in the adult world. He was provincial in a sense that hardly applies to anyone nowadays when news is almost instantaneous with the event and, on the domestic television screen, the whole pageant of contemporary celebrity, from pop singers and teenage courtesans to the heads of all the great states, is paraded in loquacious close-up. Fifty years ago not one person, adult or child, in ten thousand had any direct evidence from his own senses concerning the people who ran the country. The 'average man' was aware of statesmen, land-owning dukes, financiers and manufacturers, bishops and bankers through formal photographs and caricatures reproduced in the press, possibly as brief flickers jerking across the primitive cinema screen, or on the stage as conventionalised types in farce or musical comedy. What would now be called the image of the upper class might or might not be romanticised: it was always distorted, incomplete and unreal. Although the feudal system had long broken up in its lower strata, at the top it remained intact in the sense that wealth and power belonged to a very few. The fact that some of those few considered themselves to be 'democratic' in outlook because they knew the names of their cottagers and were affable to the shopkeepers they patronised did little or nothing to bridge the gulf of unacknowledged ignorance separating them from the mass of the people.

What the schoolboy in early 1914 thought was about to happen, as a major addition to modern history, was the same as the majority of people expected to happen. He was strongly in favour of both the much predicted events, to the scandal of his schoolfellows and of his grandfather, whose whiskered face would grow purple with rage whenever the boy, poised to evade the flourish and downswing of a heavy walking stick, appeared and shouted 'Votes for Women!' followed by 'Home Rule for Ever!' Women got the vote five years later, with practically no fuss, and three years after that Ireland, all but the Six Counties, got a good deal more than the mild measure of local government known as Home Rule, but not without the civil war which had been prophesied for the later months of 1914. The assassination of an Austrian archduke at Sarajevo, then in Servia, proved, fantastically, to be an event of greater and more immediate consequence to the British people than either the arrests of suffragettes outside Parliament, the secret arming of Orangemen in Ulster or the refusal of senior officers in the British Army to move against them. 1914 was to belong to the whole of Europe, not merely to a group of islands off the western coasts of the continent. Few suspected it in the early summer of 1914, my grandfather, I dare say, least of all.

3

The popular tradition of war, as seen through civilian eyes in Britain, makes an emphatic distinction: military battles, however picturesque and moving, are never in the same class as battles at sea. Tennyson might versify the Charge of the Light Brigade and Kipling (taking a kerbside, civilian-spectator view of a marching column) pound out a spondaic rhythm about boots, but it was Nelson and his Jolly Jack Tars (many of them kidnapped into the Navy by the Press Gang) who dominated the popular songs of the eighteenth and nineteenth centuries. 1914 changed all that, and not only because the war at sea, though immensely successful from the start, was undramatic by comparison. In 1914 Britain began to turn young men into soldiers and went on doing so, on a scale unprecedented, throughout the following four years until she had three and a half million men under arms at the end of a war in which, on the Western Front alone, two and a half million British soldiers had been killed, wounded or otherwise put out of action. More than nine hundred thousand died. It is not true that a whole generation of males was wiped out, but the incidence of death was far higher than decimation. On the Western Front out of every nine soldiers five became casualties, but if

12

only troops in forward areas are taken into account – infantry, field artillery, trench engineers and so on – it is probable that out of every nine men eight became casualties, and three or even four of those – perhaps after being wounded several times – eventually were killed or died of wounds. The war was a war not only of physical endurance but of nervous and moral endurance. For the men who survived it, it became in retrospect an experience to be thrust out of memory most of the time, an experience impossible for the mind to digest, and, for many, tolerable only when some of the less distressing events were selected for recall and dressed up with sentimental emotions.

In 1914 and early 1915 many men were so eager to enlist that the Army's organisation was overwhelmed. Seven divisions of Regulars had gone to France to fight on the left flank of the French, the Territorials were mobilised, and there was everywhere a shortage of uniforms, equipment and weapons for the volunteers. There was just as great a shortage of men able to play, even in an out of date style, the part of drill instructors and junior commanders. With so much improvisation, a few months passed before those who enlisted in newly created battalions discovered exactly what it was they had let themselves in for. They had engaged to serve, twenty-four hours a day, seven days a week, fifty-two weeks in the year, for an undetermined number of years, as private soldiers in a complex organisation incidentally designed to enforce the will of each and every superior on those in the lowest rank of all, to make them jerk into action at the word of command, stand still at the word of command, go anywhere and do anything at the word of command. In order to carry out what they had conceived, for the most part romantically and generously, as a patriotic duty, the young civilians were compelled to undergo a preliminary process not unlike what would now be called conditioning. It involved an almost total surrender of personal liberty and an immediate, unconsidered obedience to orders. Military discipline was not new in history but some of its 1914 characteristics were fairly modern and probably derived from late nineteenth-century deference to the success of Prussian methods in the field: significantly it was after 1870 that parade helmets topped with metal spikes and a jerky, noisy kind of drill were adopted by the British Army. This was the process through which first a hundred thousand, then a million, eventually several million civilians were hurriedly passed to be transformed into soldiers.

The penalties for disobedience ranged from a temporary loss of leisure, if any, a temporary loss of pay and some extra duties, through pack drill – mostly marching at speed with rifle and full equipment (which weighed about sixty pounds) to specialised forms of punitive imprisonment and, on active service, Field Punishment No. 1: this involved the offender subsisting on a diet of bread and water and, lashed by hands and ankles to a wheel or a gate, being exhibited to his comrades in one of the ancient postures of crucifixion. Ninety-nine men out of a hundred never ran any great risk of the more drastic punishments but this was only because the spirit in which King's Regulations were administered was more flexible and humane than the spirit and letter of the regulations themselves. The possibility of severe punishment hung perpetually over the private soldier and indeed some Regular N.C.O.s boasted that if they really wished to do so they could make sure that any man under them would be sent to a military prison. As soon as a private soldier realised the power of the organisation to which, body and soul, he now belonged, he realised also that, while he might learn certain ways of outwitting it, outwardly he had no choice but to submit. Any form of direct defiance was worse than useless.

It is noteworthy that while many of the songs sung by the troops were sentimental in content and in melody, few have the lilting light-heartedness so characteristic of the late Victorian and Edwardian period which immediately preceded 1914. Even ragtime, which had the attraction of novelty and a transatlantic brashness as well, was comparatively little sung by the troops, perhaps because its rhythms were not always easy to march to, but perhaps also because it was too individual, too self-assertive. The Army rarely allowed a private soldier to be an individual: he was a name and a regimental number, and on returns of strength was likely to be shown as one of so many 'rifles'. If and when he were killed or wounded, another man took over the rifle. It is all understandable but, to the private soldier of 1914–18, left alone for a few rare moments with his own thoughts, hardly reassuring.

4

The songs here set out were universally sung in British
Expeditionary Forces at one time or another during 1914–18.
They come from the ranks, especially from the private soldiers
without ambition to bear office or special responsibility. The
very roughness of the metre, the assonances, the faulty
rhyming and the occasional omission of rhyme indicate their
illiterate or semi-literate origin. They are the songs of homeless
men, evoked by exceptional and distressing circumstances; the
songs of an itinerant community, continually altering within
itself under the incidence of death and mutilation.

Like mediaeval ballads, these songs are anonymous, and
even the method of their composition is a mystery. Much
speculation and a deal of scholarship has failed to prove how
the ballads originated. One theory is that each of them was
composed by an individual poet, now unknown; and that repetition by professional minstrels merely polished the text and
altered a word here and there. Another theory holds that the
ballads were community songs, in building which each person
present would add a line or a stanza at a time. The same induc-
tions may be applied to these soldiers' songs and – although
they are so recent – with as little hope of final proof. The only
author to whom they can be attributed is 'Warrior, or Warriors,
Unknown'. Most units included at least one man with some
literary experience: a small journalist, a writer of Christmas
card verses or parish magazine poetry, or someone with a gift
for personal abuse, who would produce, for the battalion or
battery concert-party, jests and ditties about topics of the
moment or outstanding personalities of the unit. Songs of that
kind correspond to the 'family' joke abhorred by visitors. They
lack universality of spirit and application, but they may be a
clue to the origin of true Army songs, many of which are
parodies. The men who composed battalion songs, and other
men, satiric or jocular but not able to produce a complete and
original composition, would often find an opportunity so to twist
and rearrange a line of a popular concert or music-hall song as
to travesty its sentiments or satirise some aspect of the
common lot. The wit, delighted with his inspiration, would
shout it aloud, louder than his comrades singing the original

words. If the variation was appreciated, it would be taken up generally, and other minds, expanding the idea, might improve the phrase and possibly add to it.

That this is a likely origin for many of the songs may be seen from one or two aborted parodies. In 1917–18 there was current a 'ragtime number', *The Black Eyed Susans*, and it became customary at one part of the refrain to sing instead of the proper couplet:

> The Orderly Sergeant knows I'm coming,
> I can hear him softly humming.

There for some reason the afflatus ceased, and the parody was never completed. Similarly with *Colonel Bogey*, probably the most frequently heard marching tune in the Army. Some bars of the refrain went very well to a percussive repetition of the word 'ballocks', which could be hurled against the Warwickshires or any other regiment whose name would fit the metre. The rest of the tune was too intricate and, although it was known, whistled and hummed everywhere, no further words were ever attached to it. Songs that were invented were either snatches of nonsense or satire, or pseudo-ballads that told a story – usually a bawdy one. These may be more convincingly ascribed to a single author, but who that author was is now quite beyond proof. Some were inherited from the professional Army of pre-1914 and may derive from an oral tradition reaching back to the press-gangs and prisons of the eighteenth century. They sprang into being at different stages of the war – *Mademoiselle from Armenteers*, for example, is a 1915 song, *I Wore a Tunic* is 1917. The majority are period songs and became obsolete, mere souvenirs of departed comradeship and never-to-be-repeated adventures, the moment the war ended in 1918. It is as such unique memorials to a unique event that they are here collected.

5

It would be difficult to the point of impossibility to establish a date when any one of these songs was sung by one battalion, battery, brigade or division while still unknown to the rest of the B.E.F. Radio was in use, but it sent telegraphic messages only, by long and short 'buzzes', and there was no amplification by loudspeaker at the receiving end. Songs such as these were never sung in music-halls or concert halls, and never put on gramophone records. No more than a few bowdlerised fragments got into even ephemeral print. The rapid and thorough propagation of soldiers' songs through the Army was due to the intermingling of men from different units in billets and estaminets behind the line, and in hospitals, base-camps and troopships. After July 1st, 1916, the system of restoring an invalided man to his own battalion or battery broke down; 'Base Details' were sent 'up the line' to those formations which at the moment were most in need of reinforcements. A man who enlisted in the Devons might, after being wounded or sick, find himself in the Border Regiment or the Northumberland Fusiliers, and, after another wound, in a nominally Lancashire battalion composed of former Munsters, Scots Fusiliers, Middlesex, Norfolks and possibly every regiment in the Army.

Most of the songs fall readily enough into one or other of seven categories.

Satire on war, and mock heroics. Plain-speaking about war, the cold eye and the literal tongue turned upon what lies beyond the flag-waving and speech-making, the deliberate lowering of exalted spirits – this sort of realism is often supposed to be the discovery of the 1914–18 soldier. The warriors of previous ages are understood to have conducted themselves as romantically as the conditions of their warfare allowed. Seemingly, they believed the patriotic songs, and were slaughtered in very pretty attitudes, decorating the background effectively for their more fortunate comrades who survived with no more than a few romantic rents in the scarlet tunic or a becoming bandage round the head. Thus the witness of Clio. The disillusionment, the bitterness, the grousing of the soldiers of the past are not much on record and we are incited to believe (as they themselves perhaps believed, once the danger and the fatigue were over) that the martial spirit in the 'days of old' took no account of lice or the smell of corruption. It is hardly probable. As C. E. Montague pointed out, the stubborn, strictly agnostic spirit which ruled in the dangerous places of 1914–18 is to be found in Shakespeare's *Henry V*, in the foot-soldier Williams.

17

Even a Great War does not utterly transform national character: it can but expose the foundations, the conflicting stresses and inertias on which it is built. If British soldiers half a century ago were jesting about the death which slew their comrades and seemed their own certain fate, if they cheated hysteria with songs making a joke of mud and lice and fear and weariness, it must have been because their forefathers had evolved the same ironic method of outwitting misfortune. When the victims can mock Juggernaut even as they writhe under the wheels, then by so much do they subtract from his victory. That a man should be familiar with *Hush! Here comes a Whizz-Bang* or the second stanza of *If the Sergeant Steals Your Rum* did not, during a bombardment, alter or diminish the incidence of shells that burst around him, but knowledge of such songs may well have reduced the emotional distress caused by fear, and aided him, after the experience, to pick his uncertain way back to sanity again. Similarly, when the romantic conception of war proved false, out of date, useless, the man in the line was helped in his daily endurances if he could ridicule all heroics and sing, with apparent shamelessness, *I don't Want to be a Soldier* or *Far Far from Ypres I Want to Be*. These songs satirized more than war: they poked fun at the soldier's own desire for peace and rest, and so prevented it from overwhelming his will to go on doing his duty. They were not symptoms of defeatism, but strong bulwarks against it.

Satire on the military system. A great part of Army procedure was (or so it seemed to a private soldier) devised for parade purposes. Polishing brass buttons, presenting arms, adjusting alignment on the parade ground, saluting officers with the hand further away, and keeping one's thumbs in line with the seam of the trousers, all this appeared somewhat irrelevant to the main purpose of winning the war. The new recruits were assured that punctiliousness in such trifles had a miraculous moral effect, and in some unspecified manner would make them into efficient soldiers. As soldiering was a new science to them, they were compelled to believe the professors until their own experience let in a great flood of naked light and the old colonels and majors were seen to be maunderers speaking from the book, blind to reality. By that time it was too late. Military discipline in 1914–18 was so hierarchic and rigid that it could be altered only by revolution – and a revolution would have meant defeat. The British soldier continued to suffer the absurdities and irritations of a system designed, a century or more before 1914, to transform tramps and wastrels into pretty puppets. He did not suffer silently. His comments off parade, and occasionally *sotto voce* on parade, were incisive and impolite. The very discipline against which he rebelled kept his opinions out of his songs, although some indication of his thoughts and feelings about the handling of the New Armies may be found in *We Are Fred Karno's Army* and *At the Halt on the Left Form Platoon*.

Satire on superior officers. The soldier's resentment against the system to which he was subjected often took the form of reflections on a particular person in authority over him, who seemed to typify the general stupidity or who was notoriously inefficient or domineering. Superior rank was, by its own nature, a target for satire: chiefly the colonel, the sergeant-major, the quarter-master sergeant and the sergeant. The colonel figures in songs of this kind because he was the supreme authority the private soldier knew, but officers generally escaped satire; not that the private failed to recognize that they had a much more comfortable time than he, but because they belonged to the excessively privileged class, the barons, so to speak, of the anachronistic feudal system in which the private soldier was serf, scullion and load-carrier. The sergeant, however, along with the sergeant-major and the quartermaster-sergeant were close at hand, and all the rant and bluster in the world failed to conceal a single defect. With the colonel they are the comic villains of *The Old Barbed Wire*, while the C.S.M. had one song all to himself – *The Sergeant-Major's Having a Time* – and the platoon sergeant two – *We Haven't Seen the Sergeant*, and that terse objurgation which is called in these pages, *Greeting to the Sergeant*.

Panegyrics of Civilian Bliss, Past and Present. Present experience always subordinates what is distant in time or space. Yesterday is never real as today is, and if we stand in Oxford Street the most vivid imagination in the world will hardly bring

19

Whitehall before our eyes in any comparable fashion. The very fact that men became soldiers, enrolled themselves in a masculine community and were bandied about northern Europe and the least attractive quarters of Africa and Asia inevitably made their own civilian past and the normal civilian routine of England (which newspapers and letters showed to be continuing) seem unreal. Siegfried Sassoon speaks of soldiers:

> Dreaming of things they did with balls and bats,
> And mocked by hopeless longing to regain
> Bank-holidays, and picture-shows, and spats,*
> And going to the office in the train.

The poem is appropriately called *Dreamers*, for to the soldier civilian life appeared only in the disproportionate and deliciously fantastic quality of a dream. The life imposed on a man by the War was so unnatural, and at the same time involved such a complete enslavement of body and mind, that his presoldiering past became as incredible as the possibility of an undisturbed and liberated future. The most ordinary details of normal life were longed for more intensely than saints on earth have desired the benefits of their paradise. *I Want to Go Home*, the soldier sang, mockingly perhaps, but without pretences. That was what he wanted most of all, though some more obscure aspiration fixed him in his trench until certain conditions should be fulfilled. He kept the hard-flogged flesh going with ribald promises, listed in *When This Blasted War is Over*. There was little envy of civilians avoiding the perils and discomforts of war. The soldier had his opinions and stated them bluntly. After that, the matter was done with. *I Wore a Tunic* stands alone, and it had but a 'limited run'.

Celebration of Drink and other Comforts. Even teetotallers will join boisterously in the chorus of a good drinking song, and it must not be inferred from *Here's to the Good Old Beer* and *Glorious!* that it was an army of drunkards which won the War. Remarkably few soldiers were reduced to bestiality by

* Spats is short for spatterdashes, worn over shoes or over the upper parts of boots as a protection against mud or rain. They were secured with a strap under the instep and buttoned on the outer side with pearl buttons. They were made of grey or buff woollen cloth, or white or grey canvas. 'Picture-shows' were (silent) films.

20

their experience but all felt a renewed zest in animal pleasures – among which the quenching of thirst and the warming of chilled bodies rank high. Hence the celebration of beer and rum.

Nonsense and Burlesque. There is a long British tradition of nonsense, and such refrains as *Inky-Pinky Parley-Vous* and *Skibboo* are in the direct line from the Elizabethan *Hey Nonny Nonny Noes.* They are no more than singable sounds invented to go with a tripping tune. *Down by the Sea* and *Wash Me in the Water* are examples of irrational fooling: examine them and there is no content at all, but sing them in good company and they satisfy some deep, unsuspected thirst of the spirit. Such songs annihilate logic. Others burlesque the human capacity for gratifying the mind with high-falutin' sentiments, and more formal literature has produced nothing better in this kind than *She was Poor but She was Honest* and *I Have No Pain, Dear Mother, Now.*

Sex Ribaldry. Contrary to a common supposition, only a minority of Army songs are improper in subject or in language. Nevertheless when the original version of this book was published in 1930, Eric Partridge and I, after taking advice, could publish the text of certain songs, as we and other ex-soldiers remembered them, only by a fairly lavish use of printer's dashes. Since then custom and opinion have changed and, as the songs are now my responsibility, I feel justified in restoring to the text a number of words which are quite often found in print nowadays. Such words seem to me to be open to no more serious objection than that they are coarse and, in the old phrase, unfit for polite society. The words are: arse, balls, ballocks, piss and shit. One other word, not quite of the same kind, I have restored at appropriate places – bugger. In its remote origin it meant a sodomite but is never used, except perhaps by lawyers and pedants, in that sense nowadays because it has become a virtually meaningless term of abuse. That is how it was used in the Army and because it also is nowadays frequently found in print and regarded apparently as unobjectionable I have restored it.

Two other words I have jibbed at and they are replaced in the text by the traditional asterisks, although similarly precedents could be found, in books from respectable publishing houses, for printing them in full. The convention in these matters is always a current one, that is to say it is always changing and during the present century the changes have been almost all towards an increased freedom for author, publisher and printer. I myself do not believe that this freedom can ever be absolute and I therefore think it important that the code of what may and what may not be printed without objection from the Law should be specific and practicable. If, for example, it were laid down that certain words should not appear in public print – with exemptions for scientific and scholarly books – and that certain things and processes, notably sadistic practices, should not be described, authors might grumble but they would at least know where they were.

Such a code does not exist and, partly because of that, I have decided to continue to omit two words which, anyhow, I myself find disgusting. Each of these words was used in the 1914–18 Army as both noun and verb. Each is of four letters but was often adapted to make adjective and adverb by adding -ing or -ing well. The words are not old and I doubt if they came into common use, by word of foul mouth, much more than a hundred years ago. Like Blake's 'dark Satanic mills' they may be regarded as memorials to the Industrial Revolution. Senseless repetition has taken the edge off their meaning. They are synonyms for the man's part in the act of copulation and for the female genital organ. As terms of abuse they are predominantly urban. In this abusive function they probably originated with men who, finding themselves trapped in the nineteenth-century wage slavery of factory towns, spilled their resentment over into self-hatred and then turned that self-hatred, by a trick of the mind we are all capable of, into hatred for women and sex. I think I could justify the use which James Joyce made of these two words in *Ulysses*, but with other authors, notably Frank Harris, the intent, in my view, is crudely pornographic. *Lady Chatterley's Lover*, taking into account Lawrence's statement of his aims – and his lifelong deficiency of humour – must be reckoned an exception. He believed that he could use the words so that their sordid associations were sloughed off, but in my judgement he failed, and not only because *Lady Chatterley* is weak in characterisation and sloppily written. The words are beyond redemption. Like the slum property surrounding so many Satanic mills, they are overdue for demolition.

6

Immediately after the Armistice of 1918 it was an eerie experience, in Flanders or Picardy, to walk in daylight, from what had been a back area, past reserve and support trenches to the old front line, moving above ground and every now and then pausing where a few months earlier it would have been impossible to stand upright and survive. It is almost as fantastic, now that four decades and six years have gone by, to visit the same or other old battlefields, tidied up, restored to cultivation, unrecognisable, some with full-grown trees, planted since 1918, now thirty feet high where nothing but roots and stumps had been left in the rent and polluted earth. What is most disquieting on such a visit is to realise how little space – eighty miles perhaps – separated the line, the soldier's troglodyte world, the world which might have been another planet, from home, from England, from sanity.

If soldiers sang at all in the front line it was one at a time and under the breath, unless they had reached a tacit and reciprocal arrangement with the Germans opposite. When they sang on the march it was during a route march for exercise or to shift quarters, and only after the successive commands had been given 'March at Ease' and 'March easy'. These permissive orders, like the provision of a band at the head of the column, were the Army's way of encouraging troops to sing in the belief that it was good for morale. Singing, with intervals of silence or of whistling or humming, provided a distraction from the long, slow count of the heavy laden miles. How many miles could not be calculated in advance because it was very rare for troops to be told where they were going or for what purpose. If they were told, the information usually proved to be false. Many of the songs soldiers made up for their own entertainment are songs of weariness, disbelief and exasperation.

During training, in camps and billets behind the line, and whenever soldiers had the opportunity, and the money, to visit estaminets, a different sort of song was also in demand, more of a set piece for one man, or perhaps a trio, to render: such songs sometimes told a story, a ribald story as likely as not, but sometimes they were clearly incomplete, no more than snatches from substantial lays, handed down by earlier generations of pub-singers and half-forgotten. Songs of these kinds were not universal favourites and were sung, to make a change, during brief intervals in conversation and in the predominant singing of music hall songs, old and new, not otherwise connected with the Army or the War.

Every unit, almost every platoon or battery, had in its ranks a few men who cherished a repertoire of popular songs and fancied themselves as soloists or leaders of unecclesiastical choirs. Most of them could and would render, with emotional histrionics, *The Lost Chord, Trumpeter, What are you Sounding Now* and *Sweet and Low*. These were all taken very seriously, as things of beauty, joys for ever. Towards nightfall, when they were off duty and out of the line, the troops tended to become sentimental, and anyone then attempting ribaldry or even facetiousness might earn a communal reprimand. As the evening wore on, the songs chosen often had a soothing lilt of the lullaby about them and their themes were domestic – true love, home, mother and the roses round the cottage door. This may not be easy to reconcile with the coarseness of some, and the callousness of a few, of the songs here recorded. In retrospect, however, there may be something poignant in the lullaby sweetness of some of the tunes. The soldiers of 1914–18 were, after all, young men, many of them very young. Anyone in the ranks who was over thirty-five was regarded as elderly, and in the later years of the war most of the infantry reinforcements were eighteen-year-olds.

The typical British soldier – one perceives now – looked boyish when he went into the Army and, if he survived, boyish when he came out. Gallipoli, Mesopotamia, the Ypres Salient, the Somme and Passchendaele may belong to history but that history was not often perceptibly written on the faces of those who made it. That may be because it is a national characteristic of the English – and I think the Irish, the Scots and the Welsh have it also – to retain a good deal of their adolescent ways long after they are physically, and legally, mature. Or it may simply be that the convention of those days against making a fuss was more powerful than even the experience of war. In February

1964, Lord Attlee, being interviewed for television, was asked about Gallipoli, where he had served in the infantry. At once his face was transformed, and instead of an elder statesman there appeared a subaltern of 1915, complete with debonair smile and period jargon, who was disarmingly resolved to pretend that Gallipoli had been only a kind of natural history expedition, involving a certain amount of sleeping rough but on the whole quite interesting.

7

The troops of 1914–18 did little or no singing when they were in the line or on their way to the line. Coming out after a tour of duty in the trenches was another matter. Nerves began to relax after days or weeks of tension and as soon as the company had a mile or two of road behind them a kind of *sotto voce* singing or some soft whistling would begin. The tune was all that mattered then, not the words. In battle no one thought of singing. The pattern of Western Front battles, crude, cumbersome, conducted in time rather than in space, is as familiar now to most people as the shape of a mastodon to a palaeontologist. A continuous strip of No Man's Land, at places only fifty yards or less wide, wound from the Channel coast inland to the French frontier with Switzerland. In certain parts the 'front line' was nominal, defended by wire entanglements, mines, and spaced-out emplacements, keeps and redoubts, but in general it is true to say that No Man's Land was bounded on each side by systems of interconnected trenches, six, eight, ten feet deep, revetted and sandbagged and dug zig-zag to limit the effect of explosions. The trenches and emplacements on both sides were occupied continuously by infantrymen who, according to time and place of circumstance, suffered light or heavy casualties as the price of holding the ground. Battles were long in preparation, and might continue long after everyone involved in them knew that there was no hope of attaining their purpose. While the trench deadlock held, and it held for four continuous years, any advance had to be made across No Man's Land which was cluttered with formidable obstacles constructed of barbed wire, and the attackers were exposed, the moment they 'went over the top', to artillery fire from a distance and to rifle fire and especially machine gun fire at short range. On the Somme in 1916 battalions which at dawn were 800 or 900 strong were reduced by afternoon to 100 men.

The following year tactical formations were modified but the essentials of a deadlock situation remained. Preliminary bombardments intended to facilitate the attack made the ground impassable to the attackers who, because they had been subjected to a counter-bombardment, were generally disorganised and often demoralised before they began. The War had become an enormous institution with the prestige of a barbaric religion. It demanded unquestioning devotion and, as if the serpentine trench lines of the Western Front were a fire-breathing monster, it demanded daily sacrifices of human lives. At Passchendaele many infantrymen who were wounded or whose strength gave out drowned slowly in liquid mud. Millions of shells burst on the Western Front but the machine gun still commanded the devastation. The defence was broken only twice. At the end of 1917, attacking without the dubious benefit of a preliminary bombardment, British tanks broke through in front of Cambrai to a depth of five miles. Open country lay beyond, with the prospect of a decisive war of manoeuvre, but G.H.Q. had provided no reserves to follow up. The following spring the Germans attacked, using gas shells and infiltration tactics, and forced the British Fifth Army into a prolonged retreat. The Germans got so far and no further, perhaps because they were without cross-country vehicles. The British and French had acquired a new ally, the United States, coming belatedly into the War and deploying troops slowly but providing, as it were, a vast overdraft of manpower. It was, many consider, because they knew this that the German armies were at long last forced out of the trench systems where so many millions had died, and compelled to sue for a Cease Fire.

The carnival celebrations of 'The Armistice' - a word often pronounced with the second syllable accented - neatly timed for the eleventh hour of the eleventh day of the eleventh month of 1918, were held, spontaneously enough, in London, Paris, New York and other cities. On the Western Front the advancing troops were too tired for junketing and too sceptical: there had been false alarms of peace before. The Allies halted: the Germans withdrew out of sight and out of range of rifle, machine gun and artillery fire. This agreed 'disengagement' brought about a sudden relief from mental and nervous tension, after four and a half years, which constituted for most of the surviving soldiers the first sign that their soldiering days were almost over. There were some minor celebrations, however. One battalion, marching into a liberated village, found themselves greeted by the inhabitants waving Union Jacks. The flags, it appeared, had been sold to the villagers, under some duress, by the quarter-master sergeant of the German rearguard just before it left. And at one hospital, not far from Etaples, a Scottish R.A.M.C. officer recklessly signed an order – which was duly posted in the wards – declaring: 'To celebrate the conclusion of hostilities every patient will be allowed an extra piece of bread and jam with his tea.'

Part One

SOLDIERS' SONGS

SOLDIERS' SONGS 1914-18

Edited by John Brophy and Eric Partridge

I. Songs Predominantly Sung on the March

Fred Karno's Army
Air: 'The Church's One Foundation'

WE are Fred Karno's army,
The ragtime infantry:
We cannot fight, we cannot shoot,
What earthly use are we!
And when we get to Berlin,
The Kaiser he will say,
'Hoch, hoch! Mein Gott,
What a bloody fine lot
Are the ragtime infantry!'

This varied in a few details from unit to unit. Australians and
New Zealanders, for example, sang 'A.N.Z.A.C.' for 'ragtime infantry', and 'rotten lot' was often substituted for the
sarcastic 'fine lot', in the penultimate line. Fred Karno was a
popular comedian whose performance, 'The Mumming Birds',
was a crescendo of imbecility and absurd incompetence. It was
a sketch in which several minor comediant appeared, among
them, at one time, Charlie Chaplin and Harry Weldon – both
of whom continued and made famous the pathetic-comic
tradition of ineffectiveness.

Après la Guerre
Air: 'Sous les Ponts de Paris'

APRÈS la guerre finie,
Soldat anglais parti;
Mam'selle Fransay boko pleuray
Après la guerre finie.

Après la guerre finie,
Soldat anglais parti;
Mademoiselle in the family way,
Après la guerre finie.

Après la guerre finie,
Soldat anglais parti;
Mademoiselle can go to hell
Après la guerre finie.

Brutal and cynical: a traditional masculine jest. The tune was
delightful and gay; the words went without much thought,
and more often than not were omitted in favour of whistling.

We've Had No Beer

Air: 'Lead, Kindly Light'

WE'VE had no beer,
We've had no beer today,
We've had no beer!
We've had no beer,
No beer at all today,
We've had no beer.

This was sung lugubriously and low, often at the end of a long route march. With a variation, *We've Had No Duff*, it belongs properly to the period of training in England. The song is so simple in structure that innumerable variations could be made to suit the occasion. Really indignant battalions would go through the whole range of monosyllabic drinks, stanza by stanza, adding to the list of deficiencies *stout*, *gin*, *ale*, *wine*, *port*, etc. In France the song was usually forgotten except when an expected issue of rum failed to appear.

At the Halt on the Left

Air: 'Three Cheers for the Red, White and Blue'

AT the halt on the left, form platoon!
At the halt on the left, form platoon!
If the odd numbers don't mark time two places,
How the hell can the rest form platoon?

This was a pre-War Regular Army and Territorial song, taken up by the New ['Kitchener's'] Army early in 1914. It conveys with some precision the querulous tone as well as the drill-book phraseology of an exasperated officer or N.C.O. endeavouring to teach this complicated evolution. To form platoon a column of men four abreast was, as a preliminary, required to adjust itself into a column two abreast. The alternate men – the 'odd numbers' – had to mark time, i.e. lift their feet without moving forward – while the others, the 'even numbers', slipped into place beside them. Then the whole platoon turned and began to swing round into line.

Some units added:

> If he moves in the ranks, take his name! (*bis*)
> You can hear the Sergeant-Major calling:
> 'If he moves in the ranks take his name.'

She Married a Man

Air: ?

THE squire had a daughter, so fair and so tall,
She lived in her satins and silks at the hall,
But she married a man who had no balls at all.
    No balls at all,
    No balls at all,
    She married a man who had no balls at all.

Almost certainly a pre-War folk-song turned to Army use
and profit. The verse tune is faintly reminiscent of *Bonnie
Dundee*.
    It may be related to, or derived from, an old civilian
song about Sammy Hall who 'only had one ball', which
Charles Whibley says was the song sung by Captain Costigan
in the 'Cave of Harmony' at the beginning of Thackeray's *The
Newcomes*. Originally it was a scoundrel's funeral oration, *Sam
Hall*, or *the Body Snatcher*, but its military popularity caused
it often to be known as *Captain Hall*. Each verse ended with
        Damn your eyes, blast your soul,
        Damn your eyes.

According to other accounts *Sammy Hall* dates from 1848,
when it was sung by W. G. Ross, a Scotch low comedian. An
old version and an account of the song's reception are given in
Hayward's *The Days of Dickens*, and a twentieth-century
American version appears in Godfrey Irwin's *American Tramp
and Underworld Slang*.

Yes! And We Can Do It!

Air: 'In and Out the Window' [Nursery Song]

BREAKING out of barracks!
Breaking out of barracks!
Breaking out of barracks!
    As you have done before.

Parading all unbuttoned!
Parading all unbuttoned!
Parading all unbuttoned!
    As you have done before.

Take his name and number!
Take his name and number!
Take his name and number!
　　As you have done before.

Up before the C.O.!
Up before the C.O.!
Up before the C.O.!
　　As you have done before.

Fourteen days detention!
Fourteen days detention!
Fourteen days detention!
　　As you have done before.

Pack-drill, bread and water!
Pack-drill, bread and water!
Pack-drill, bread and water!
　　As you have done before.

　　Yes, and we can do it!
　　Yes, and we can do it!
　　Yes, and we can do it!
　　As we have done before.

To appear on parade with a button unfastened was to be
'naked' – a punishable offence. The officer who detected the
offence could – and often did – order an N.C.O. to 'take his
name and number', i.e. to make a note in his notebook of the
man's regimental number and name.

A variant, though not clearly connected with the main text,
was a single stanza, to the same tune, sung to reprove some-
one boasting or exaggerating:
　　　His comrades don't believe him,
　　　His comrades don't believe him,
　　　His comrades don't believe him,
　　　　He's such a bloody liar.

Tiddleywinks, Old Man

Air: 'Hornpipe'

TIDDLEYWINKS, old man,
Find a woman if you can,
If you can't find a woman,
Do without, old man.
When the rock of Gibraltar
Takes a flying leap at Malta
You'll never get your ballocks in a corn beef can.

The text is slightly bowdlerised. This nonsense song is a
pretty nasty scrap of folklore, and was sung chiefly by those
who wished to show off their own toughness. Generally, the
words stopped after the first line and the rest of the tune was
whistled.

We're Here Because

Air: 'Auld Lang Syne'

WE'RE here
Because
We're here
Because
We're here
Because we're here.

Sung with great gusto because – ninety-nine times out of a
hundred – the men who sang it had no idea why they were
'here', or where 'here' was, or how long they would continue
at it.

Nobody Knows

Air: ?

NOBODY knows how tired we are,
Tired we are,
Tired we are;
Nobody knows how tired we are,
And nobody seems to care.

Often 'dry', was substituted for 'tired'. An end-of-the-march
song.

Down by the Sea

Air: ?

Down by the sea
  (Down by the sea!)
Where the water-melons grow
  (Where the water-melons grow!)
Back to my home
  (Back to my home!)
I dare not go
  (I dare not go!)
For if I do
  (For if I do!)
My wife will say:
  (My wife will say!)
'Have you ever seen a cow with a green eye-brow,
Down where the water-melons grow?'

The repetitive lines were intoned very softly, and the whole piece of nonsense was sung slow and sweet, till the last two lines, which went with speed and gusto. Although most soldiers did not realize it, this was almost certainly a pre-War American ditty.

She Was So Good

Air: ?

She was so good and so kind to me,
Just like one of the family,
I shall never forget
The first time we met,
She was—
She was—
She—

       was so good and so kind to me, etc, etc,
       (and so on interminably, or as long as
       patience held out).

Almost certainly, in pre-War days, a folk-recitative.

We Beat 'Em

Air: 'Coming Through the Rye'

WE beat 'em on the Marne,
We beat 'em on the Aisne,
They gave us hell at Neuve Chapelle
    But here we are again.

Barney

Air: ?

I TOOK my girl
For a ramble, a ramble,
Adown a shady lane.
She caught her foot
In a bramble, a bramble,
And arse over ballocks she came.

    Oh, Barney,
    Oh, Barney!
    Oh, bring back my Barney to me-ee-ee.
    Oh, Barney,
    Oh, Barney!
    Oh, bring back my Barney to me.

Variation:

Oh, Sergeant,
Oh, Sergeant,
Oh, bring back my rations to me.

The variation confirms this as an authentic soldiers' song, for the original form of the chorus is a well-known air: *Bring back my Bonnie to me;* see, e.g., the old *Scottish Students' Song Book.* The reference to 'ballocks' in the context is anomalous to the point of lunacy. Mounted units had several variants of which one went:

    Sergeant,
    Sergeant,
    Bring back my stirrups to me.
    I stuck it as long as I could.
    Sergeant, Sergeant,
    My ballocks are not made of wood.

John Brown's Baby

Air: 'John Brown's Body'

JOHN BROWN's baby's got a pimple on his – shush!
John Brown's baby's got a pimple on his – shush!
John Brown's baby's got a pimple on his – shush!
 The poor kid can't sit down.

The Moon Shines Bright

Air: 'Pretty Red Wing' (Sentimental ballad: pre-1914)

THE moon shines bright on Charlie Chaplin,
His boots are cracking
For want of blacking,
And his khaki trousers
They want mending,
Before we send him
To the Dardanelles.

Some units sang (line 4) 'baggy trousers', and it is possible
the word khaki was introduced only after the film *Shoulder
Arms* had reached English cinemas. Almost certainly this song
was sung by children before being taken up by the troops.

Behind The Lines

Air: ?

WE'VE got a sergeant-major,
Who's never seen a gun;
He's mentioned in despatches
For drinking privates' rum,
And when he sees old Jerry
You should see the bugger run
Miles and miles and miles behind the lines!

Here's to the Good Old Beer

Air: ?

HERE's to the good old beer,
Mop it down, mop it down!
Here's to the good old beer,
Mop it down!
Here's to the good old beer,
That never leaves you queer,
Here's to the good old beer,
Mop it down!

Here's to the good old whisky,
Mop it down, mop it down!
Here's to the good old whisky,
Mop it down!
Here's to the good old whisky,
That makes you feel so frisky,
Here's to the good old whisky,
Mop it down!

Here's to the good old porter,
Mop it down, mop it down!
Here's to the good old porter,
Mop it down!
Here's to the good old porter,
That slips down as it oughter,
Here's to the good old porter,
Mop it down!

Here's to the good old brandy,
Mop it down, mop it down!
Here's to the good old brandy,
Mop it down!
Here's to the good old brandy,
That makes you feel so randy,
Here's to the good old brandy,
Mop it down!

41

Here's to the good old stout,
Mop it down, mop it down!
Here's to the good old stout,
Mop it down!
Here's to the good old stout,
That makes you feel blown-out,
Here's to the good old stout,
Mop it down.

Here's to the good old rum,
Mop it down, mop it down!
Here's to the good old rum,
Mop it down!
Here's to the good old rum,
That warms your balls and bum,
Here's to the good old rum,
Mop it down.

Here's to the good old port,
Mop it down, mop it down!
Here's to the good old port,
Mop it down!
Here's to the good old port,
That makes feel a sport,
Here's to the good old port,
Mop it down!

Here's to the good old gin,
Mop it down, mop it down!
Here's to the good old gin,
Mop it down!
Here's to the good old gin,
That fills you up with sin,
Here's to the good old gin,
Mop it down!

Rolling Home

Air: ?

ROLLING home,
Rolling home,
Rolling home,
Rolling home,
By the light of the silvery moo-oo-oon!
Happy is the day
When you draw your buckshee pay
And you're rolling, rolling, rolling, rolling home.

Often sung quietly and with much sentiment. In the evening or towards the close of the afternoon, the words would sometimes be omitted and the air whistled and hummed.

I have no Pain, Dear Mother, Now

Air: 'My Love is Like a Red, Red Rose'

I HAVE no pain, dear mother, now,
But oh! I am so dry.
Connect me to a brewery
And leave me there to die.

This tune was the regimental march of the Loyal North Lancashires, but to these words it was known throughout the Army. The first two verses are a quotation from an old sentimental recitation. There is said to exist a Ph.D. thesis (American, presumably) on 'The Influence of *Bell's Standard Elocutionist* and similar Books on lower-middle-class and working-class Culture'.

43

The Old Black Bull

Air: A traditional Somerset tune

THE old black bull came down from the mountain,
Euston, Dan Euston.
THE old black bull came down from the mountain
A long time ago.

Chorus:
  A long time ago,
  A long time ago
  The old black bull came down from the mountain
  A long time ago.

There were six fine heifers in the pasture grazing,
Euston, Dan Euston.
There were six fine heifers in the pasture grazing,
A long time ago.

Chorus:
  A long time ago, etc.

And he pawed on the ground and he pissed in the fountain,
Euston, Dan Euston, etc.

Chorus:
  A long time ago, etc.

Now the old black bull's gone back to the mountain,
Euston, Dan Euston, etc.

Chorus:
  A long time ago, etc.

And his head hung low and his back was broken,
Euston, Dan Euston, etc.

Chorus:
  A long time ago, etc.

Sung especially in 'Mespot'. Pre-1914, when it was local to
Somerset.

What Did You Join the Army For?

Air: 'Here's to the Maiden of Bashful Fifteen'

WHAT did you join the Army for?
Why did you join the Army?
What did you join the Army for?
You must have been bloodywell barmy.

This tune was the regimental march of the King's (Liverpool)
Regiment, with whose Regular battalions it may have
originated. Another version ran thus:
What did we join the Army for?
Why did we join the Army?
Skilly and duff, skilly and duff,
Surely to God we've had more than enough!

Raining

Air: 'Holy, Holy, Holy' (Hymn tune)

RAINING, raining, raining,
Always bloodywell raining.
Raining all the morning,
And raining all the night.

Grousing, grousing, grousing,
Always bloodywell grousing.
Grousing at the rations,
And grousing at the pay.

Marching, marching, marching,
Always bloodywell marching,
Marching all the morning,
And marching all the night.

Marching, marching, marching,
Always bloodywell marching;
When the war is over
We'll damn well march no more.

In the first stanza, *lousing* or *boozing* was sometimes substituted for *raining*.

45

They were only Playing Leap-Frog

Air: 'John Brown's Body'

THEY were only playing leap-frog,
They were only playing leap-frog,
They were only playing leap-frog,
(*Prestissimo*) When one grasshopper jumped right over
the other grasshopper's back.

Oh, it's a lie, Oh, it's a lie,
Oh, it's a lie, Oh, it's a lie,
For you know, you blighter, you're telling a lie,
You know you're telling a lie.

They were only playing leap-frog,
They were only playing leap-frog,
They were only playing leap-frog,
(*Prestissimo*) When one staff-officer jumped right over
the other staff-officer's back.

Oh, it's a lie, etc.

We were only drawing water,
We were only drawing water,
We were only drawing water,
(*Prestissimo*) When the sergeant-major came and stole
the handle off the pump.

Oh, it's a lie, etc.

A pre-War University parody parodied by the Army. Some
regiments sang this in reverse order: with 'They were only
playing leap-frog' as the chorus.

46

We Haven't Seen the Sergeant

Air: 'He's a Cousin of Mine' (Music-hall song: War period)

WE haven't seen the sergeant for a hell of a time,
A hell of a time, a hell of a time.
He came up to see what we were doin';
Number Eight Platoon will be his bloody ruin.
Oh, we haven't seen the sergeant for a hell of a time,
Perhaps he's gone up with a mine.
He's a sergeant in the Rifle Brigade,
Well, strafe him, he's no cousin of mine.

Compare these sentiments with *Greeting to the Sergeant* (page
67). For 'Number Eight' substitute any other number up to
Eleven – higher numbers won't fit the metre. For 'Rifle
Brigade', substitute the name of any other regiment. For
'sergeant', some units sang 'Kaiser'; and for 'well' of the last
verse, 'Gott'.

I Wore a Tunic

Air: 'I Wore a Tulip' (Sentimental ballad: War-time)

I WORE a tunic,
A dirty khaki-tunic,
And you wore civilian clothes.
We fought and bled at Loos
While you were on the booze,
The booze that no one here knows.

Oh, you were with the wenches
While we were in the trenches
Facing the German foe.
Oh, you were a-slacking
While we were attacking
Down the Menin Road.

A late-in-the-War song, and almost the only one which
displays resentment against those who evaded military
service.

In the Evening by the Moonlight

Air: ?

WHEN you're coming from the firing line,
When you're coming from the firing line,
You can hear them shuffling along;
You can hear the Sergeant-Major calling,
'Come along, boys! Get into some sort of line,
Fill up the last blank file.'
In the evening, by the moonlight,
When you're coming from the firing line.

The tune was charming and plaintive, punctuated with
delicately spaced pauses.

The Son of a Gambolier

Air: ?

Chorus: OH, I'm the son, the son of a gun,
The son of a gambolier,
Oh, I'm the son, the son of a gun,
The son of a gambolier.
Come all you gay young fellows
That drink your whisky clear,
I'm a rolling rag of poverty,
I'm a bloody old Engineer.

Said variously to be a regimental song of (*a*) the Royal
Engineers, (*b*) a London Territorial Regiment. It was nevertheless well-known to many units on the Western Front.

We Know Our Manners

Air: ?

WE are the regimental boys,
We never make a noise,
We know our manners,
We can spend our tanners,
We are respected everywhere we go.

Believed to be of Cockney origin.

Marching Order

Air: ?

HERE comes Mary,
Covered all over with Marching Order! Marching Order!
Marmalade and jam.

This was a kind of chorus tacked irrelevantly on to other songs.

Mademoiselle from Armenteers

Air: French Music-hall Tune

MADEMOISELLE from Armenteers,
Parley-vous!
Mademoiselle from Armenteers,
Parley-vous!
Mademoiselle from Armenteers,
She hasn't been —— for forty years,
Inky-pinky parley-vous.

This song was adopted in 1918 by American troops who that
year arrived in France and during the peace-time years that
followed innumerable stanzas were invented and perpetuated
at and for American reunions of 'veterans'. The stanza given
above constituted the complete version of the song as sung by
British troops in 1914–18 – but three other songs, of which the
third may most closely resemble the prototype, were in
favour. They are set out on the following pages. In all versions
the final line was sometimes begun with 'Ninky' instead of
'Inky'.

Madame, Have You . . .?

Air: 'Mademoiselle from Armenteers'

MADAME, have you any good wine?
Parley-vous!
Madame, have you any good wine?
Parley-vous!
Madame, have you any good wine
Fit for a soldier of the line?
Inky-pinky parley-vous?

Oh, yes, I have some very good wine,
  Parley-vous!
Oh, yes, I have some very good wine,
  Parley-vous!
Oh, yes, I have some very good wine
Fit for a soldier of the line,
  Inky-pinky parley-vous!

Madame, have you a daughter fine?
  Parley-vous!
Madame, have you a daughter fine?
  Parley-vous!
Madame, have you a daughter fine
Fit for a soldier of the line,
  Inky-pinky parley-vous?

Oh, yes, I have a daughter fine,
  Parley-vous!
Oh, yes, I have a daughter fine,
  Parley-vous!
Oh, yes, I have a daughter fine
Far too good for a bloke from the line,
  Inky-pinky parley-vous!

The Sergeant-Major's having a Time

Air: 'Mademoiselle from Armenteers'

THE Sergeant-Major's having a time
  Parley-vous!
The Sergeant-Major's having a time
  Parley-vous!
The Sergeant-Major's having a time
Swinging the lead behind the line,
  Inky-pinky parley-vous!

The Sergeant-Major's having a time
  Parley-vous!
The Sergeant-Major's having a time
  Parley-vous!

The Sergeant-Major's having a time
Swigging the beer behind the line,
      Inky-pinky parley-vous!

The Sergeant-Major's having a time
      Parley-vous!
The Sergeant-Major's having a time
      Parley-vous!
The Sergeant-Major's having a time
—— the girls behind the line,
      Inky-pinky parley-vous!

Skibboo

Air: Variation of 'Mademoiselle from Armenteers'

A GERMAN officer crossed the Rhine, ⎫ *bis*
      Skibboo! Skibboo! ⎭
A German officer crossed the Rhine,
He was on the look-out for women and wine.
      Skibboo, skibboo,
      Ski-bumpity-bump skibboo!

Oh, landlord, have you a daughter fair! ⎫ *bis*
      Skibboo! Skibboo! ⎭
Oh, landlord, have you a daughter fair,
With lily-white breasts and golden hair.
      Skibboo, skibboo,
      Ski-bumpity-bump skibboo!

Oh, yes, I have a daughter fair! ⎫ *bis*
      Skibboo! Skibboo! ⎭
Oh, yes, I have a daughter fair,
With lily-white breasts and golden hair.
      Skibboo, skibboo,
      Ski-bumpity-bump skibboo!

But my fair daughter is far too young, } *bis*
        Skibboo! Skibboo!
But my fair daughter is far too young
To be mucked about by a son of a gun.
        Skibboo, skibboo,
        Ski-bumpity-bump skibboo!

Oh father, oh father, I'm not too young, } *bis*
        Skibboo! Skibboo!
Oh father, oh father, I'm not too young,
I've been to bed with the parson's son.
        Skibboo, skibboo,
        Ski-bumpity-bump skibboo!

It's a hell of a song that we've just sung, } *bis*
        Skibboo! Skibboo!
It's a hell of a song that we've just sung
And the fellow that wrote it ought to be hung,
        Skibboo, skibboo,
        Ski-bumpity-bump skibboo!

The origin of all these 'Mademoiselle' and 'Skibboo' songs
may be an untraceable parody, perhaps written for performance at 'men only' smoking concerts, of a German song
by the poet J. L. Uhland, 'The Landlady's Daughter'.

II. Songs Sung on the March, but more often in Billets and Estaminets

Wash Me in the Water

Air: Salvation Army hymn tune

WASH me in the water
That you washed your dirty daughter
And I shall be whiter
Than the whitewash on the wall.
Whiter
Than the whitewash on the wall.
Oh, wash me in the water
That you washed your dirty daughter,
And I shall be whiter
Than the whitewash on the wall.

Said to have been sung by the Regular Army before 1914 but
well known up and down the Western Front throughout 1914–
18. A variant for 'your dirty daughter', when no officers
were present, was 'the Colonel's daughter'.

Hush! Here comes a Whizz-bang

Air: 'Hush! Here Comes the Dream Man'
    (Pantomime song: pre-1914)

HUSH! Here comes a whizz-bang,
Hush! Here comes a whizz-bang,
Now you soldiers, get down those stairs,
Down in your dug-outs and say your prayers.
Hush! Here comes a whizz-bang,
And it's making straight for you:
And you'll see all the wonders of No Man's Land
If a whizz-bang (bump!) hits you.

The Old French Trench

Air: ?

OH what a life, living in a trench,
Under Johnny French in the old French trench.
We haven't got a wife or a nice little wench,
But we're still alive in the old French trench.

A 1915 song, apparently, to judge from the reference to Sir
John French, who commanded the B.E.F. then.

The Bells of Hell

Air: 'She Only Answered "Ting-a-ling-a-ling" '

THE bells of hell go ting-a-ling-a-ling
For you but not for me:
And the little devils how they sing-a-ling-a-ling
For you but not for me.
O Death, where is thy sting-a-ling-a-ling,
O Grave, thy victor-ee?
The bells of hell go ting-a-ling-a-ling,
For you but not for me.

Believed to be founded on a Salvation Army song.

I Don't Want to Die

Air: ?

I WANT to go home,
I want to go home,
I don't want to go in the trenches no more,
Where whizz-bangs and shrapnel they whistle and roar.
Take me over the sea
Where the Alleyman can't get at me.
Oh my,
I don't want to die,
I want to go home.

This was one of the most famous of war songs.

We are the Boys who Fear no Noise

Air: ?

WE are the boys who fear no noise
When the thundering cannons roar.
We are the heroes of the night
And we'd sooner —— than fight,
We're the heroes of the Skin-back Fusiliers.

Sometimes the first two lines were chanted *piano* and followed
by 'Ah! Ha! Ah! Ha! Ha!', *staccato* and *fortissimo*.

If the Sergeant Steals Your Rum

Air: ?

IF the sergeant steals your rum,
Never mind!
If the sergeant steals your rum,
Never mind!
Though he's just a bloody sot,
Just let him take the lot,
If the sergeant steals your rum,
Never mind!

If old Jerry shells the trench,
Never mind!
If old Jerry shells the trench,
Never mind!
Though the blasted sandbags fly
You have only once to die,
If old Jerry shells the trench,
Never mind!

If you get stuck on the wire,
Never mind!
If you get stuck on the wire,
Never mind!
Though the light's as broad as day
When you die they stop your pay,
If you get stuck on the wire,
Never mind!

When this Blasted War is Over

Air: Hymn, 'Take it to the Lord in Prayer'

WHEN this blasted war is over,
Oh, how happy I shall be!
When I get my civvy clothes on,
No more soldiering for me.
No more church parades on Sunday,
No more asking for a pass,
I shall tell the Sergeant-Major
To stick his passes up his arse.

When this blasted war is over,
Oh, how happy I shall be!
When I get my civvy clothes on,
No more soldiering for me.
I shall sound my own revally,
I shall make my own tattoo:
No more N.C.O.s to curse me,
No more bleeding Army stew.

Some units sang this additional stanza:

N.C.O.s will all be navvies,
Privates ride in motor cars;
N.C.O.s will smoke their woodbines,
Privates puff their big cigars.
No more standing-to in trenches,
Only one more church-parade;
No more shivering on the firestep,
No more Tickler's marmalade.

When the Stew is on the Table

Air: 'When the Roll is Called up Yonder'

WHEN the stew is on the table,
When the stew is on the table,
When the stew is on the table,
When the stew is on the table, I'll be there.

When the beer is in the tankard,
When the beer is in the tankard,
When the beer is in the tankard,
When the beer is in the tankard, I'll be there.

He's a Ragtime Soldier

Air: 'Ragtime Lover'

HE's a ragtime soldier,
Ragtime soldier.
Early on parade every morning,
Standing to attention with his rifle in his hand.
He's a ragtime soldier,
As happy as the flowers in May
(I don't think!),
Fighting for his King and his Country,
All for a shilling a day.

Send Out the Army and the Navy

Air: Music-hall tune

SEND out the Army and the Navy,
Send out the rank and file,
Send out the brave Territorials,
They'll face the danger with a smile
(I don't think!).
Send out my mother,
Send out my sister and my brother,
But for Gawd's sake don't send me!

This song, very popular and very typical, was overlooked when the first edition was prepared. Mr J. B. Priestley, in a review, promptly called attention to the lapse.

Far, Far from Ypres

Air: 'Sing Me to Sleep' (Sentimental ballad: pre-1914)

FAR, far from Ypres I long to be,
Where German snipers can't snipe at me.
Damp is my dug-out,
Cold are my feet,
Waiting for whizz-bangs
To send me to sleep.

Pronounce 'Ypres' – 'Eepree'.

Old Soldiers Never Die

Air: 'Kind Thoughts Can Never Die'

OLD soldiers never die,
Never die,
Never die,
Old soldiers never die –
They simply fade away.

Old soldiers never die,
Never die,
Never die,
Old soldiers never die –
Young ones wish they would.

Plum and Apple

Air: 'A Wee Deoch an' Doris'

PLUM and Apple,
Apple and Plum.
Plum and Apple,
There is always some.
The A.S.C. get strawberry jam
And lashings of rum.
But we poor blokes
We only get
Apple and plum.

'Plum and Apple' in the early years of the War was the only
kind of jam which reached the fighting troops.

Glorious

(*Chant*)

GLORIOUS! Glorious!
One bottle of beer among the four of us.
Thank Heaven there are no more of us,
Or one of us would have to go dry.

Another version, belonging to the later years of the War, ran:

> Glorious! Glorious!
> One shell hole among four of us.
> Soon there will be no more of us
> Only the bloody old hole.

Good-bye, Nellie

Air: ?

GOOD-BYE, Nellie,
I'm going across the main.
Farewell, Nellie,
This parting gives me pain.
I shall always love you
As true as the stars above.
I'm going to do my duty
For the girl I love.

Sung with great sentiment, and no notion that it was ridiculous. Possibly pre-1914, but a persistent favourite with the troops.

The Old Barbed Wire

Air: ?

IF you want to find the sergeant,
I know where he is, I know where he is.
If you want to find the sergeant,
I know where he is,
He's lying on the canteen floor.
I've seen him, I've seen him,
Lying on the canteen floor,
I've seen him,
Lying on the canteen floor.

If you want to find the quarter-bloke,
I know where he is, I know where he is.
If you want to find the quarter-bloke,
I know where he is,
He's miles and miles behind the line.
I've seen him, I've seen him,
Miles and miles behind the line,
I've seen him,
Miles and miles and miles behind the line.

If you want to find the sergeant-major,
I know where he is, I know where he is.
If you want to find the sergeant-major,
I know where he is,
He's boozing up the privates' rum.
I've seen him, I've seen him,
Boozing up the privates' rum,
I've seen him,
Boozing up the privates' rum.

If you want to find the C.O.,
I know where he is, I know where he is.
If you want to find the C.O.,
I know where he is,
He's down in the deep dug-outs.
I've seen him, I've seen him,

Down in the deep dug-outs,
I've seen him,
Down in the deep dug-outs.

If you want to find the old battalion,
I know where they are, I know where they are.
If you want to find the old battalion,
I know where they are,
They're hanging on the old barbed wire.
I've seen 'em, I've seen 'em,
Hanging on the old barbed wire,
I've seen 'em,
Hanging on the old barbed wire.

III. Chants and Songs rarely, if ever, Sung on the March

It was Christmas Day in the Workhouse

Recitative

IT was Christmas Day in the workhouse,
That season of good cheer.
The paupers' hearts were merry,
Their bellies full of beer.
The pompous workhouse master,
As he strode about the halls,
Wished them a Merry Christmas,
But the paupers answered 'Balls!'
This angered the workhouse master,
Who swore by all the gods
That he'd stop their Christmas pudden,
The dirty rotten sods.
Then up spake a bald-headed pauper,
His face as bold as brass,
'You can keep your Christmas pudden
And stick it up your arse!'

A short variant ran:

It was Christmas Day in the harem
And the eunuchs were standing around.
In strode the bold, bad Sultan
And gazed on his marble halls.
'What would you like for Christmas, boys?'
And the eunuchs answered, 'Balls!'

Pre-1914, part of the lore of the 'working class', and popular
with the troops because it expresses the resentment of the
helpless against circumstance and against those with power
over them.

Old Mother Riley

Air: ?

OLD MOTHER RILEY had a little kid,
Poor little blighter, he wasn't very big.
He wasn't very big
And he wasn't very small.
Poor little blighter, he only had one ball.

Probably derived from the old Victorian ballad, *Sammy Hall*
– see page 35.

My Nelly

Air: 'Three Blind Mice'

My Nelly's a whore!
My Nelly's a whore!
She's got such wonderful eyes of blue.
She uses such wonderful language too,
Her favourite expression is, 'Ballocks to you!'
My Nelly's a whore.

Casey Jones

Air: 'Casey Jones' (American railroad song: about 1905)

CASEY JONES,
Standing on the fire-step,
Casey Jones,
With a pistol in his hand.
Casey Jones,
Standing on the fire-step,
Firing Very lights into No Man's Land
　　(La-diddy-dah-dah – Dah! – Dah!)

Dan

Air: ?

DAN, Dan, the sanitary man,
Working underground all day
Sweeping up urinals,
Picking out the finals,
Whiling the happy hours away –
　　Gor blimey!
Doing his little bit
Shovelling up the shit,
He is so blithe and gay.
And the only music that he hears
Is poo-poo-poo-poo-poo all day.

Presumaly *'finals'* meant (football) final editions of evening
newspapers.

I've Lost My Rifle and Bayonet

Air: 'Since I Lost You' (Sentimental ballad: pre-1914)

I'VE lost my rifle and bayonet,
I've lost my pull-through too,
I've lost my disc and my puttees,
I've lost my four-by-two.
I've lost my housewife and hold-all
I've lost my button-stick too.
I've lost my rations and greatcoat –
Sergeant, what shall I do?

Pull-through was a long cord for cleaning the barrel of a rifle. It was looped at one end and around this loop was wrapped a small piece of flannel – *four-by-two* – soaked in oil. *Housewife* or *hussif* was a small cloth compendium in which were kept needles, cotton, wool, etc. *Hold-all:* a coarse linen receptacle, tabbed and pouched to hold in due order knife, fork, spoon, toothbrush, and other articles. *Button-stick:* a thin strip of brass split down the centre, the split ending in a small circular hole. The button-stick was placed behind several brass buttons at once, the tunic being rucked up to bring the buttons close together. *Soldier's friend* – a pink metal-cleaning paste – could then be smeared over them all without staining the khaki. *Disc* was an identity disc, a small medallion of brass or red or green composition on which were stamped a soldier's name, regiment, number and religion, so that, if he were killed or rendered unconscious, he could be identified.

Michael Finnigan

(*Chant*)

POOR old Michael Finnigan,
He grew whiskers on his chinnigan.
The wind came out,
And blew them in again,
And that was the end of poor Michael Finnigan.

Pre-1914. Probably a children's chant in street games.

I Don't Want to be a Soldier

Air: 'On Sunday I Walk Out With a Soldier'

I DON'T want to be a soldier,
I don't want to go to war.
I'd rather stay at home,
Around the streets to roam,
And live on the earnings of a well-paid whore.
I don't want a bayonet up my arse-hole,
I don't want my ballocks shot away.
I'd rather stay in England,
In merry, merry England,
And —— my bloody life away.

This song was a soldier's parody of the song noted above; the
original, we are told, belonged to a revue, *The Passing Show
of 1914*, and was sung at the London Hippodrome.

Can We Clean Your Windows?

(*Chant*)

CAN we clean your windows, mum?
We'll make 'em shine,
Bloody fine:
We'll make 'em shine,
Bloody fine.
Not today.
Run away!
'All right,' says poor old Jim,
As he threw down his bucket,
And he called out, 'Drat it!
Can we clean your windows, mum?'

Greeting to the Sergeant

(*Chant*)

You'VE got a kind face, you old bastard,
You ought to be bloodywell shot:
You ought to be tied to a gun-wheel,
And left there to bloodywell rot.

Never Trust a Sailor

Air: 'Oh Susannah'

ONCE I was a skivvy
Down in Drury Lane,
And I used to love the mistress
And the master just the same.

One day came a sailor,
A sailor home from sea,
And he was the cause
Of all my miseree.

He asked me for a candle
To light him up to bed.
He asked me for a pillow
To rest his weary head.

And I being young and
Innocent of harm
Jumped into bed
Just to keep the sailor warm.

And next morning
When I awoke
He handed me
A five-pun' note.

Take this, my dear,
For the damage I have done.
It may be a daughter
Or it may be a son.

If it be a daughter
Bounce her on your knee.
If it be a son
Send the bastard out to sea.

Bell-bottomed trousers
And a coat of navy blue,
And make him climb the rigging
As his daddy climbed up you.

Never trust a sailor
An inch above your knee.
I did and he left me
With a bastard on my knee.

This brutal ballad, to a gay tune, is pre-1914 in origin. The contemptuous word for a domestic servant – 'skivvy' – sets the period.
Sometimes called *The Servant Girl of Drury Lane* or *Never Trust a Sailor*, but the melody is now better known (because of radio and television) under the euphemistic title: 'With a Banjo on my Knee.'

She was Poor, but She was Honest

Air: Old ballad melody

SHE was poor, but she was honest,
Victim of the squire's whim:
For he wooed and he seduced her,
And she had a child by him.

Oh, it's the same the whole world over,
It's the poor gets all the blame,
While the rich gets all the pleasure,
Oh, isn't it a bleedin' shame!

Then she came to London city
To recover her fair name:
But another man seduced her,
And she lost her name again.

Oh, it's the same, etc.

What right had he with all his money
To go with her that was so poor,
Bringing shame on her relations,
Turning her into a whore.

Oh, it's the same, etc.

See the little country cottage
Where her sorrowing parents live:
Though they drink the fizz she sends them,
Yet they never can forgive.

Oh, it's the same, etc.

Now she's standing in the gutter,
Selling matches penny-a-box:
While he's riding in his carriage
With an awful dose of pox.

Oh, it's the same, etc.

See him in the grand theayter,
Eating apples in the pit:
While the poor girl what he ruined
Wanders round through mud and shit.

Oh, it's the same, etc.

See him in the House of Commons
Making laws to put down crime:
While the victim of his passion
Slinks around to hide her shime.

Oh, it's the same, etc.

Now she's living in the cottage
But she very rarely smiles:
And her only occupation's
Cracking ice for grandpa's piles.

Oh, it's the same, etc.

Pre-1914. Never sung seriously: always as a travesty of a
street ballad, with an excessive Cockney accent, and a whine
in the voice.

Part Two
SOLDIERS' SLANG

GLOSSARY OF SOLDIERS' SLANG

Including Rhyming Slang, Invective, Catchwords and Technical Language in use on the Western Front and other Fronts 1914–18

Edited by
John Brophy and Eric Partridge

A.: (Cf. *Brass Hats* p. 91). Adjutant's Branch, that part of the Staff which dealt with the personnel, training and discipline of the Army. See *G and Q*, I.

Also worn on the regimental shoulder-colours by hose Australian troops who had served at Anzac, i.e. Gallipoli.

A.A.A.: Ack Ack Ack. Represents 'full stop' on buzzer (*q.v.*); used in all signal messages.

ABDUL: Turk, individual or collective. (Cf. *Johnny*.)

ABORT: German for water-closet or latrine. The word occurs frequently in books written by ex-prisoners of war.

ABOUT TURN: The village of Hébuterne.

ACCESSORY: Such poison gas as was discharged in preparation for an attack.

ACE: A fighting air-pilot of outstanding ability. Obviously, from cards. Originally from French *as*.

The French Ace was René Fonck; the English, Major E. W. Mannock, who brought down 73 machines; the Canadian, Colonel W. A. Bishop, 72 machines; the American, Captain E. V. Rickenbacker, 26; the German, Baron Manfred von Richthofen, 80 machines. Richthofen was himself brought down at Sailly-le-Sec, near Amiens, on April 21, 1918, by Capt. Roy Brown, a Canadian aviator. Eric Partridge, who was on infantry observation nearby, remembers that, in this sector, this feat was the great topic of conversation for quite a day.

ACK EMMA: Air Mechanic, in the Royal Air Force. Also a.m. = morning. (Cf. *Pip Emma*.)

ADDRESSED TO: Aimed at, of bullet, bomb, or shell.

ADJUTANT: In the eighteenth century also called *Aide-Major*. As Captain Francis Grose (see entry in Bibliographical Note on page 237) who, having held two different and lengthy adjutancies, should know, says: 'There is scarce any duty going forwards in a regiment, without the adjutant having some share in it.' Major-General Voyle: 'The duties of an adjutant are unremitting,' for he is 'appointed to assist the commanding officer [of a battalion] in the execution of all details of duty and discipline.' The usual rank held by an adjutant in 1914–18 was that of Captain.

ADJUTANT'S NIGHTMARE: A confidential Army Telephone Code Book (= *Bab Code* or *B.A.B.*). Very complicated and frequently revised. A bright idea of 1916.

ADRIAN HUT: Seemingly not an English structure, but a French one occasionally used by or for the English troops. Its distinguishing feature was a widening near ground level to allow additional floor-space.

ADRIFT: Absent without leave.

AERODART or *Fléchette*: A steel dart or arrow used by both French and German aviators. According to the French Official Report issued on January 7, 1915, 2,000 were dropped on wagons and infantry at Nampoel on Christmas Day, 1914. Their use was soon discontinued. Weighing not more than one pound (some weighed very much less), they were made of highly tempered steel, pointed at one end and milling-fluted at the other. Their striking velocity had to be only 400 feet per second to enable them to traverse a man's body from head to foot.

'A' FRAME: A wooden frame, shaped like the letter A; inverted and fitted in the bottom of water-logged trenches. Planks were then stretched from one cross-piece to the next, to make a rough pathway.

AFTERS: Pudding.

AIDE-DE-CAMP: A junior officer employed as a general's 'handy man'.

AID POST: The R.A.M.C. went as far forward as Advanced Dressing Stations, which might be in support or in reserve trenches. The battalion M.O. and his orderlies and stretcher-bearers dealt with casualties in the front line itself and passed them back to the R.A.M.C.

AGONY: A newly-arrived officer showing nervousness or confusion.

AK DUM: Among Regulars: instantly. From Hindustani. In 1914–18 it also meant a German notice-board, which more often than not was headed *Achtung*.

ALBATROSS: A kind of aeroplane.

ALL CUT: Excited; in a pother, upset; confused.

ALLEY: Run away! Clear out! Or in full, *Alley tootsweet*. From the French *Allez tout de suite*. Often also *alley at the toot*.

ALLEYMAN: A German. French *Allemand*. Not much used after 1916.

ALL KIFF: All right, all correct. Usually as an affirmative. Probably cognate with the French argotic *kif-kif*, similar, the same, equal.

ALL THE BEST: A form of farewell, chiefly among younger officers. Later, over a drink, as a variant of 'Good health'.

ALLY SLOPER'S CAVALRY: The A.S.C. (cf.) – Army Service Corps – responsible for all road transport behind the lines. Ally Sloper was a comic character in a popular paper (pre-War) called *Ally Sloper's Half-Holiday*. The A.S.C. were so named by the infantry and artillery because, having good pay, comfort and comparative safety, they were hardly considered to be soldiers at all. (Cf. *R.A.M.C.*) A variant was *Army Safety Corps*.

AMIENS HUT: A very uncomfortable frame-and-canvas tent-hut seen at base-camps in 1915–16.

AMMO: Short for ammunition.

AMMONAL: An explosive used in Mills grenades and in charges placed in mines.

AMMOS: The stock active-service boots. From the technical term, *Ammunition Boot*; cf. the old *(Am)munition loaf*. Sometimes called *Kitchener's Boots*.

ANGEL FACE: A young or boyish-looking officer (usually a Probationary Flight Officer). Air Force term.

ANGELS OF MONS: These supernatural interveners on the battlefield – intervening on behalf of the British – were fictitious. They occurred in a story by Arthur Machen printed in a London evening paper. Very soon large numbers of people were convinced that the intervention was a part of military history. The late Eric Kennington, asked if he believed in the Angels of Mons once replied: 'Madam, I was one of them!'

ANNIE LAURIE: Lorry. For a note on this kind of usage, of which many examples follow, see the Glossary at R – RHYMING SLANG.

ANTI-FROSTBITE: In the winter of 1914–15 this commodity, which looked rather like lard, was supplied in two-pound tins; it evidently contained pork fat, for the tin was marked 'Not to be given to Indian troops'. Afterwards, *Whale Oil* was issued; it arrived in rum-jars. Owing to its foul smell, little was used as H.Q. intended; the order was that, before going out to a Listening Post (*q.v.*) or on patrol, each man was to be stripped and rubbed down with whale oil by an N.C.O.!

ANTONIO: A Portuguese soldier. Sometimes '*Tony*.

ANY MORE FOR ANY MORE: A jocular shout by the Orderly Man (cf.) when he had given every man his share of a meal, and still had some stew or tea or rice remaining. Also used by the man running a Crown and Anchor board or a House outfit, inviting others to join in before the game began.

ANZAC: Short for A.N.Z.A.C. – Australian and New Zealand Army Corps. Hence for the district in Gallipoli near Anzac Cove, where the Australian and New Zealand landing was made. The name was made popular by journalists at the time of the Gallipoli campaign, and afterwards applied as a synonym, singular and plural, for Australian or New Zealand troops. Rarely, if ever, used by English soldiers, who preferred *Aussie* or *Digger* (cf.).

A.O.C.: The Army Ordnance Corps.

A.P.M.: Assistant Provost Marshal. A sort of Head Constable of Military Police. A harrier of too lively subalterns, an eagle eye for omitted salutes, surreptitious drinks, overstayed passes. It is said that A.P.M.'s often acted as guides for Generals wishing to see the night-life of the large towns in France and Belgium. For the hardened type of *A.P.M.*, see C. E. Montague's *Rough Justice* (Chatto & Windus, 1926). Cf. *Red Caps* and *Battle Police*.

Grose, in his *Military Antiquities of the English Army*, 1786, writes:

'At present the chief duties of the provost marshal . . . are: the keeping of all prisoners, particularly those concerned for great offences, apprehending deserters, marauders, or soldiers straggling beyond the limits of the camp. At night, by his rounds or those of his deputies, preventing any disturbances among the petty sutlers in the rear, and apprehending all soldiers out of camp after gun-firing. Causing the butchers to bury all their offal; also to kill all glandered horses, and to bury them, and all others dying in the camp, in order to prevent infection. To enable him to perform those duties, the provost marshal has a sergeant's and sometimes a subaltern's guard; and occasionally to give him the more authority, has the rank of captain; besides which, he is permitted to make out a contingent bill, for his fees for executions, and other expenses attending his office.'

APPLES AND PEARS: Stairs.

APRÈS LA GUERRE: A magical phase used by soldiers jokingly for the indefinite and remote future, and as a depository of secret sentiment, longing for survival and for the return of peace. The two usages can be seen in the ribald ditty composed by some unknown warrior – 'Après la guerre finie' (page 33), and a later music-hall song, fairly popular in 1917–18, of which the refrain began, 'Après la guerre, There'll be a good time everywhere: smiling faces, gladsome missus,' etc. (Cf. *Blighty*.)

ARBEIT: A work-camp for prisoners of war in Germany.

ARCHIE: Short for Archibald: facetious name for an anti-aircraft gun; also for its shell bursts. It has pride of place in *The Wipers Times*, No. 2, i.e. February 26, 1916, when this gun was a new feature at the Front.

ARCHIE, TO: To shell aircraft.

AREA COMMANDANT: A sort of super *Town Major* (cf.) in charge of an area of some square miles behind the lines and responsible for the provision of adequate camps and billets, and for amicable adjustments of disputes with French residents.

AREA SHOOT: The bombardment of a given area in order to make it untenable or untraversable by the enemy.

ARGUE THE TOSS: To dispute loudly and long, especially when such argument was an annoyance to others not involved (e.g. *Chew the Fat*).

ARM: To chance your arm: to take a risk in the hope of achieving something worth while. Possibly a metaphor from boxing; more probably from the fact that badges of rank (stripes) were worn on the sleeve.

ARMOUR-PIERCING BULLETS: The Germans were the first to use such bullets, which could penetrate plates guarding loopholes; the plates were about 20″ × 15″ and were inserted between sandbags in the parapet of a trench, fire bay, or sniper's post.

ARMSTRONG HUT: Serving many purposes, this small and collapsible structure was made of wood and canvas.

ARMY: The British Expeditionary Force was divided into four or five Armies, each composed of a variable number of Army Corps.

ARMY CORPS: Made up of a number of divisions which varied as occasion demanded.

ARMY FORM S.H. One T.: *Bumf*, q.v. Variants: *Army Form Nought*, often abbreviated to *A.F.O.*; *Army Form O.O.* or *O.O.O.*

ARMY ROCKS: Socks.

ARSTY: Slowly! Slow down! From Hindustani *ahisti*. The opposite to *jeldi, jildi, jillo*.

ARTILLERY DUEL: Technically, this was a contest between the artillery of each side, in which practically all guns available were employed continuously. In practice, the German artillery battered the British infantry, and the British artillery the German infantry, until supplies of ammunition ran short. It was a pleasant sport for the gunners. Cf. also *Counter Battery Fire*.

A.S.C.: The Army Service Corps—for supply and transport.

ASCOTS, THE: A fancy name for A.S.C.

ASIATIC ANNIE (or ANN): A Turkish big gun at Gallipoli.

ASQUITHS: 'Wait and see' matches, i.e. French matches. The terse allusiveness is typical of British Army Slang. Compare the name applied to the Middlesex Regiment some years after 1918—*Colonel Barker's Own*. This was an allusion to a woman who successfully passed herself off as a man.

ASSAULT COURSE: A bayonet-fighting ground.

AS YOU WERE: An order at drill or on parade, meaning 'reverse the previous order'. It was also a way of acknow-

ledging a mistake, and sometimes used off parade to over-
take and correct an erroneous assertion of one's own.

A.T. CART: Army Transport Cart. A light all-metal cart,
not much used outside India.

AUSSIE: Used by Australians originally as an affectionate
diminutive of *Australia*. Applied by British troops to
Australian soldiers, in both singular and plural. (Cf. *Anzac*
and *Digger*.)

AVEC: Spirits. *Café avec* was coffee with rum or brandy.

AWKWARD SQUAD: A small group of men (as in *squad-drill*)
detailed for intensive instruction in those parts of foot or
arms drill in which they were backward.

AYRTON FAN: A loose flapping piece of canvas on a wooden
handle; used to disperse gas.
     Variant *Ayrton Flapper Fan*; colloquially, *Flapper Fan*;
slangily, *Flapper*. Devised by Mrs Hertha Ayrton, who in
1915 presented the invention to the War Office; over
100,000 were used on the Western Front.

B. or BEE: The former in writing, the latter in speech. A
frequent euphemism for *bugger*.

BABBLING BROOK: Cook. *Babbler*, an Army cook, derives from this.

BABY: The small Sopwith aeroplane of the Royal Naval Air
Service in the first year of the War; later the R.N.A.S.
used *Camels* or Sopwith scouting 'planes.

BABY CRYING: Defaulters' bugle call. Regular Army.

BABY'S HEAD: Meat pudding.

BACKS TO THE WALL: This special order was published on
Thursday, April 11, 1918, by F.M. Sir Douglas Haig.
One paragraph read: 'With our backs to the wall and
believing in the justice of our cause, each one of us must
fight to the end.'

BAG OF RATIONS: Contemptuously for a fussy or over-enthu-
siastic person, particularly if he were of superior rank.

BAGS OF: Plenty, lots. E.g. 'Got any bully?' – 'Yes, bags of
it.' And especially *bags of room*.

BALACLAVA HELMET: A woollen, 'pullover' head-covering
leaving only the face exposed. Worn in really cold weather.
It looked like a medieval helmet of chain mail. In the
modern form it presumably originated at the time of the
Crimean War. Cf. *Cap Comforter*.

BALL AND BAT: Hat.

BALL OF LEAD: Head.

BALLOON: 'What time does the balloon go up?' was a favourite way of asking the time fixed for any special parade or 'stunt'.

BALLOON OBSERVATION: Large balloons, shaped rather like vegetable marrows, were flown at intervals of a mile or so close behind the lines. Each carried an observer in a basket below and was secured to the ground by cable. They were flown in daylight and fine weather and were often shot down by hostile fighter aircraft.

BALLOONATICS: Those operating, or in charge of, observation balloons.

BALOO, or BERLOO: Bailleul. Probably Albert, Armentières, Amiens, Bailleul, and Ypres were the towns most familiar to the British soldier on the Western Front.

BANDAGEHEM, DOSINGHEM, MENDINGHEM: Certain hospital stations in Flanders, on the analogy of such place-names as Ebblinghem.

BANDOLIER: A canvas bag divided into compartments, capable of carrying 100 rounds of ammunition. Carried slung over the shoulder.

BANDOOK: A rifle. Pronounced *bundook*. From the Arabic for a fire-arm, originally for a cross-bow. Some Egyptians still call Venice 'Bundookia' – the place of the big guns. British soldiers, however, took the word from Hindustani. (Cf. *Hipe*.)

BANGALORE TORPEDO: A device (introduced on the Western Front in 1915), consisting of explosive tubes for clearing a way through a wire entanglement.

BANJO: A shovel. Australianism.

BANTAMS: Certain battalions of very short men. An official order of January 31, 1916, reads thus:

'. . . It is notified that until further orders only men who are between 5 feet 1 inch and 5 feet 4 inches in height are to be considered eligible for Bantam Battalions. The minimum chest measurement (fully expanded) for these men will be: For men from 19 to 21 years of age, $33\frac{1}{2}$ inches, and for men of 22 years and over, 34 inches.'

BARBED WIRE: Entanglements of barbed wire were erected in front of the trenches by both sides. Men were frequently caught in these when patrolling or raiding at night, and during daytime attacks, when they became easy targets for machine-guns. The dead bodies could not fall to the ground, but hung sagging in limp and often grotesque attitudes among the wilderness of wire. Hence it became a common euphemism to say that a dead man was 'hanging on the old barbed wire'. The phrase was often used by survivors at roll-call after an attack, when the name of a man was called without any response from him. (Cf. the song, 'The Old Barbed Wire', page 61, and *Concertina Wire, Trip Wire.*)

BARKER: A sausage; from a once popular song about the Dutchman's dog. A revolver; this dates from 1815 or earlier; an eighteenth-century synonym was *barking iron*.

BARPOO: Silly; insane. *To go barpoo*, to go mad or merely to lose one's nerve; (Air Force) to crash.

BARRAGE: A concentration of heavy artillery fire in front of advancing or retreating troops to afford them protection. Also, facetiously, for any excessive quantity. 'We've had a perfect barrage of orders today.' A *creeping* barrage was one which moved forward (or back) a time intervals. A *box barrage*, one surrounding a small area; used especially for raids. *Lifting the barrage* meant advancing the target area aimed at; as the range increased, the gun barrels would be elevated.

BARROW WALLAH: A big man (or thing); *choter wallah*, a small man (or thing). Regular Army terms from India.

BASE-WALLAH: A soldier perpetually at the Base, and so living comfortably and safely. (Cf. *Wallah.*)

BAT OUT OF HELL: *To go like a . . .*, at extreme speed. Flying term.

BAT, TO SLING THE: Seldom *talk the bat*. To speak the language of the foreign country where one happens to be.

BATCHY: Silly; unnerved; mad.

BATHMATS: Duckboards, *q.v.*

BATMAN: Officer's servant; used contemptuously of a sycophantic private. Often shortened to *Bat*. Originally a soldier who looked after an officer's *bat-horse*, pack-horse.

Used as early as 1809. In the Regular Army, only of the R.S.M.'s servant.

BATT: Short for battalion. (Cf. *Divvy* = division.)

BATTER, TO GO ON THE: To have a binge, *q.v.* Regular Army. In 19th century general slang (of a man) to give oneself up to debauchery and roistering, (of a woman) to go on the streets (Hotten).

BATTLE ASSEMBLY: Short for *Battle-Assembly Position*, the point of departure for an attack.

BATTLE BOWLER: Officers' slang for steel helment. (Cf. *Tin Hat.*)

BATTLE ORDER: A reduced infantry equipment, the pack or valise being left in store and the haversack moved into its place on the back. The weight thus taken away in order to make the tired infantryman more mobile was replaced by a still greater weight of spades, picks, bombs, extra bandoliers of ammunition, sandbags, etc. (Cf. *Pack.*) For months on end fighting soldiers were almost always tired out.

BATTLE POLICE: Military policeman employed on special duty behind the lines during an attack. They were armed with revolvers and had authority to stop unwounded stragglers and turn them back (if necessary using the revolvers) to the danger area where military police never appeared. (Cf. *Red Caps* and *A.P.M.*)

BATTLE SURPLUS: Often called *First Reinforcements*. Another name for *Cadre, Nucleus, Skeleton Battalion*.

BATTY: Demented, mad; or merely eccentric. Presumably from 'bats in the belfry'.

BAY: Short for *Fire-Bay*. That part of a fire trench which was manned. It usually had a *Firestep* (*q.v.*) and faced the nearest enemy position. (Cf. also *Traverses.*)

BEACHY BILL: A big enemy gun at Gallipoli.

BEAT: See *Dead Beat.*

BEAT TO A FRAZZLE: Exhausted – dead beat. From dialect *via* the U.S.A.

BEATEN TO THE WIDE: See *Dead Beat.*

BEEF HEARTS: Beans. With a rhyming pun on farts.

BEES AND HONEY: Money.

BEETLE-CRUSHERS: Army boots; cf. *Ammos* and *Footslogger*.

BEETLE OFF: An echo-allusive variant of *buzz off*.

B.E.F.: British Expeditionary Force. In Northern France and Flanders.

BEFORE YOU COME UP: 'Come' is the normal illiterate error for 'came'. This is the classic crushing retort of the private soldier, the unanswerable argument from experience and seniority. It means – 'I was in the front line before you arrived from the Base, I know more than you are capable of knowing, I've suffered more than you, I've done more than you, I'm a better soldier than you and a better man. And I refuse to believe a word you say.' Later, many elaborations were invented such as, 'Before you knew what a button-stick was'; 'Before your (regimental) number was dry'; 'Before you was breeched' or 'Before you nipped'. Variants were, 'I was cutting barbed wire while you was cutting your milk teeth.' 'While you were clapping your hands at Charlie,' i.e. Chaplin, and: 'When you were off to school with a bit of bread and jam in your hand.' The most vivid variants were: 'Before your ballocks dropped', 'Before you lost the cradle-marks off your arse', and 'When your mother was cutting bread on you'.

BE GOOD: An almost nonsensical exclamation, used in parting company, chiefly by officers, with facetious intent. Sometimes given in full – 'Be good. And if you can't be good, be careful.' Originally of sexual meaning. (Cf. *Cheero* and *Chin-Chin*.)

BELL TENT: Named not from its shape, which was conical, but after its inventor. It was supported by a central pole and stay ropes. A Bell tent held sixteen men in some discomfort and lacked head room. (Cf. *Bivvy*.)

BELLY BAND: Woollen belt worn next to the skin. (Cf. *Louse Trap*.

BELLY-FLOP: Verb and noun. To fall flat as part of extended-order drill or in the hope of saving one's life if a shell seemed to be coming uncomfortably close.

BENT: Spoiled, ruined, e.g. 'a good man bent' or even 'good tea bent'.

BERM: Ledge in the parapet of a trench, on which bombs, ammunition, etc., could be stored. It is not an Army term specifically but an excavator's term generally: it is the name for the untouched space between the lip of an excavation and the edge of the spoil-heap (as, e.g., between the trench and its parapet or its parados), left to prevent spoil from falling in again. The storage of ammunition, etc., was incidental and in some units it was discouraged.

BERT: Albert, the town.

BEVVY: Drink, especially beer; from beverage.

BIG BERTHA: Specifically the heavy German gun that bombarded Paris in the spring of 1918; generally, any very big German gun.

BIG BOYS: Big guns; cf. *big stuff*, heavy shells.

BIG NOISE: A Staff Officer, General, Politician, or Distinguished Foreign Personage visiting the troops. From the loud and important voices used by such persons. Of American origin.

BILL ADAMS: Like his 'sister' Fanny, Bill Adams was enlisted to do euphemistic duty for — *all, bugger all, damn all*, i.e. nothing or, at the most, extremely little.

BILLET: Noun. A house, barn or stable, in which troops were housed. Most billets had been abandoned by the civilian owners; further behind the lines, where civilians remained, camps were usually available. Also used as a verb.

BILL HARRIS: Bilharzia, a disease prevalent in Egypt, contracted from the water of the Nile.

BILLJIM: An Australian. (Composite word.)

BILLY WELLS: A big gun, or its shell. Probably from the name of Bombardier Wells, a British champion heavyweight boxer who served 1914–18 as a P.T. (*q.v.*) instructor.

BINGE: An expedition deliberately undertaken in company for the purpose of relieving depression, celebrating an occasion or venting high spirits, by becoming intoxicated. Music and singing were essential components of a *binge*. More an officers' word than a private soldier's. (Cf. *Zig Zag, Tight, Blotto, Blind*.) Possibly derived from eighteenth century slang *Bingo*, meaning brandy. Grose also gives *Bingo Boy:* a dram drinker, *The Bing Boys*, a wildly popular musical comedy of 1916–17, made temporarily famous the song, 'Another little drink wouldn't do us any harm.' 'Binge' is said to have been university slang before 1914. (Cf. *Blind, Blotto, Squiffy, Tight, Zig Zag*.)

BINT: A young female. The Arabic *bint:* daughter: a woman, as distinct from a lady.

BIRD: A young woman, especially in an amorous context, respectable or otherwise. The word (an abbreviation or variation of the Regency terms *lady-bird, dicky-bird,* a prostitute) is typical of a common male attitude to women, classifying them either with pets or with creatures hunted for 'sport'. (Cf. *Skirt, Tart, Piece, Square-pusher.*)

BIRD-CAGE: (Cf. *Cage.*) The term *the Bird-Cage* was applied also to the entrenched camp built around Salonika by the Allies in 1915–16. Both terms were sometimes applied to the point occupied by a sniper.

BIRDLIME: Time. It was also used for a Recruiting Sergeant.

BISCUITS: Small square mattresses, three making a bed for one man, in camp or barracks. Very hard: hence the name.

BISKIWITS: Variant *Biskwitz.* Prisoners-of-war. German for maize biscuits obtainable – at times – from the canteen.

BITCH, TO: To spoil, ruin. From civilian slang.

BIVVY: Bivouac. A makeshift tent to hold a few men: a waterproof sheet (or sheets) supported by a central ridge pole three feet or so above the ground. Bivouacs provided a pleasant feeling of privacy and airiness – in summer. The word was also used loosely for a small dug-out or other form of temporary habitation. (Cf. *Dug-out* and *Bell-Tent.*)

BIVVY, TO: To stop, or halt, for the night.

BLACK HAND GANG: A party selected, from volunteers when possible, for some hazardous enterprise such as a trench raid.

BLACK MARIA: Perhaps from the London police-van, although the Germans used *schwarze Marie* for a heavy naval gun (see Graff and Bormann's *Schwere Brocken*, 1925: a German glossary of soldiers' slang). *Black Maria* was the 1914–15 name for the 1916–18 *Coal-Box*: generally, for any big German high explosive howitzer shell, or for its burst.

BLANKET DRILL: The afternoon siesta, much prized by some 'old' soldiers with years of service in India behind them.

BLANKETS: The 10's in cards. 'Suggested by the regulation method of folding or rolling Army blankets in tens before removal for convenience of transport.' Fraser and Gibbons.

BLIGHTY: England, in the sense of home. In this one word was gathered much of the soldier's home-sickness and affection and war-weariness. Far more than the actual distance separated him from England. He had entered another mode of existence, ugly, precarious, insane, bearing hardly any resemblance to his normal life, which now had become to him abnormal and incredible. *Blighty* to the soldier was a sort of faerie, a paradise which he could faintly remember, a never-never land. The word was further used as an adjective, not merely for things English and homelike, but as a general expression of approval. E.G. 'This is real Blighty butter' – meaning ideal, as good as English. It was also used of a wound (cf. *Blighty One*). The word is thought to be a corruption of the Hindustani *bilaik*: foreign country, especially England. It often occurs in the adjectival form *bilaiti*; e.g. *bilaiti bègun*: foreign egg-plant, i.e. tomato. (Cf. also Arabic *beladi* = my own country.)

An alternative derivation is from *Vilayat*, Persian for strange or foreign. From this arose an Urdu corruption, *Belait*, which soldiers distorted to *Belati*, and eventually to *Blighty*.

BLIGHTY BAG: Received at a Casualty Clearing Station to hold a wounded man's personal belongings, for there he was parted from his rifle and equipment.

BLIGHTY ONE: A wound sufficiently serious to take the sufferer back to England. To most of the combatant troops on the Western Front to get a blighty one' was a hope and a dream and, if and when it came true, the wounded man would be openly envied. It was in general the only honourable release and many men – perhaps all men at certain times – felt ready to lose a leg or an arm in exchange for a permanent return to Blighty. (Cf. *Lucky One*.)

BLIMP: Air Force slang for the type of small, dirigible white airship used principally for anti-submarine surveys over the Channel. In the 1930s the cartoonist David Low invented a Colonel Blimp, rotund of face and figure, as a symbol of reactionary stupidity.

BLIND: Adjective: helplessly drunk. Noun: a drinking expedition, undertaken deliberately in order to become intoxicated. A more brutal term than *binge* (cf.) and presumably derived from the power of liquor to derange the eyesight (cf. *Binge, Blotto, Squiffy, Tight, Zig Zag*). Verb: to curse and swear furiously, especially to insult another person. Perhaps from the oath – *Blind your eyes,* a variation of *Blast your eyes!* Also, the technical adjective for a 'dud' shell.

BLIND TEN, TWENTY, THIRTY: The even 10, 20, 30, etc., especially at the game of House, *q.v.*

BLIP: Air Force term for switching an engine on and off.

BLOB: A glass of beer.

BLOCK: One's head. To 'do one's block' meant 'to lose one's senses.' (Cf. *Doolally.*)

BLOKE: An *officer's bloke* was his batman, while *my bloke* is 'the officer whose servant I am.'

BLOODY: The soldier's favourite adjective and adverb. For an examination of this word see Eric Partridge's edition of Grose's Classical Dictionary of the Vulgar Tongue. In 1914–18 there were certain well-observed formalities in cursing; e.g. a man could be, and often was, called with little offence *bloody bastard,* or *bloody* ——, but not, unless the word *silly* was added, *bloody bugger.*

BLOTTO: Drunk. Perhaps facetiously derived from the absorbing qualities of botting-paper. The *O.E.D.* actually defines blotting-paper as 'bibulous'. (Cf. *Binge, Blind, Squiffy, Tight, Zig Zag.*

BLOW A MINE: To spring a mine and explode it.

BLOWN TO BUGGERY: Destroyed by shellfire.

BLUE, IN THE: Lost: gone astray or wrong; out of touch.

BLUE CROSS GAS: German sneezing gas; from the mark on the shells.

BLUE UNCTION: Blue ointment used to exterminate 'crabs'.

BLUES: Regulation dress for patients in military hospital – flannel jacket and trousers, with white or cream shirt and a red tie. It was very conspicuous so that Red Caps could track down absentees from hospital and civilians and publicans would have no excuse for standing treat – an illegal practice in wartime – to 'wounded heroes from the front'.

BLURRY: In speech, a slurring of *bloody*: in newspapers and books a common euphemism.

BOB-DOWN MAN: Anti-aircraft sentry. (Cf. the catch-phrase 'Bob down, you're spotted'.

BOB TACK: Brass polish.

BOBBERY: Regular Army word from Hindustani: a row, a disturbance, noisy quarrel.

BOBBING ON: Anticipating (something unpleasant). Cf. *Sweating on*.

BOBBY'S JOB: An easy one; especially, a safe one. Bobby in this context = policeman.

BOCHE: (Also spelt *Bosche* in English.) French slang for 'German', taken into English: individual or general, noun and adjective. Practically never used by the 'other ranks' who preferred Jerry. 'Boche' was first used in the phrase *tête de boche*, in which the great philologist, Albert Dauzat, believes 'boche' to be simply an abbreviation of *caboche* – a head, such redundancies being not uncommon in speech. *Tête de boche* was used as early as 1870 of obstinate persons. In 1874 French typographers, it is recorded, applied it to German compositors. By 1883 (states Alfred Delvau's *Dictionnaire de la Langue Verte*) the phrase had come to have the meaning of *mauvais sujet* and was so used especially by prostitutes. The Germans, having among the French a reputation for obstinacy and perhaps as 'bad lots', from *Allemands* became *Alleboches* and *Allboches*. About 1900 *Alboche* was shortened to *Boche* as a generic name for Germans. During the war propagandist posters revived the memory of *Alboche* by making it *Sale Boche*. Déchelette in his fascinating *L'Argot des Poilus* (1918) has his own theory of the origin of the word: that it comes by anagram from *schwob* (cf. English slang *swab*), a term of contempt applied by Alsatians to Germans in the late nineteenth century. The extent to which this word has fascinated the French may be gauged from the publication of R. Lestrange's *Petite Monographie du mot Boche*, 1918. (Cf. *Fritz, Hun, Jerry*.)

BOMB: See *Grenade, Mills bomb, Stick bomb, Egg bomb*.

BODY SNATCHERS: Stretcher-bearers.

BOKO: For the French *beaucoup*. Also pre- and post-1914 general slang for nose.

BOLO: A spy; from Bolo Pasha, shot for treason in 1918.

BOMBARDIER FRITZ: Variant *pom Fritz*, i.e. *pommes de terre frites*, chips.

BOMBERS: Experts with hand grenades. Sometimes called *The Suicide Club*.

BOMBING-POST: A 'strong point', manned by bombers, in a fire trench. Usually not very strong.

BOMB-PROOF: Spinter-proof only.

BOMB-PROOF JOB: Employment at the Base or on the Lines of Communication.

BOMB-STOP: A traverse, *q.v.*; also a barricade in a trench part of which was occupied by the enemy.

BOMBING or BUMMING THE CHAT: Talking too much, holding the floor; bragging; 'telling the tale'; deceiving with plausible speech.

BON: Exclamation or adjective signifying pleasure or approval. Taken over from the French. Typical uses were 'That's bon!' 'We've got a bon dugout here.' 'The rations are bon,' and, simply, 'Bon!' The reverse was not *pas bon* but *no bon*; often vigorously reinforced as in 'These trenches are no bloody bon'. (Cf. *Bon Time*.)

BON FOR THE BUST: Good to eat; of great food-value. Said to have been first used by French civilians trying to sell chocolates to the troops, who adopted the phrase.

BON TIME: A period, brief or not, when unexpected happiness came the way of the soldier: 'We had a bon time at St Pol.' 'Dick says he's having a bon time with the V.A.D.'s.'

BONCE: The head, e.g. 'I'll give you a crack on the bonce.'

BONE, TO: To borrow with dubious intent; to steal; also, to arrest. From eighteenth-century thieves' cant.

BONE-ORCHARD: Cemetery. Pre-1914 civilian.

BONGO BOOSH: A tasy morsel. French *bonne bouche*.

BONK, TO: To shell; generally in the passive.

BONZA: Good. (Australian, from mining.)

BOON: Military prison; guard-room. An American import.

BOOBY-ACK: Bivouac. Pre-1914.

BOOBY-HUTCH: One of the primitive, built-up (not dug-out) trench-shelters before 'Elephants' (corrugated iron trench-shelters) came into use.

BOOBY-TRAP: German explosive devices to catch the unwary; left in trenches, farms, villages, before they were evacuated. Not much heard of till March, 1917. Bitterly resented.

BOOKRI: Crooked; wrong.

Booze: Pre-war Cockney. Verb: to drink to excess or, in another sense, simply to drink. Noun: intoxicating liquor, especially beer. (Cf. *Mop Up, Tight, Blotto*.) Originally Elizabethan from Dutch.

Boozer: A public-house or tavern; also a man who drank habitually and excessively.

Bo-Peep: Sleep.

Bosum Chums: Lice.

Bottle and Glass: Rhyming slang for *arse*. Two other nouns, barred in polite society are skilfully represented in rhyming slang: *Berkeley* or *Berk* (pronounced to rhyme with 'Turk', is short for *Berkeley Hunt*; *Hampton* short for *Hampton Wick*.

Bow and Arrow: Sparrow.

Bowler Hat, to get a: To be sent home, to be 'sacked'. Officers' slang; applied only to officers holding a command of some importance.

Bow Street: The orderly room. From the old and famous London police-court.

Box Open, Box Shut: A phrase used when offering cigarettes, the inference being that the donor's generosity was limited by hard circumstances. Those who were quick or near got a cigarette. Most soldiers kept a permanent tin, round or flat, into which were emptied the paper packets of 'issue' or canteen cigarettes, which otherwise would have been crushed to uselessness. As the soldier had to carry his whole store about with him, a box that would hold a hundred was more useful than a gold, silver, or gunmetal pocket case.

Bracketing: Trial shots to right and left, in front and behind the target, by the Artillery. (Cf. *Registering*.) In the Navy: *straddling*.

Brag: A card game not quite obsolete in 1914–18 and reputed have been so designated by 'The Old Bragg's' (28th Foot, now 1st Gloucesters), who may have invented it. Philip Bragg was colonel of the regiment in 1734–59. *Bank* (sometimes called *Banker*) was also popular. The most popular of Army gambling games were *House* and *Crown-and-Anchor*.

Brassard: Armlet. A white band with red (Geneva) cross woven on it. Used as a badge of recognition by personnel of military and international ambulances in time of war. Other brassards were used by officers of various branches (A., G. & Q.) of the General Staff. Regimental Police and others.

BRASS HATS: Generals and Senior Staff officers. So called because of the lavish display of gold lace on their caps. A less derisive variant: *Tabs*.

BRASS OFF, TO: Regular Army for to grumble.

BREAD AND JAM: A tram.

BREAK THROUGH: Noun and verb. An attack which penetrated the enemy's three successive lines of defence and created a possibility of open warfare. It rarely happened after 1914 on the Western Front.

BREAMY: Bad, chiefly in 'That's breamy'.

BREATHER: A short pause or period of rest in drill or during a piece of hard work, during which the men's breathing could slow down to normal.

BREEZE TO: The Regular Army variant of the civilian *blow*, to boast.

BREEZE-UP: Variation of *Wind-up* (cf.).

BRIDE AND GROOM: Broom.

BRIEF: A pass; furlough.

BRIGADE: An infantry brigade consisted of about 4,300 men in all, on the basis of 4 battalions at full strength and various complementary troops. In 1917–18 a brigade generally consisted of only 3 under strength battalions.

BRIGADIER-GENERAL: The officer commanding a brigade; the term used in 1914–18. *Brigadier* is the current equivalent. *Colonel-Commandant* pleased nobody and was soon discarded.

BRITISH WARM: An overcoat reaching only to the knees and close-fitting at the waist; worn by mounted troops and officers generally.

BROCK'S BENEFIT: The rockets and flares sent up at night from the opposing front lines, both for the detection of foes in No Man's Land and as signals. From civilian displays of fireworks and a manufacturer's name.

BUCK: Exaggeration or—usually as 'old buck'—insolence.

Also nickname for any man named Taylor. (Cf. *Nicknames*.)

BUCKLE: Short for *buckle-my-shoe*, a roundabout way of saying 'Jew'.

BUCKSHEE: Surplus; free; adjective applied to anything come by with unexpected ease, e.g. 'There's some buckshee rum going (cf.) tonight.' Also used as an adverb, e.g. 'I got this bread from the cookhouse, buckshee.' It was also used as a noun, meaning an extra share or surplus. 'Now the rice has gone round, what about a bit of buckshee?' A development of the Persian *bucksheesh*: a gratuity, a tip, but Regular soldiers pre-1914 took the word from Hindustani.

BUDDOO: Arab. *Bedu* or (plural) *Beduin*. Used by troops in Mesopotamia and Palestine.

BUGGER ALL: Nothing. An Australian soldier is said to have described the Egyptian desert as 'miles and miles and bloody miles of bugger all.'

BULL: Bullshit; not spit and polish but any kind of pretentiousness or incredible nonsense. (Cf. *Eye wash*.)

BULL-RING: Training grounds at the Base, where up-the-line soldiers, just out of Base hospitals and convalescent camps, were put through arduous 'courses' by P.T. and other instructors who had rarely, if at all, been under fire. From Spanish bull-fights because of the cruelty involved and the fact that the training ground was often sited on sand. The most notorious was at *Etaples* (cf.).

BULLY-BEEF: Corn or corned beef is beef cooked, preserved and tinned. Chiefly from the Argentine Republic. When the Company cooks got it, it was served in stew. When the cooks' 'services were not available', it was eaten cold or fried in the lid of a canteen. (Cf. *Emergency Rations, Orderly Man, Cooker* and *Canteen*.) Frequently abbreviated to *Bully*.

BUMF: Toilet paper or newspaper used for that purpose. Short for *bum-fodder*, an expression dating back to the seventeenth century (Urquhart). Also used, however, in a specifically military sense (chiefly officers' slang) for orders, instructions, memoranda, etc., especially if of a routine nature, e.g., 'Bags of bumf from Division (H.Q.).'

BUMP: The near-by explosion of a shell. Used as a verb almost always in the passive voice, e.g. 'We fairly got bumped last night.'

BUND: A bank or dam, e.g. Zillebeke Bund. Flemish.

BUNDLE OF TEN: A packet of cigarettes; from the Army roll of blankets.

BUNG, BUNGY, BUNG-HOLE: Cheese.

BUNK IN WITH: Share a bivvy or a funk-hole. Canadian.

BURBERRY: The town of Burbure on the Western Front. After a well-known make of rainproof 'trench coat' for officers.

BURGLARS: Bulgarians.

BURGUE (or BURGOO): Oatmeal porridge. Pronounced by English troops with a hard *g* and the final vowel sound – *ew*; by Australians with a hard *g* but with the last syllable – *oo*. First recorded use 1750. Found in Marryat 1833 and Sala 1863. Occasionally applied by Australians to stew. From *burghul*, Turkish and Arabic for wheat-porridge.

'BUS: Royal Air Force slang, affectionate and facetious, for an aeroplane. As the term is of R.N.A.S. origin, perhaps it is from *buss*, a smack, a small boat.

BUSHEL AND PECK: The neck.

BUSINESS: The French town, Busnes.

BUTCHER'S: Short for *Butcher's Hook*, a look; especially in 'Let's have a butcher's.' (Cf. *Dekko, Look See.*)

BUTTERFLY BOAT: A leave boat.

BUTT-NOTCHER: A sniper. Some snipers kept a tally of the successes they claimed by notching the butts of their rifles.

BUTTON-STICK: See note on p. 66.

BUY, TO: To believe an unlikely story.

BUZZ, TO: To send a message on the Buzzer.

BUZZER: A telegraphic instrument (portable telephone D, mark D3) which could also be used for spoken messages.

BYNG BOYS, THE: The Canadians; from the name of their 1917 commander, Lord Byng, and prompted by the popular revue *The Bing Boys.*

C3: Early in the war only men fit for active service were accepted. Afterwards recruits were enlisted for Home, Garrison and Base duties, and were graded according to physical fitness, A1, B2, B3. C3 was the lowest category. Wounded men were also classified during convalescence in this manner. *C3* thus became a term of contempt – *not* applied to a man who *was C3*, but, by analogy, to a thing or an action.

CA NE FAIT RIEN: See *San Fairy Ann.*

CABLE-TRENCH: One in which telephone wires were buried, the operation being *to lay a cable*; often a very unpleasant job, for the cable-trench, being preferably straight, could easily be enfiladed while it was being dug.

CADRE: A nucleus of a hundred or less officers and other ranks from a battalion. As the war progressed it was found that a battalion put into an attack would almost certainly lose anything from 50 to 90 per cent of its strength in casualties – far more than in the old-fashioned 'decimation' – one in ten. It was extremely difficult to build up the shell-shocked and dispirited remainder, even with reinforcements, into an efficient battalion. Hence arose the practice of keeping a cadre out of the action so that a continuity of organization could be preserved.

CADY: Hat. Pre-1914 civilian, but often used by soldiers in off-parade reference to service caps. Rhymes with 'lady.'

CAGE: A barbed-wire enclosure close behind the lines to hold recently taken prisoners of war. A temporary prison for our own men was sometimes called *the bird-cage*. Shakespeare used *cage* = prison in 1593 and the word was good English in the seventeenth century; during the next century it became slang and finally was degraded to the status of cant.

CAGNAS: Barracks. In use among Canadian troops; a development from French soldiers' slang *cagna(t)*, a trench-shelter or (less often) a room; originally an Annamite word.

CAIN AND ABEL: Table.

CAKE WALK: Any enterprise turning out to be unexpectedly easy. From a pre-1914 popular dance of American Negro origin.

CAMEL: A Sopwith scouting 'plane.

CAMEL CORPS: Infantry; from the heavy weights loaded on to their backs.

CAMELLIA: A member of the Imperial Camel Corps in Palestine and Egypt. An Australianism.

CAMOUFLAGE: French, now fully adopted into English. The act of concealing positions from enemy observation; or the means employed for the purpose. Guns were painted in parti-colours and roads were hung with wire-netting on which fluttered 'scrim', small pieces of brown and green rag. The practice was initiated by Solomon J. Solomon, R.A., in 1916. Not to be confused with the *Dazzle-Painting* used on ships; this latter was invented by Lieut.-Commander Norman Wilkinson. Soldiers adopted 'camouflage' as a useful variant of *eye-wash* (cf.).

CAMOUFLET: First recorded in English in this form in 1836, but centuries earlier as *moflet*, this word denoted the blowing-in of enemy galleries by counter-mining.

CANARY: An instructor at the Bull Ring; so called from the yellow brassard he wore.

CANE, TO: To shell, especially to shell heavily.

CANISTER-SHOT, CASE-SHOT: Old-fashioned military terms sometimes applied to shrapnel.

CANNED UP: Drunk.

CANNON-FODDER: All combatant soldiers below the rank of, say, major: especially the infantry. A journalistic expression, only used with the implication of quotation, by soldiers. Of German origin.

CANTEEN: A tin receptacle carried in the infantryman's equipment, enclosed in a cotton cover, immediately under his valise (cf. *Pack*). The artillery, cavalry, and other mounted troops had a canteen shaped like a cylinder; the infantry *canteen* was, looked at from above, about three-quarters of an oval. It was in two parts, one fitting into the other. In his *canteen* the soldier received, at different times, from the orderly man all his cooked food – stew, tea, soup, rice, porridge in the lower and deeper section, bacon in the shallower top. When cooked food was not available, he cooked his own in his canteen over a fire or a *'Tommy'* *Cooker* (cf.). Also cf. *Orderly Man, Dixie, Dish Out.*

In another sense a canteen was an officially-appointed bar and grocer's shop and tobacconist's, organized by the unit. There were sometimes two, a dry and wet canteen; but usually only one – the dry. Both tended to run short of supplies and to lead a very intermittent existence. They really flourished only during periods of Divisional Rest out of the line. See also *E.F.C.*

CANTEEN MEDALS: Beer stains on the breast of a tunic. Pre-1914 Regular Army.

CANTEEN RAT: An old soldier who constantly hung about in or near the canteen in the hope of being stood a drink.

CANTEEN STINKER: An inferior cigarette.

CANTEEN WALLAH: A man addicted to beer. (Cf. the civilian *pub-crawler*.)

CAP BADGE: A piece of bone; a bone with but little meat on it; a bone found in a stew.

CAP COMFORTER: A sack, about 18 inches long, of khaki knitted wool used for storing odds and ends and, off parade and in the line, in a rolled up form, as a cap for cold weather, patrols, fatigues and so on.

CAP OFF: When a man was reported by an N.C.O. or an officer as having committed a military crime, such as appearing on parade with a button unfastened or his hair more than one-eighth of an inch long, he was ordered to present himself next morning to his Company Commander (or, if his were a repeated or more serious offence, to his Commanding Officer). To be more precise, he did not present himself but was presented: two men acting as escort, one in front and one behind; the Sergeant-Major ordering them in after this fashion: 'Cap Off!' – to the prisoner. 'Prisoner and escort, right turn! quick march! left wheel! right turn! halt!' So, capless, beltless, flanked on either side by his escort, his heels together, his thumbs in line with the seams of his trousers, his eyes staring to his front, the offender heard the charge against him read out in cumbersome and almost meaningless phrases. He was asked what he had to say in defence or mitigation, but was usually too bewildered (or too old a soldier) to utter a word. If he did attempt an explanation, he might be cut short by a bored officer, or else by a bellow from the sergeant-major ordering him to look to his front or to straighten his pose. Once the machinery of military law was set in motion, there was little injustice done, except what is inherent in its rough-and-ready methods. Injustices began before that. If a private soldier incurred the dislike of an unscrupulous superior, his life might be made a misery and there was no way of escape for him from a thousand daily vexations and petty punishments.

The convention of compelling a prisoner to remove his cap was universal: in some battalions he was allowed to hold it in his hand, in others the escort or the sergeant-major took charge of it for fear (it was rumoured) the prisoner lost his temper and flung the cap at his judges. The prisoner was compelled to enter without a belt or 'side-arms' (i.e. bayonet) for a similar reason. This may have been due to prudence in the C.O., but more probably was intended to prevent a desperate man steeping himself in further crime. For the procedure of an English court-martial, see A. P. Herbert's *The Secret Battle*; for that of a German, see A. J. Evans's *The Escaping Club*. (Cf. *Orders* and *High Jump*.)

CAPE OF GOOD HOPE: Soap.

CAPTAIN COOK: A book.

CARACHOU: Good. From Russian. Frequently used by prisoners of war in Germany.

CARL: *Carl the caretaker*, or *Hans the Grenadier, is in charge* was applied to a quiet sector of the line.

CARNEY: Sly; artful. A development from dialectal *carney*, 'soft, hypocritical language. Also, to flatter, wheedle, or insinuate oneself' (Hotten).

CARPET-SLIPPER BASTARD: A heavy shell passing far overhead, therefore with but a faint noise.

CARRIER PIGEONS: Used extensively during the War. The unit of the Pigeon Service was a *Loft*. In the Museum of the Royal United Services Institution, London, is to be seen 'the V.C. Pigeon'.

CARVING KNIFE: Wife; cf. *Trouble and Strife*.

CASABIANCA: The last one, especially of cigarettes. From the poem 'The boy stood on the burning deck
        Whence all but he had fled.'

CAT WALK: Pathway of bricks across French and Belgium farm fields; often only one brick wide.

CATAPULT: The West Spring Gun used in the front line for throwing grenades; the springs were tautened with a winch. Often the bombs only just cleared the parapet and burst short of the enemy position.

CATEGORY MAN: One pronounced unfit for active service.

CATSOOD: i.e. *quatre-sou'd*. Drunk. *Catsoos* = a drink.

C.B.: Confined to barracks. A minor punishment, applicable only out of the line. A soldier on C.B. had to report, during what would normally be his free time, to the guard-room at regular intervals. He was also liable for extra fatigues.

C.C.S.: Casualty Clearing Station. Tents or huts behind the lines where operations were performed, and wounded were classified into dangerous, slight and 'return to England' cases.

CHALK FARM: Arm; cf. *Fire-Alarm*.

CHAR: Tea. From the Hindustani. Compare Arabic *chai*.

CHARGER: A metal clip holding five rounds of ammunition for a rifle.

CHARLIE CHAPLIN: A C.C. moustache, worn by some officers; about half an inch in width. The *Tooth brush* moustache, which averaged more than twice the width of a C.C. and covered most of the upper lip, was rather the 'property' of the rank and file. From October, 1916, the other ranks could grow a moustache or not as they pleased.

CHARLIE CHAPLIN'S ARMY CORPS: Canadian Casualty Assembly Centre at Shorncliffe, England.

CHARMING WIFE: A knife.

CHATT: The louse. The word may be used in the singular, but the insect was found (or it escaped) in hordes. *Chatt* is given by Grose, who suggests it may be derived from *Chattell*, i.e. something personal, carried about. From this noun developed the verb, meaning to rid oneself of some of the parasites by searching uniform and underwear, especially along the seams, and cracking the lice between the thumb-nails. They squelched blood, not their own! Another and better method was to take off the garment and run the seams over a candle flame. A vivid crackling noise announced the death of both *chatts* and their eggs. *Chatts* were not fleas or bugs; they did not jump but crept. They were a pale fawn in colour, and left blotchy red bite marks all over the body except in the hair of the head. They also created a distinctive sour, stale smell. Living in the same clothes without a bath for weeks on end, it was impossible for a private soldier not to become *chatty*, and the most thorough *chattings* were little more than demonstrations of ill-will. A bath and a change of clothing at a *delousing station* (cf.) was the only remedy – and this happened rarely. As time went on, *chatting* became part of normal routine during quiet and rest periods; indeed, it was almost a social occasion, and in huts or dug-outs during the winter, and outdoors if there was summer sunshine, groups of men could be seen with their shirts or trousers or tunics laid over their knees, cracking lice and jokes together. What became of the uncountable millions of the parasites after the War ended no one knows. It was alleged that they were indigenous to the soil of Northern France and Flanders, but they flourished also in Gallipoli. On the other hand, captured German dug-outs on the Western Front sometimes had a species of small red lice crawling over their walls and blankets. Déchelette in his dictionary of French soldiers' slang has this priceless remark: '*Les gaux [poux] craignent la solitude et ont un profond sentiment de la famille.*' He adds: '*Les gaux ont une chambre à coucher bien chaude, bien douillette, où la table est toujours mise. Alors, dans leurs nombreux loisirs, ils suivent les conseils du créateur: ils multiplient.*' He notes that lice quitted a man soon after he was killed, i.e. when the corpse became cold.

CHEERIO: See *Cheero*.

CHEERO: A salutation. Perhaps derived from the pre-1914 Cockney *what cheer!* The word was later developed, chiefly by officers, into *Cheerio*. (Cf. *Chin-Chin* and *Be Good*.)

CHERRY NOB: Military policeman; cf. *Red Cap*.

CHERRY RIPE: Pipe.

CHESTNUTS: Bullets. Cf. French *pruneaux, châtaignes, marrons*, of which the first and third were also compounded with *pralines* to mean the same thing.

CHEVRON: The original *chevrons* were always called *stripes* (c.f.). Later in the war a system was instituted by which soldiers wore on the lower right sleeve small *chevrons*, about an inch wide; one of these indicated that the wearer had seen active service, and one more was added for each completed year of active service. 1914 was denoted by a red *chevron*; later years by blue. (Cf. *Gold Stripe*.)

CHEW THE FAT: To sulk, to be resentful. Especially to grumble or argue at length. e.g. 'Stop chewing the fat and get the job done!'

CHEW THE RAG: To argue endlessly or without hope of a definite agreement. This phrase and the preceding one belong to the Regular Army; the distinction between them cannot precisely be defined.

CHINA: Short for *China plate*, rhyming slang for mate. *Old* was frequently added to the vocative.

CHIN-CHIN: Comes from the Chinese; spoken as a vague toast just before drinking liquor, implying general goodwill, satisfaction and hope. (Cf. *Cheero* and *Be Good.*)

CHINESE ATTACK A feint attack.

CHINK: A Chinese. There was a large Chinese Labour Corps employed behind the lines and at the Bases on the Western Front. They were liked because they were good-natured and amusing, but they were not often to be seen actually at work. (Cf. *Goody-la! Ruski, Macaroni, Froggie, Pork-and-Beans, Aussie, Yank.*)

CHINNY: Sugar. From Hindustani.

CHIN-STRAP: Except by mounted troops the *chin-straps* of khaki field-service caps were never used. A steel helmet, however, was liable to fall off and the chin-strap was often lowered round the jaw. Many a man, however, preferred to keep it hanging loosely on the back of the neck for fear a bullet or fragment of shrapnel, striking the helmet, should cause the strap to choke him or break his jaw. The phrase *to come in on your chin-strap* meant to finish a march or a carrying party so fatigued that (figuratively) only the *chin-strap* kept the body upright.

CHIPS: Pioneer Sergeant. In nautical and civilian slang, *chips* = a carpenter.

CHIT: (From Hindustani *chitthi.*) Any sort of handwritten message or authorization.

CHOKEY: Prison; guard-room. From Hindustani.

CHOW: Food. Adopted from sailors' slang and originating in the East.

CHRONIC: Very bad: adjective or adverb. Taken probably from medical idiom, without any idea of its meaning, merely with a vague association of unhappiness. Used especially in the phrase, 'The pain's something chronic.' (Cf. *Proper*.)

CHUBARROW: Shut up! Hold your tongue! Often shortened to *Chub*. (From Hindustani *chuprao*.)

CHUCK A DUMMY: To faint on parade.

CHUM: More popular, at least with non-Cockney troops, than either *mate* or *pal*. Used also as a vocative, especially in addressing strangers, e.g. 'Give us (i.e. me) a light, chum?' Almost invariably used in the opening phrase when speaking to a man just wounded.

It dates back to the seventeenth century, when it was applied to intimate friends at Oxford or Cambridge. *The Dictionary of the Canting Crew*, 1690, defines 'chum' as 'a chamber-fellow, or constant companion'. The word appears also in the dictionaries of Dr Johnson and Captain Grose.

CHUM, LONG-EARED: A mule. *Long-faced chum* = a horse. But *long-haired chum* = a girl, a sweetheart.

CHUPATTY: Usual nineteenth-century spelling *chow-patty*; Hindustani *chapati*. The N.E.D.: 'A small cake of un-leavened bread, generally made of coarse wheaten meal, flattened with the hand, and baked on a griddle'. One hardly ever saw an Indian soldier without some chupatties; he managed to cook for himself even at Gallipoli.

CHUPRASSY: Hindustani *chaprasi*, the wearer of a *chapras* or official badge. In civilian use, a messenger, etc.; in Army use, an Indian orderly.

C.-IN-C.: Commander-in-Chief.

CIRCUS: A combination of German fighting aeroplanes under Count von Richthofen, which at one period was all-conquering. So called from their habit of circling round and round one British or French machine at a time, from the bright colours in which the machines were painted, or from the fact that these squadrons moved from sector to sector of the front.

CIVVIES: Civilian clothes. Dates in the Army from ca. 1850.

CIVVY: Civilian: adjective or noun. A word freighted with much emotion, envy, fond memories and eternal hope. See the songs, 'When this Blasted War is Over' (page 57) and 'I Wore a Tunic' (page 47).

CLACK: A rumour. ? Scottish.

101

CLICK: To strike up a temporary acquaintance for sentimental purposes with a stranger of the opposite sex in the street or other public place. A modern use of the word, easily understood, from the slight noise made when two parts fit easily together. *Clicking* always began with a mingling of glances: it was at once realized that two moods and two desires fitted, for the moment, perfectly. *To click for* something fortunate was another variation, e.g., 'Bill's clicked for leave.'

CLICKETY-CLICK: 66, especially in the game of House. Onamapoeic.

CLIENT FOR ROUEN: A 'venereal' case.

CLINK: The guard-room in which offenders against military law were detained pending trial by the C.O. or Court Martial. The *Clink* was a criminal's name for a prison in Southwark. Grose suggests the clinking of fetters as the origin. (Cf. *Jug.*)

CLOBBER: Clothing; especially when off the body. Also equipment in general. A gipsy and costermonger word.

CLOCK: Face. Used in derision or boisterous fun. (Cf. *Dial.*)

CLOD: To shell. Nearly always intransitive.

CLOTHES PEGS: Legs.

CLUTCHING HAND, THE: The quartermaster sergeant.

COAL UP!: Pay-day. *Coal* or *cole*, thieves' cant for money in the seventeenth and eighteenth centuries, was revived by Barham in the *Ingoldsby Legends*.

COAL-BOX: The shellburst of a 5.9 or heavier shell. From the black smoke. Sometimes used of the shell itself. (Cf. *Johnson* and *Crump.*)

COBBER: A comrade, a friend; used also as a vocative. An Australianism and, like *cliner* = sweetheart, derived from Hebrew; *chaber*, a comrade, appears also in Yiddish.

COCK AND HEN: Ten.

C.O.: Commanding Officer. Usually in the infantry a Lieutenant-Colonel in command of a battalion. Cf. O.C.; O. i/c.

C.O.D.: A blessing on an outgoing, a comment on an incoming shell. 'Cash on Delivery.' (Cf. the French *Colis-Postal* (*franco de port et d'emballage*) used of German five-inch shells.

COFFIN-NAILS: Cigarettes, especially cheap ones. Pre-1914. Sometimes abbreviated to *Nails*.

COLCO-PARI: How much? Salonican front.

COLD FEET: Cowardice, temperamental and permanent, or of a temporary bout of fear. (Cf. *wind-up*.)

COLD, HAVE SOMEONE: To have the upper hand of.

COLD MEAT TICKET: *Identity disc* (cf.).

COLD STORAGE: Cells, prison.

COLNEY HATCH: Mad, from the lunatic asylum north of London. As rhyming slang = a match.

COLT GUN: The Canadian Corps used the Colt machine-gun for some time.

COLUMN OF BLOBS, or LUMPS: Column of Route which was both a drill order and a marching formation. (Cf. *Route*.)

COME THE ACID: To swank. *Put the acid on* meant to ask for money or some other favour.

COME THE BAG: To make oneself a nuisance or objectionable in almost any way.

COME THE OLD SOLDIER: To dodge unpleasant duties; to bluff; to boast.

COME UNSTUCK: To fail; to be reduced in rank. By the other ranks used in a general sense; by officers only in the second sense, not uninfluenced by the French *dégommé*, ungummed, *i.e.* reduced in rank.

COMFORTER: See CAP COMFORTER.

COM TRENCH: Communication trench. See C.T.

COMIC CUTS: An Intelligence summary or report. Officers' slang.

COMMANDEER: To take possession of, more or less legitimately, as in the case of an officer 'commandeering a billet'.

COMMO: Communication Trench. See C. T.

COMPANY: In an infantry battalion at full strength, about 240 men; on active service often 150 or less.

COMPLAINTS: A private soldier had to make his *complaints* through his platoon sergeant, though he could request to be taken before his Commanding Officer. In practice, it was wiser not to make *complaints*.

COMPLAINTS, ANY: The standardized enquiry made by the orderly sergeant, accompanying the orderly officer on a round of barracks or huts or tents at dinner time.

Comsah: Generic name for anything. Alternative to *Oojah* (cf.). From the French comme ça.

Con Camp: Convalescent camp, to which men discharged from an overseas hospital were sent, and where they sometimes recuperated.

Concertina Wire: Wire used for entanglements; when touched, it coiled about the intruder. Sometimes barbed, sometimes not.

Conk (out), To: To fail, of an engine. Hardly, if at all, used in 1914–18 in the sense of to die.

Conshie, properly *Conscie*: From popular journalism. A conscientious objector to military service. Some refused to bear arms: others went further and refused to participate in manual or clerical labour behind the lines or at home. Some were suspected of hypocrisy by the fighting troops, some were admired by them.

Consolidate: To maintain an advantage, especially to curry favour with authority in order that a cushy job might be continued. From the technical *consolidate* – to fortify and make secure a captured trench or other position.

Contemptibles, Old: The original Expeditionary Force. Journalese, allegedly from a speech by the Kaiser in which he referred to the 'contemptible little British Army'. The phrase should perhaps have been rendered as 'contemptibly small'.

'Continental News, The': A defeatist (nominally neutral and impartial) newspaper issued by the enemy to prisoners of war.

Contour-Chasing: Flying very low. Air Force.

Convoy: Noun and verb. To protect vessels carrying troops or supplies by having ships-of-war accompany them.

Cooker: Travelling field-kitchen, wheeled and pulled by horses and mules. In these company cooks made tea, stew, porridge, rice, etc., and sometimes took the 'cookers' remarkably close to the front line. (Cf. *Dixie, Orderly Man, Burgue*.)

Cookhouse Official: A baseless rumour.

Cook's Tour: A visit to the front, made, during a quiet period, by Members of Parliament, journalists and other civilians.

Cooler: The guard-room; cells. Originally American thieves' slang.

Coop: The same. Dates from ca. 1860.

COOT: A louse. Pre-war cockney: said to be derived from the name of a titled lady who suffered in this way. (Cf. *Chat.*) Adjective: *cooty.*

CORDITE: Explosive used as propellant for shells and bullets. Malingerers extracted the strings of cordite from the .303 rifle-cartridge and chewed them, thus acquiring a high temperature: the effect did not last long and the ruse was not often successful.

CORDUROY ROAD: See *Wooden Track.*

CORKSCREW-STAKE: A metal stake for supporting barbed-wire, shaped not unlike a corkscrew. It did not have to be knocked into the ground but was screwed in, with little or no noise.

CORP: Familiar for Corporal. Used only in the vocative.

COSH: An improvised wooden club, twelve inches or more long, the head weighted with lead, used by night raiders especially when they were seeking to bring back prisoners. See *Knobkerry.*

CORPSE FACTORY: Many people believed that the Germans were driven to obtaining fats by melting corpses. This particular rumour perhaps arose from the fact that many of the German dead were sent to Germany for burial.

CORPSE TICKET: *Identity disc.* cf.

CORRECT: The correct number; the required quantity. (*Up*) *to correct,* to the correct number, etc. See *Roll Call.*

COUNTER-BATTERY FIRE: Almost half the artillery's fire is said to have been directed at enemy gun positions.

COVERING FIRE: Rifle and machine-gun fire given from another position, in front or on the flank, to keep the enemy inactive while a party of troops moved forward or back or performed some special task.

COUNTERSTRAFE: To *strafe* in retaliation. An officers' (and artillery) expression.

COURSE: A 'refresher' *course* of instruction given behind the lines to which selected officers, N.C.O.'s and men were sent on occasion. There were *courses* in bombing, Lewis-gunnery, signalling, physical training, map reading, and other subjects: it was soon fairly obvious that the courses were devised more for the recreation of these soldiers who had had long spells of duty in the line than for the direct improvement of efficiency.

105

COVERING PARTY: A body of rifleman or bombers lying out in front of a working party in order to protect them from enemy interference.

COW: Milk. Canadian term.

COXEY'S ARMY: A ragtime army. Canadian term.

CRAB GRENADE: An oblong, flat German hand-grenade.

CRABS: A variety of lice or perhaps an alternative name for them. (Cf. *Chatt*.)

CRAPPO: One kind of improvised trench-mortar used by the French. French *crapaud*, a toad. But the French themselves used *crapaud* of a German grenade, the *Diskushandgranate*, and had the analogous terms *crapouillot* and *tortue*.

CRATE: An aeroplane (British).

CRATER: Especially a shell- or mine-crater. The great mine-crater at La Boisselle, blown on July 1, 1916, at the beginning of the Somme push, contained 27 tons of gun-cotton; it was said to be the largest crater on the Western Front. *Crater* is recorded in 1839 in this military sense of a cavity caused by an explosion.

CRAWLING WITH: Infested with lice or, metaphorically, with people disapproved of, e.g. crawling with Red Caps.

CREASED: Unconscious; knocked out.

CREATE: To grumble; make a fuss. Short for *create a disturbance*. The word has passed into civilian slang.

CREEPING BARRAGE: Not only used in a technical sense but applied metaphorically in convalescent camps where men were divided into four groups according to physical fitness. A man had to show that he could march a certain distance before progressing from one group to another. The weakest marched or walked so slowly that the term 'Creeping barrage' was applied to them.

CRICKET BALL: A kind of hand-grenade.

CRIME SHEET: A record of a soldier's trials and punishments under Military law.

CROAKER: The Medical Officer. Possibly from *to croak*, to die. Alternatively a variant of *quacker* or *quack*, civilian slang for any medical man.

CROWD: Like *Crush*, *Outfit*, *Mob*, and *Push*, a colloquial synonym for any Army unit.

CROWN AND ANCHOR: Prohibited but not very actively discouraged, this gambling game was extremely popular in

1914–18. It needed dice and a cloth, marked out in squares; stakes were set down on the squares. One variation or another of the following patter was used by the man acting as Banker.

'Lay it down, my lucky lads; the more you put down the more you pick up. You come here on bicycles, you go away in Rolls Royces. The old firm, all the way from 'Olloway. What about the lucky old mud-hook? The old mud-hook's badly backed. Any more for any more before we turn 'em up? Lay it down, my lucky lads, thick and heavy. Have you all finished, have you all done? Right, up she comes. Two jam tarts and the lucky old sergeant-major.' Mud hook = anchor. Jam tart = heart. Sergeant-major = crown.

CRUCIFIX CORNER: On the Western Front almost any cross-roads or intersection of roads with a Calvary.

CRUMMY: Itchy because of louse-bites. (Cf. *Chatt.*)

CRUMP: Synonymous with *Coal-box*. Also as verb, to shell with 'heavies'.

C.S.M.: Company Sergeant Major.

C.T.: Communication Trench, i.e. one not facing the enemy and not prepared for defence.

CUBBY HOLE: A small dug-out or shelter. Perhaps from fox-hunting. Or from *cupboard*. (Cf. *Dug-out.*)

CUCKOO: Only in the phrase, 'lousy as a cuckoo'.

CULLY: A pal. From thieves' cant; very old.

CUP AND WAD: Tea and a bun: at canteen or Y.M.C.A., Church Army or Salvation Army hut.

CURTAIN FIRE: A concentration of shell fire between a body of troops and the enemy. Not necessarily for an attack or withdrawal. (Cf. *Barrage.*)

CUSHY: Soft; comfortable; luxurious. Especially, safe where danger was the general rule. Other people were always getting cushy jobs. Typical uses were, 'This is a cushy sector'; 'He's been having a cushy time.' (From Hindustani.)

CUTHBERT: A fit man of military age ensconced in a Government office; also, any other shirker. Journalese.

DAB ON THE DOOK: A tip; literally a pat on the hand. From Cockney, rhyming slang where *dooks* is a corruption of *dukes*, short for *Duke of Yorks* = forks, *forks* being slang for fingers, *fingers* being synecdoche for a hand.

DADOS: Deputy Assistant Director of Ordnance Services; one to each division.

DAG UP: To smarten up one's appearance.

DAISY ROOTS: Boots.

DAMN ALL: Nothing. Used to give emphasis. E.g. 'I worked my guts out all day and what did I get? – damn all!' A bowdlerization. (Cf. *Bugger All* and *Sweet Fanny Adams*.)

DAPS: Slippers. Regular Army.

DARKY: Prefix or synonym for the surname Smith. Probably of Cockney origin. (Cf. *Nicknames*.)

D.C.M.: Most civilians knew that this stood for Distinguished Conduct Medal. To some soldiers its first connotation, however, was District Court Martial.

DEAD BEAT: Utterly fatigued; worn out and past caring. Frequently varied to *Beaten to the Wide*. Probably from the old days of penal flogging for slight offences. (Cf. *Chin Strap*.)

DEAD, ON THE: Teetotal. Regular Army.

DEAD SOLDIER: A bottle of beer or other 'booze' that has been 'killed', i.e. emptied.

DEAD NUTS: Enthusiastic, keen, desirous, e.g. 'He's dead nuts on vin blanc.'

DEATH SENTENCE: The Army Act provided for the sentence to be carried out by either shooting or hanging. Sunrise was the customary hour. In *Statistics of the Military Effort of the British Empire during the Great War*, 1914–1920, published by His Majesty's Stationery Office in 1922, there is the following record.

DEATH SENTENCES CARRIED OUT
in the British Army, 1914–1920

Offence	Officers	Soldiers	Total
Mutiny	—	3	3
Cowardice . . .	—	18	18
Desertion . . .	2	264	266
Murder	1	36	37
Striking or Violence . .	—	6	6
Disobedience . . .	—	5	5
Sleeping on post . .	—	2	2
Quitting post . . .	—	7	7
Casting away arms . .	—	2	2
	3	343	346

DEBUS: To get, or be got, out of a bus – a rare form of military transport in 1914–18. The infantry occasionally travelled by train. (Cf. *Homforty*), but almost always marched.

DECEAUVILLE: Light tramway behind the lines; used to bring up R.E. stores, etc. It may be obscurely connected with the cant word *daisyville*, *deuseauville*, the countryside.

DEKKO: Look! Watch! (From Hindustani imperative of *dekhna*.) Also used as a noun, e.g. 'Let's have a dekko at the wire.' (Cf. *Butcher's, Look See.*)

DE-LOUSING STATION: Huts where troops out of the line or proceeding on leave could have a bath and exchange their lice-ridden clothing, not for new but for old garments which had been baked in ovens at a temperature which, it was believed, was sufficiently high to kill off lice. (Cf. *Chatt.*)

DEMOB: Demobilisation. A magic word after November 11, 1918.

DEMONSTRATION: A 'show' bombardment, i.e. not one to prepare for or to support an attack. Often used figuratively.

DEPOT: The headquarters of a regiment in 'Blighty'; also a place for military stores.

DERBY MEN: Men recruited under a voluntary scheme instituted, (just before conscription became law) by Lord Derby. It was understood that young, unmarried men were to be called up for service first.

DER TAG: German for 'The Day' which meant variously: 'The day when we Germans declare war on' or 'conquer England', 'come into our own'. Popularized by journalists; used by officers, often facetiously for any much-desired date or goal.

DESERT, SWING IT ACROSS THE: To malinger; to get oneself into hospital. Used in Egypt, Palestine, Mesopotamia.

DEVIL-DODGER: A scripture-reader or a chaplain.

DEVIL'S WOOD: Delville Wood, on the Somme.

DHOBI: Laundryman. From India: Regular Army.

DIAL: Face. (Cf. *Clock.*)

DICKY DIRT: Shirt.

DIG ONESELF IN: Figuratively, to hold on to a cushy job.

DIGGER: Used by Australian Troops as a vocative for either a personal friend or a stranger, e.g. 'Hello, digger, what about a drink?' Derived from the first days of the goldfields in Australia when the word was used to distinguish the holder of mining rights over a few square yards from a 'squatter' or farmer. In time, *the diggers* became a fairly common term for Australian troops and (among British troops) sometimes for New Zealanders. Later in the war it was sometimes used as a vocative by English soldiers in place of the commoner 'chum'.

DINGBAT: A batman. Australianism.

DINGO: Slightly insane. Probably from the French slang *dingot* = mad, eccentric. *Dingot* is an altered abbreviation of *louftingue* = mad. But Dauzat gives: '*La 'dingue' est la fièvre paludéenne* (marsh fever) *qui rend 'dingot', c'est-à-dire toqué.*'

DINGHY: Dengue, a disease only too well known in Macedonia.

DINKUM: Australian slang. An adjective meaning good, satisfactory, genuine, excellent, delightful. Among Australian troops 'The Dinkums' were those who had been in Gallipoli.

DINKY: A mule.

DINKY-DOO: The number 22, especially at the game of House. Onomatopoeic.

DIPPY: Temporarily insane; foolish; unduly simple. E.g. 'You're a bit dippy this morning, aren't you?' Perhaps from 'dipsomania'. (Cf. *Doolally, Tapped, Touched.*)

DIRECTION-BOARDS: Wooden signboards at cross-roads and sap-heads or trench-entrances.

DIRT: Shells.

DIRTY WORK AT THE CROSS-ROADS TONIGHT: A pre-1914 catch-phrase from melodrama. Used by the troops figuratively and sometimes for enemy shellfire concentrated on cross-roads.

DISH OUT: To distribute in equal portions. Cooked food was 'dished out' by the orderly men of the day; other rations by the corporal of the section. Sometimes this was an argumentative process. Used by officers of an indiscriminate award of decorations. (Cf. *Orderly Man, Dixie.*)

DITCHED: Out of action, especially of a tank.

DIVISION: Three brigades of infantry plus artillery, engineers etc. Nominally 12–20,000 men. Commanded by a major-general. (Cf. *Army, Army Corps, Brigade.*)

110

DIVISIONAL COMIC CUTS: Soldiers' term for cheering communiqués issued from Divisional Headquarters, in which some of the information was known to be false and the rest was suspect. *Comic Cuts* was, pre-1914, a cheap humorous periodical for the very young.

DIVVY: Division. Also: to divide, to share, usually as divvy up or divvy out.

DIXIE: A large iron pot, oval, with an iron lid and a thin white metal handle devised to bite into the hands carrying it. Stew, rice, porridge, soup and tea were boiled in the *dixie*; bacon and biscuit-pudding were cooked in the lid. The word is not from the United States but India: *degschai*, a cooking-pot. (Cf. *Orderly Man, Canteen* and *Bully-Beef.*)

DO: Noun. An attack or raid. (Cf. *Stunt, Show.*) Also, a party or celebration with liquid and other refreshments.

DO A GUY: To desert. Extension of an Americanism.

DO AN ALLEY: To go; to depart rapidly, from the French 'aller'.

DO DOWN: To over-charge.

DO IN: To kill; to murder. Pre-1914.

DO ONE'S BIT: (to win the war). To enlist and, more especially, to serve on one of the fronts overseas.

DOCK: Hospital, used only in the phrase *in dock*. The metaphor is taken from ships going into dock for repairs.

DOCTOR, THE: The No. 9 pill; also the number 9 in House, in which a variant was *Doctor's Shop*. (Cf. *Sick.*)

DODGING THE COLUMN: The art and science of advoiding unpleasant and especially dangerous duties. The phrase originated in India and South Africa where a column was a mobile body of troops sent forward into hostile country. (Cf. *Swinging the Lead* and *Wangle.*)

DOG: Swank. An Australianism, as in 'carrying too much dog'.

DOG AND MAGGOT: Biscuit and cheese. Regular Army.

DOG FIGHT: A fight between two small groups of airplanes.

DOG'S LEG: A lance-corporal's stripe.

DOING IT: Doingt, a town near Péronne.

DOINGS: A general term, like *oojah* and *cumsah* (cf.) for anything which the speaker is too lazy to mention by its proper name. E.g. 'Hand me the doings, will you?' Also,

111

specifically, for the front line, an attack or a bombardment. E.g. 'We're going up into the doings tonight.'

DOLLY: Nickname for anyone named Gray. From a popular song of the South African War period. (Cf. *Nicknames*.)

DOOLALLY: Mad, insane, not normal. More literally, sunstroke. From Deolali(e), name of a sanitorium in Bombay. A variation was *doolally tap*, e.g. 'Ever since his mate went west, he's been doolally tap.' *Tap* is the Hindustani for fever; in Macedonia a slight sunstroke was called *Balkan-tap*. (Cf. *Tapped*, *Touched* and *Dippy*.)

DOOR KNOB: A bob, i.e. a shilling.

D.O.R.A.: The Defence of the Realm Act: a multiplicity of regulations affecting everyone in Great Britain. (Cf. *Blues*.)

DOUGH: Money. Pre-1914 American.

DOUGH-BOYS: American soldiers; their own name. They disliked being called *Yanks* and *Sammies*.

DOWN: *To get down to it* meant, to go to sleep, to lie flat and get under a blanket.

DOWN THE LINE: Away from the front line towards the Base.

DRAFT: A miscellaneous body of men selected from a depôt in England or at the Base abroad to proceed as reinforcements to a unit up the line. Once arrived at its battalion or battery or other headquarters the *draft* would be split up and absorbed into various subdivisions of the unit. A peculiar awareness of their own impermanent association pervaded *drafts*; old soldiers were cynical and depressed, new soldiers curious and elated, and every *draft* was actuated by intense emotions and – leaving England at least – often by liquor.

DRILL ORDER: Infantry equipment much reduced for drill parades. (Cf. *Battle Order*, *Marching Order*.)

DRUM FIRE: Concentrated artillery fire in one sector, the guns of each battery firing not in salvoes but one after another, so that on each target there was always a shell bursting or about to burst. *Drum* from the continuous *roll* of such a bombardment.

DRUM UP: To make tea in a *canteen* (cf.). Pre-1914 navvyese: the drum is the navvy's 'billycan'.

DUBBIN: Issued for the 'water-proofing' of boots, but with a piece of four-by-two (cf.) for a wick, dubbin made a passable nightlight.

DUCKBOARD: A device for flooring trenches and making foot-tracks across marshy ground. A *duckboard* consisted of two narrow planks about eight feet long, across which were nailed horizontal wooden slats, about eighteen inches to two feet wide. *Duckboards* were most useful, but they were heavy to carry, and (having been carried and put down) they tended to slip under foot in the dark, so that the loose end rose suddenly and violently. Duckboards, however, made good firewood (illicit) and roof-props for trench shelters (semi-illicit).

Also used for the ribbon of the Military Medal; from its arrangement of colours.

DUCKBOARD GLIDE, DOING THE: Walking quietly along the tracks at night. From pre-1914 popular songs and dances such as the Palais Glide.

DUCKBOARD HARRIER: Runner (qv.).

DUCKBOARD PATROL: Where the front line was thinly held, the unmanned trench between posts would be patrolled from time to time, especially at night, by parties of two, three or four men moving as quietly as possible along the duckboards and hoping not to be fired on by the next post.

DUD: A shell which failed to explode. Perhaps from the subdued thud, heavy in itself but so much less than the expected explosion. Also used for an inefficient person. E.g. 'The new sergeant's a bit of a dud on parade.'

DUFF: Pudding, especially boiled suet pudding. Also noun from verb = to do a job incompetently. The latter meaning derives from Cockney slang of ca. 1850; *duff*, to trade in inferior goods; *duffing* fiddles, razors, etc., were made for sale, not use.

DUG-OUT: A shelter from shell-fire and the weather, made by digging into the wall of a trench or down from the trench-floor. Dug-outs were of three kinds. *Cubby-holes* dug into the side of the trench, in which one or at most two men could sleep without much comfort. *Shelters*, also dug into the trench wall but rather bigger and shored up with wooden props and corrugated iron. Sometimes these shelters had no more protection overhead than a layer of sandbags or a few duckboards or pieces of corrugated iron.

Deep Dug-outs: these afforded real protection, but their construction was not encouraged except at H.Q. of various kinds. A *deep dug-out* had a stairway shaft leading six, ten, or more feet underground into one or more rooms which might be walled with boards and contain wire-netting beds – and even electric light. It was a great luxury to capture an undamaged German dug-out, even though its entrance faced the wrong way and might admit a shell-burst. The best *deep dug-outs* had at least two entrances, so that if one collapsed, there was still a way of escape. Among the most famous were the Catacombs, near Armentiéres, and the Canadian dug-out near Ypres.

Also a facetious name among officers for an oldish officer returning from retirement to active service and displaying little efficiency.

DUG-OUT DISEASE: Chronic fear of death and danger which kept those, whose rank permitted any choice, safe in their *dug-outs.* (cf.).

DUG-OUT KING: Familiar way of referring to an officer or N.C.O. who took advantage of his rank and office to remain in his dug-out whenever the trench above was under bombardment. Some of this genus never showed their heads above ground from the moment of entering a position till it was time to leave.

DUKE OF FIFE: A knife; cf. *Duke of York,* a fork.

DULAY, DUPAN: Respectively milk, bread; from *du lait, du pain,* in the belief that these two pairs of words were just two words. E.g. 'Pass the dulay', 'give me a bit of dupan'. Cf. the immortal warning in a farm billet: 'Madame, madame! dulay promenade', i.e. 'the cow's got loose'.

DULLMAJOR: An interpreter in prison-camps in Germany.

DUMB INSOLENCE: A military crime. Allowing a derisive or disbelieving or amused or uninterested expression to appear on one's face when spoken to by a superior officer. There was little hope in pleading 'Not Guilty' to such a charge.

DUM-DUM: i.e. a *dum-dum bullet,* one that, on impact, expanded. Each side charged the other with using such soft-nosed bullets. The name comes from India.

DUMMY: A dummy figure to deceive snipers.

DUMMY-TRENCHES: New trenches dug to 'disguise' the preparation of an offensive elsewhere. They were intended to be observed by the enemy.

DUMP: A place, in the open, behind the line, where all sorts of military requisites were stored. Divisional Dump was jocularly called 'Divisional Toy Shop'.

DURATION: The duration of the war. Always, of course, until the end, a period unfixed and apparently unlimited. The volunteers of 1914–15 enlisted for 'three years or the duration of the war' – an ambiguous phrase which caused endless argument among optimists who expected the end to come, each successive year, by the following Christmas. 'Roll on, Duration' (i.e. God end the war and make me a civilian again) was a frequent exclamation in moods of depression.

DUSTY: All men named Miller would respond if addressed as *Dusty*. (Cf. *Nicknames*.)

EARS PUT BACK, GET YOUR: Your hair needs cutting.

EASY: *To stand easy* was a relaxation on parade. One might move the arms, talk, and turn the head, but not move away. An *easy* was a period of rest during drill. *Go easy*: a typically English protest against excess of labour, of speed, of eating or drinking, of swearing, of almost anything. (Cf. *Steady on*.)

E.F.C.: Expeditionary Force Canteens. Independent of any unit. Huts erected for the sale of groceries, cake, cigarettes, tobacco, etc., at the Base and behind the lines.

EGG: A bomb (not a grenade); aeroplanes *dropped*, minelayers *laid eggs*.

EGG BOMB: A very small hand grenade, about the size of an egg, first used on the Somme in the summer of 1916. A smart tap on the heel of a boot severed a wire and started the detonator fuse before the bomb was thrown. An egg bomb could be thrown further than other grenades but was less deadly. (Cf. *Mills Bomb* and *Stick Bomb*.)

EGGS AND CHIPS: Probably the most popular dish in France. Sold in almost all estaminets and eventually in Salvation Army, Church Army, and other refreshment huts behind the lines. So far as is known, a wartime invention due to the scarcity and high prices on one hand of bacon, and on the other of steak. In 1930 the dish was still to be found on public menus in England and in France. (Cf. *Estaminet.*)

ELEPHANT: A small hut of semi-circular section, built of curved pieces of corrugated iron, with or without floorboards. Trench shelters reinforced with such sheets of iron were also sometimes called *elephants*. (Cf. *Nissen* and *Dug-out.*)

EMBUS: To put, or be put, into a bus; cf. *debus*.

EMBUSQUÉ: An officers' usage. A shirker in a soft job; especially, and generally, if that job were in Paris or London. In French soldiers' slang, *embusqué* is just anyone with a good job. According to Déchelette, the only soldier who could not be said to have, at some time or other, been *embusqué* was a soldier already dead.

EMERGENCY RATIONS: A tin of bully-beef, with packets of tea, sugar and biscuits, carried by every infantryman and officially not to be touched except in emergencies and under special orders. Often called *Iron Rations*.

EMMA: A favourite German name for a cannon; so was *Bertha*.

EMMA GEE: At first signalese, then general, for M.G., i.e. machine-gun.

EMMA PIP: M.P., i.e. a military policeman.

EMPLACEMENT: A platform, or a pit, or simply a place, for a gun or guns.

ENFILADE: Noun and verb: to bombard a trench from end to end with shells, or to sweep it with bullets, from a position on or towards a flank.

ENTANGLEMENTS: Wire entanglements, generally in No Man's Land (cf.), for the defence of a trench or other strong point. Some entanglements were designed only to delay, others to debar. They were erected at night by a *wiring-party*.

ENTRANCE FEE: Just sufficient money to enter a canteen and order one drink.

EPSOM RACES: Braces.

EQUIPMENT: Worn by the infantry: belt, shoulder braces, pouches. See *Marching Order*.

ERSATZ: Properly the German reserve. Used by some British troops (who probably took it from newspapers) as meaning an inferior substitute.

116

Esma: Listen! Arabic. Used in Egypt and by Regulars who had served there.

Esses Emma: Signalese, later fairly general, for S.M., i.e. the sergeant-major.

Estaminet: There is no equivalent in Great Britain. On the Western Front an *estaminet* was not a pub. Neither was it a café or a restaurant. It had some of the qualities of all three. It was never large and was found only in villages and very minor towns. It had low ceilings, an open iron stove; it was warm and fuggy; it had wooden benches and table. It sold wine, cognac and thin beer, as well as coffee, soup, eggs and chips and omelettes. The proprietress (a proprietor was unthinkable) had a daughter or two, or nieces, or younger sisters who served at table and made no objection to tobacco smoke and ribald choruses in English and pidgin French. No doubt some estaminets overcharged but in general they provided for the soldier off duty behind the line many and many a happy hour. The name had a magical quality in 1914–18 – and still has for those who survive. (Cf. *Eggs and Chips*.)

Etaples: A small town just inland from Le Touquet, the site of many infantry base depôts and hospitals. The cemetery with its crosses reached to the horizon, and the tented depôts in bad weather were cheerless. Discipline at *Etaples* was so repressive that in 1917 a mutiny, said to have been provoked by military police, broke out. An account of this may be found in *Memories and Base-Details* by Lady Angela Forbes, who during the War ran an officers' club at Etaples; also in the columns of the *Manchester Guardian* on several dates during February, 1930. For some unguessable reason, *Etaples* was always pronounced 'Ee-tapps', with the accent on the first syllable. (Cf. *Ypres.*)

Evacuation Party: One that provided covering fire for the withdrawal of the main body of troops, as at Gallipoli.

Evaporated Vegetables: Shipped out in hermetically sealed tins: unpalatable and disliked: first used in the summer of 1915 and soon discontinued.

Expanded Metal: Employed in the revetting of trenches.

Eyeties: Italians. Sometimes spelt *Ityes*.

EYE-WASH: Official deceit or pretentiousness, especially an appearance of virtue designed to conceal a disgraceful reality. Threats of punishment which could hardly be carried out were *eye-wash*; published despatches from the front were *eye-wash*; the Orderly Officer's *Any Complaints* (cf.) was *eye-wash*. Some of the Regular Army's tradition of smartness (now called 'Bull') came under this heading. The term is perhaps taken from an oculist's lotion for bathing the eye, which often caused temporary blindness or at least, blurred sight; it may date from pre-1914 when officers adding colours to their sketch-maps in the hope of concealing inadequacy as maps were said to use *eye-wash*. In officers' 1914–18 slang: artificial tidiness, e.g. arranged for an inspection. (Cf. *Hot Air*.)

F.A.: Sometimes lengthened into Sweet F.A. or bowdlerized into *Sweet Fanny Adams* (cf.). Used to mean 'nothing' where something was expected. E.g. 'Got any fags?' – 'Sweet F.A.!' (Cf. *Bugger All*.)

Also, of course, abbreviation of *Field Artillery*, used by Gunners – infantrymen would say, R.F.A. for Royal Field Artillery.

FAG: Cigarette. Pre-war civilian slang; diminutive of *fag-end*. In respectable print at least as early as 1888, in dialect at least as soon as 1890. *Fag-end* was applied to stumps of cigars and ends of cigarettes picked up in the streets. Certain brands of cigarettes, of inferior quality, were issued to the troops at irregular intervals, among the best known being 'Red Hussar', 'Ruby Queen', 'Oros' (usually called 'Horrors'), and 'Flag'. (Cf. *Gasper, Smoke, Woodbine* and *Issue*.)

FAIR DOOS: Justice, especially in sharing out rations, duties, etc. E.g. 'Now then, Corp. Let's see *all* the butter; fair doos!'

FAIRY LIGHT: Very light, *q.v.*

FANCY RELIGION: Not C. of E., R.C., or Presbyterian.

FANNY: A member of 'The First Aid Nursing Yeomanry' – a pre-war woman's horsed ambulance unit, which early in the War acquired motor ambulances and sent detachments both to the B.E.F. and to the French Army.

FANNY ADAMS: See *F.A.*

FANTI: Mad. (From Hindustani.) (Cf. *Doolally.*)

FASCINES: Bundles of tightly bound faggots (tree branches) carried by tanks in some operations to drop into shell holes or wide trenches so that wheeled transport could cross them.

FASHY: Angry; annoyed. From the French *fâché*. A variant was *fashy avec*.

FATIGUE: A pre-war Regular Army term implying chores and other necessary jobs of work. Privates on *light-duty* (cf.) were invariably used for fatigues, but all had to take a turn at it. Fatigue duty included all sorts of employments from peeling potatoes and skinning rabbits to scrubbing huts, from carrying sacks of flour to watering the Colonel's garden in barracks. (Cf. *Sanitary Fatigue.*) Sometimes facetiously pronounced *fattygew*.

FATIGUE DRESS: Without puttees, belt or equipment, in order to work.

FED UP: A pre-1914 phrase originally implying satiation; later it came to mean disgusted; weary; disillusioned; grumbling; impatient; discontented. A curious phrase of uncertain origin. Elaborated with into – 'Fed up, —— up and far (away) from home.'

FEEL OUT: Of artillery 'feeling' for the right range and direction.

FEEL TO YOUR RIGHT: A frequent command from N.C.O.'s or officers, when on route march, to close the fours to the side of the road to allow vehicles to pass.

FEMALE TANK: See *Tank.*

FERNLEAVES: New Zealanders.

FEU DE JOIE: Originally a bonfire. Since ca. 1800 a salute by musket or rifle fire. Each man in succession, along a rank, fires a single shot. In 1914–18, successive single firing along a pre-determined length of the front line. In the Gallipoli campaign the Turks were once sorely puzzled by this device at Hellas.

FIELD CASHIER: A paymaster at the front.

FIELD DRESSING: Two small bandages and safety-pins carried by every man inside his tunic for immediate application to a wound. *Shell Dressing:* the same, only larger, and with a phial of iodine.

FIELD GREY: Colour of the German service uniform. Also, a German soldier.

FIELD GUN: Roughly, any British gun of a size less than the 60-pounder.

FIELD OFFICER: One of a rank above a captain but below a general.

FIELD POSTCARD: A stereotyped postcard on which various formulae of communication were printed: words not needed were to be crossed out. Often called a *Whizz-Bang* because, needing almost no censoring, it reached its destination quicker than a letter. The troops made rather a point of mailing field postcards on coming out of battle. Some ingenious fellows tried to convey messages by deleting odd letters or by crossing-out those letters they really wished to be read.

FIGHTING ORDER: Same as *Battle Order* (cf.).

FINI KAPOUT: French slang used in the same sense as *napoo* (cf.) but not so popular. *Kapout* is the German pronunciation of the Latin *caput* = head. In surrendering to the French Germans would often say, 'Kamarade, pas kapout,' i.e. Don't shoot, don't kill me! To which the answer was often, perhaps, 'Fini kapout.' Dauzat gives: 'Capout: tué . . . véritable mot passe-partout, qui signifie tour à tour "fini, abîmé, cassé, tué.' Professor E. Weekley suggests Fr. *capot*.

FIRE ALARMS: Arms.

FIRE-BUCKET: A brazier for coke used in cold weather: usually a punctured bucket.

FIRESTEP: The step running along the forward side – the fire bay – of a trench on which soldiers stood to keep watch or to fire.

FIRE-TRENCH: Usually the front trench. The parts which were manned on Stand To (*q.v.*) were *fire-bays*.

FIRING SQUAD: A squad detailed to shoot a condemned man; for a good account see C. E. Montague's *Rough Justice* (Chatto & Windus, 1926). They used rifles already prepared and waiting for them and were told that only some of the rifles had been loaded with live cartridges, the others carrying blanks. The idea was to obviate feelings of guilt. It is believed that, often, no blank cartridge was employed. If the condemned man were merely wounded it was an A.P.M.'s job to give him the coup de grâce with a shot or shots from his revolver.

FIVE NINE: Variant: *five-point-nine*; a much hated, very destructive German high-explosive shell; also the gun that fired it.

FIXED RIFLE: A sniper's rifle so clamped as to cover a selected point in the enemy's trench, sap, latrine, etc.

FLAG-WAGGING: Signalling by the semaphore code. *Flag-Wagger*, often just *Wagger*, a signaller.

FLAMMENWERFER: Or *Flame-Projector*. The flame was rather a *Liquid Fire*. It was first used on February 26, 1915, by the Germans against the French 15th Corps in the Bois de Malancourt; first against the British on July 30, 1915, a little north of Hooge. (See *The Wipers Times*, March 20, 1916). The British first employed it (*Blazing Oil*, the same thing) at Hill 70 on August 15, 1917. The Flammenwerfer was carried and operated like the Vermorel Sprayer (*q.v.*) and seems to have been difficult to use; a hand pump on the right side had to be worked and the hose held in the left-hand. Liquid fire assaults were carried out more often from fixed positions as with Gas (see *Gas Cylinders*). Specially constructed saps were dug in advance of the main front-line trench and cylinders distributed at intervals. Sometimes the manual F.-W. was carried forward by special troops in the advancing wave after the main projection had ceased.

FLANK BARRAGE: On, not necessarily from, a flank.

FLAPPER: Pre-1914 civilian and middle-class slang for what would now be called a teenage girl, age 15–18; from the 'pigtail' of braided hair she wore and swung about on occasion. The name survived through 1914–18. N.B. *Ayrton Fan, q.v.*

FLAPPER'S DELIGHT: A young subaltern, cf. London slang of the 1950's–60's, *Deb's Delight*.

FLARE PISTOL: A pistol to project a flare; used in urgent need or as a pre-arranged signal of an objective gained. (Cf. *S.O.S., Three Blue Lights, Very Light.*)

FLASH: A small piece of coloured cloth sewn on at the shoulder, etc., of the tunic to differentiate between battallions, brigades, divisions.

FLEA-BAG: An officer's sleeping bag, comfortable and warm. The principle was to retain the natural heat of the body. Some of the other ranks procured or made sleeping-bags for themselves; Eric Partridge made his out of a blanket laced with twine (through holes punctured with a fork or some equally suitable instrument) at the foot and for about forty inches up the side. John Brophy felt the cold less and did without – or perhaps he had an idea that if he damaged a blanket by such treatment the cost would be stopped out his pay.

FLIGHT: The R.F.C. (later R.A.F.) unit: five or six fighter aircraft.

FLIP: Air Force noun and verb: fly, flight.

FLOATERS: Suet dumplings served in stew and floating on the top.

FLOG: To sell Government property to civilians surreptitiously and, of course, illegally. Rations and blankets were the chief commodities, and Quartermaster-Sergeants were popularly supposed to have a large deposit in the bank as a result of successful and methodical *flogging*.

FLY-CATCHERS: Officially *Fleet Fighters*; fast protective fighter.

FLY-SLICER: A cavalryman. It dates from eighteenth century.

FLYING ARSEHOLE: Observer's badge, R.A.F.; the *O* with a wing.

FLYING BEDSTEAD: A military bicycle or motor-cycle; both pretty substantial.

FLYING DARTS: Released from aircraft against ground troops. Used in 1914–15. See *Aerodart*.

FLYING MATINÉE: A trench raid – especially one by day.

FLYING PIGS: Trench mortar bombs. (Cf. *Trench Mortar*.)

FLYING TRAPEZE: Cheese.

F.M.O. or F.S.M.O.: See *Marching Order*.

FOKKER: A distinctive kind of German fighting aeroplane, but the word was often used loosely for any enemy aeroplane. Named after the Dutch inventor.

FOOTBALLS: Trench mortar bombs so called because of their size and shape. (Cf. *Minnie Trench Mortar*).

FOOT-SLOGGER: An infantryman. Grose's *Classical Dictionary of the Vulgar Tongue*, 3rd edition, 1796, gives for *foot-warbler* – 'a contemptuous appellation for a foot soldier, commonly used by the cavalry.' Variants in the 1890s were *mud-crusher*, *beetle-crusher*, *worm-crusher*, of which the first two were occasionally heard in 1914–18. By *foot-warbler* Grose means *foot-wabbler* or *wobbler*.

FOR IT: Due for trouble, especially for a visitation of wrath from on high. 'All right, my lad, you're for it,' meant 'You'll be punished.' (Cf. *Orders, High Jump,* and *On the Mat.*)

FOUR-BY-TWO: See Note on page 66. Sometimes *Two-by-Four*. Among Cockneys *Four-by-Two* was rhyming slang for Jew.

FOUR-LETTER MAN: An unpleasant or untrustworthy character, a S.H.I.T.; after 1918 the expression came to mean a pervert; 'homo' for 'homosexual'.

FOUR TWO: Variant: four-point-two; a German shell.

F.P. No. 1: Field Punishment No. 1. Notorious because part of the punishment consisted in the offender being lashed, like one crucified, to a gun-wheel by wrists and ankles for one hour in the morning and one in the evening for as many days as were specified up to twenty-eight. The intention was to humiliate as well as to exhaust him, and in the past it may have been that his comrades were expected to jeer at him. It has been stated that some unfortunate men were so lashed to guns *in action!* Unlikely but not impossible. Generally F.P. No. 1 was awarded only rarely, and, by an open conspiracy, often the period was arranged to fall while the unit was in the line, where such punishment was quite impracticable. The general routine seems to have been, even behind the line, to omit the lashing to the wheel. The remainder of the punishment consisted of *pack-drill* (cf.) and a diet of bread and water.

F.P. No. 2: Field Punishment No. 2. Not so vindictive as F.P. No. 1, but nevertheless severe.

FRANCE AND SPAIN: Rain.

FRATERNIZATION: The only properly attested instance of fraternization with the enemy occurred on the Western Front: Christmas Day, 1914. G.H.Q., it is said, went to a deal of trouble to prevent any recurrence in the three succeeding Christmas seasons.

FRAY BENTOS: The name of one brand of Bully-beef (*q.v.*) often used for any Bully-beef. Also, facetiously, as an approximation to 'très bien', especially in reply to an enquiry about one's health and well-being. 'Oh, I'm Fray Bentos.' (Cf. *Trez Beans* and *Bully-Beef*.)

FRIENDLY, A: A distant shell, whether 'ours' or 'theirs'.

FRIGHTFULNESS: Originally *German frightfulness*, journalese; but adopted widely by officers, little by the ranks, to signify cruelty, tyranny, injustice, bullying, and cognate horrors. Used jocularly.

FRIGO: Frozen or chilled meat. It is a French slang word, abbreviated from *viande frigorifiée*.

FRITZ: Diminutive of *Friedrich*. German soldiers, singly or collectively. After 1915 less frequent among private soldiers than *Jerry* (Also cf. *Boche, Hun.*)

FROG: As in *Sword-Frog, Bayonet-Frog*. Loops attached to a belt into which bayonet and scabbard were slid.

FROG AND TOAD: Road.

FROG IN THE THROAT: A boat.

FROGGIE: A French soldier. From schoolboy slang and the English amusement at the French habit of eating frog's legs. Rather old-fashioned by 1914. Sometimes abbreviated to *Frog*. Grose, however, gives *frog-eater* = a Dutchman!

FRONT: To people in Britain the Front meant Northern France and Belgium. Across the Channel it meant the forward area, not the front-line trenches especially. Used in the Boer (and perhaps earlier) wars, so probably derived from *frontier*. Used in Italian and French 1914–18. Dauzat says that *front* 's'est popularisé aussitôt après l'invasion [allemande de la France], le jour où le front du combat n'a plus coïncidé avec la frontière. L'usage a rapidement déformé le sens stratégique, en englobant sous ce nom toute la zone des armées, profonde de 50 à 60 kilometres.' (Cf. *Line.*)

F.S.M.O.: Field Service Marching Order. Often qualified to F.M.O. – Full Marching Order. (Cf. *Marching Order, Pack.*)

FULL PACK: (Cf. *Marching Order, Pack.*)

FUNCTION, TO: Used by officers in almost any intransitive sense of *to make, do, act.*

FUNK-HOLE: A term, dating from the South African War, for a dug-out or other shelter. No disparagement of the occupants was implied by the civilian slang word, funk, for coward or cowardice.

FUNKY VILLAS: The village of Fonquevillers.

FURIOUS JOY: Feu-de-joie, *q.v.*

FURLOUGH: The official word for *leave*; the French was *permission*.

FURPHIES: Rumours. Australian slang, from the name of the maker of sanitary carts at a Melbourne camp in 1914, when the destination of the A.I.F. was still unknown, and rumours abounded.

'G' AND 'Q': Short for General Duties and Quartermaster's Department. Those branches of a divisional (or corps or army) staff which attended to fighting and operations, and that which looked after *matériel* and the maintenance of the troops. Each branch was visibly distinguished by differently coloured brassards worn by officers. See also *A.* and *I.*

GADGET: Naval, then Army technical, then general slang for any mechanical instrument or contrivance. The War brought it into general use.

GAFF: Any 'window-dressing' raid or small attack. Also an entertainment, especially a concert. Nineteenth-century slang – penny gaff.

GALLOWS: Assault-course erections from which depended straw-filled sacks or dummies to be spitted in bayonet-fighting practice.

GAMBARDIER, GAMBOLIER: One of the Royal Garrison Artillery (usually *R.G.A.*). See Mark Severn's *The Gambardier* (Benn, 1930).

GAME: 'It's a game!' meant, 'It's ridiculous! There's no sense in it.' Frequently applied to the War as a whole and to the methods and outlook of the Army.

GANGWAY FOR A NAVAL OFFICER!: A facetious way of asking for a passage through a group of soldiers, or of announcing *sotto voce* the approach of some self-important person.

GARNISONLAZARETT: A German military hospital.

GAS ALARM: A motor horn operated by a rubber bulb, or a mechanical (Klaxon) horn or an empty shell-case to be struck with a stick. It was a sentry's duty to give the alarm on the advent of gas or gas-shells, when all except the very sceptical put on their respirators. The sound of the Klaxon carried further than that of bulb-horn or shell-case; the Klaxon was most in use after June, 1917.

GAS ALERT: A variant of *gas alarm*; also the period of time during which troops wore or carried at the ready the gas-helmet. 'At the alert' meant carrying the helmet in its bag high on the chest so that it could be put on in a second.

GAS-BAG: Facetious for the anti-gas respirator and the bag in which it was carried. The bag was of cotton cloth, khaki in colour, angular and flat. See *Respirator* and *Gas Masks*.

GAS-CYLINDER: One containing poison gas for dispersal from the front-line; in favourable conditions more deadly than gas shells.

GAS-GUARD: A sentry given the task of looking for, and smelling for, gas and if necessary sounding a *Gas Alarm, q.v.*

GAS MASK: Before the invention of the Box-Respirator (the Large Box-Respirator), which was to be modified as the Small Box-Respirator (S.B.R.) the B.E.F. had five successive types of anti-gas mask.

1. *White Gauze Pad.* About 6 inches square, with elastic band. Within three days of the first German gas attacks there was forthcoming enough of these pads to equip all the British troops then (Spring, 1915) in France. The pads were made mostly by civilians in Britain after an urgent appeal in the Press: voluntary unpaid labour.

2. *Block Gauze Pad.* This was larger; tied with tapes, it had an extra flap of gauze to reach up and cover the eyes. Like all the following, it was factory-made. (1915 only.)

3. *P. Helmet.* With mica eye-pieces; made from standard Grey Flannel Army shirt-material (P = *Phenol*, 1915–16).

4. *P.H.* or *Tube Helmet.* Same as (3), except that it had a metal tube, rubber tipped, to be held between teeth for exhalation. (1917.)

5. *P.H.G. Helmet.* This improvement on the *P.H.* was made of heavier flannel; it had glass eye-pieces with sponge rubber around them, to fit close to the cheek. (1917.) See also *Gas Bag* and *Respirator*.

GASPER: A cheap – ten-for-sixpence – cigarette. Pre-1914 civilian slang. Used almost exclusively by officers.

GASPIRATOR: Gas mask, *q.v.*

GAS-PROJECTOR: It cast a small cylinder of poison gas over any distance up to about 1,000 yards. Not to be confused with *Gas-Cylinder*, *q.v.*

GAWD (or GOD) FORBID: A kid, i.e. a child.

GEAR: Personal equipment. 'That's the gear' = That's fine. Military extensions of a very old word, lately (1964) revived by 'teenage' boys for their smart and expensive clothing.

GEESE: The Portuguese, who, as Britain's oldest ally, maintained a sizeable force on the Western Front.

GENTLE ANNIE: A variant of *Asiatic Annie*, *q.v.*

GERMAN BANDS: Hands.

GERRY: See Jerry.

GERTY LEE: The number 33, especially at House.

GET AWAY WITH IT: To commit a transgression of military law and then by bluff, bribery, deceit, blackmail or luck to escape punishment.

GET 'EM: To be scared. 'Them' probably meant 'the Willies', civilian slang for uncontrollable nerves. (Cf. *Wind-up* and *Windy*.)

GET OFF: Synonymous with *click* (cf.).

G.H.Q.: General Head-Quarters, i.e. the headquarters of the Commander-in-Chief. On the Western Front after 1915 it was at Montreuil-Sur-Mer.

GIPPO: See *Jippo*.

GLASS HOUSE: Detention-barracks, guard-room, cells. Pre-1914 Regular Army.

GLORY HOLE: Any small dug-out or smallish billet.

GO OVER: I.e. go over the top – to climb out of a trench and advance in an attack on the enemy position.

GO UP: Go up the line, i.e. into the trenches, or to move from the Base to a forward area. (Cf. *Line*.)

GOING: Available, e.g. 'Is there any rum going tonight, Sergeant?'

GOLD STRIPES: Thin gold stripes worn on the lower left sleeve, one for each occasion the wearer had been wounded (*not* for each wound). Instituted in 1916.

GONE DIS: The original and usual meaning was that the cable or telephone line had 'gone disconnected'. *Dis* was a fateful word for the linesman (a signaller). It always meant urgent work, probably in the dark and under fire, for shelling was the normal reason for telephone lines 'going dis'. 'We are dis to Brigade' was a Battalion H.Q. signaller's way of announcing that the only means of communication with Brigade H.Q. would be by *runner* (*q.v.*).

GONE PHUTT: Ceased, collapsed, lost favour, e.g. 'I used to get buckshee tea from the sergeant-cook, but that stunt's gone phutt now.' *Phutt* is Hindustani. The *O.E.D.* gives the first use of *phutt* as by Stevens, of a shell burst, in *With Kitchener to Khartoum* (1898).

GONG: Medal or decoration. Regular Army.

GOODY-LA!: Chinese Labour Corps for 'Good!' Taken over by British troops for facetious use, it became a catch word. Also in the negative *No Goody-la*. (Cf. *Bon*.)

GOOSEBERRY: A reel of barbed wire; also a cluster of wire used as an entanglement.

GORBLIMEY: Field Service caps softened by removing the wire frame. Early in the war a soft cap was issued with earflaps attached; these, when not in use, could be buttoned on top. *Gorblimey* is a Cockney expression and was probably used before the war in ridicule of civilian peaked caps of startling colour and worn at an angle. A pre-1914 civilian (probably children's) song, revived in John Brophy's novel *Waterfront* (1932) and the film based on it (1948) and later by Mr Lonny Donegan, ran something like this:

> My old man's a fireman,
> Now what do you think of that?
> He wears gorblimey trousers
> And a little gorblimey hat.

GORGEOUS WRECKS: A volunteer defence corps in England. Over-age civilians who underwent some military training, spare-time, and wore a brassard with the Royal Monogram G.R. – *Georgius Rex*. Later became more official.

GOTHA: Any big German bombing 'plane of the types made at Gotha.

GRAFT: Manual labour. Sometimes it was *hard graft*.

GRASS-CUTTERS: Small bombs dropped by aircraft on camps and bivouacs behind the line, bursting when they hit the ground and scattering shrapnel pellets at a low level, i.e. to kill rather than to destroy material things.

GREEN CROSS SHELL: A German gas-shell (trichlormethyl chloroformated; introduced in 1917. It was lethal. (Cf. *Blue Cross*.)

GREEN ENVELOPE: A form of envelope not subject to the ordinary regimental censorship. The writer signed a declaration on the outside that the contents gave no military information. Green envelopes were issued sparsely and infrequently, but some could be obtained by bribery or by barter.

GRENADE: Grenades were invented as long ago as 1594, and were first projected from hand-mortars. The name is from the city of Granada, in Spain. *Granatenwerfer* (or Granatwerfer, for short) was the German for a grenade-thrower, i.e. the mortar.

The *Newton Bomb* and *Mortar* was named after its inventor; Colonel Newton of the Second Army Workshops.

The *Hale's Hand Grenade* and *Rifle Grenade* were invented by Frederick Marten Hale. (He also invented the Hale Aircraft Bomb as early as 1913.) Hale's Bombs were the only ones available to the British Forces when the War began. The first Zeppelin to be destroyed in the War by aircraft (in its hangar at Dusseldorf, by Lieut. Marix on October 8, 1914) and the first Zeppelin to be brought down in mid-air, 1915 were destroyed by this bomb. Hale died in 1931. See also *Mills Bomb, Stick Bomb, Egg Bomb.*

GREYBACK: Soldier's shirt of regulation grey flannel. It was grey all over and through and through and had sharp-edged *tin* buttons.

GRIFFIN: Confidential information, or warning of trouble to come, e.g. 'The S.M.'s just given me the griffin about Bill's court-martial.' A variation was, *the straight griffin.* Pre-1914 origin.

GROUND FLARE: Sometimes lighted by the foremost troops during an attack to show to aircraft the progress made.

GROUSE: Noun and verb. Grumble: First recorded example in print, 1892, but Eric Partridge thinks it probably originated at the Crimea and Indian Mutiny period and may be linked with the Old French *groucier*.

GRUB STAKE: One man's share of the rations. From a West American mining term recorded as in use in 1884.

G.S.: General Service, referring to a waggon or some other machine or instrument of war. Also service at the front. Also G.S. = General Staff, meaning privileged and dandified, as in an officer's comment, 'I had on my tin hat and respirator and pistol: oh, devilish G.S. and soldierly!' Sometimes used as a contemptuous way of saying that an officer was supercilious or fussy.

G.S. HAIRY: A draught horse belonging to the Army.

GUARD ROOM: The room, hut or tent occupied by the main guard in barracks or camp, the tour of duty being normally 24 hours. Sometimes applied to the place in which prisoners under close arrest were confined.

GUARDSMAN'S WRIGGLE: Exaggerated salute affected by the Guards. Variants, 'tickling his ear', 'Guardee wriggle'.

GUM BOOTS: Waders, used in very wet trenches. (Cf. *Thigh boots*.)

GUN FIRE: Tea served (sometimes) to troops before the first parade of the day, which was normally before breakfast. A derivation from the morning gun of a garrison town may be correct, but *gunpowder*, which, at least as early as 1800, meant a fine green tea, had by 1860 come to mean a coarse or common tea; *gun fire* may well have arisen by analogy.

GUP: News; rumours. Regular-Army term; from Hindustani.

GYPPY: Familiar for an Egyptian Arab. (Cf. *Abdul, Johnny, Fritz, Jerry, Pork-and-Beans, Froggie, Yank*.)

HAIR-BRUSH: In full, *hair-brush grenade*, a hand-grenade used early in the War, from its shape.

HAIRPIN, THE: A British trench-sector so shaped, near the Hohenzollern Redoubt. Notorious in 1915–16.

HAIRY: A draught horse; sometimes loosely for any horse or even a mule.

HALES BOMB: See *Grenade*.

HALF A DOLLAR: A collar.

HALF A MO: A cigarette. ('Mo' = moment. From a celebrated 1914 cartoon by Bert Thomas, showing a Cockney private, in mid-battle, pausing to light a cigarette and exclaiming politely: 'Arf a mo', Kaiser!'

HALF-INCH: Pinch, i.e. steal.

HANS WURST: The German equivalent of Tommy Atkins; variants: *Hans, Gemeine(r)*, more especially of the infantry private soldier. The commonest German slang equivalents of *footslogger* were *Dreckfresser*, mud-eater; *Kilometerfresser*, kilometre-glutton; *Fusslatsche*, foot-shuffler; *Lakenpatscher*, rather like our *mud-crusher*; *Kilometerschwein*; *Sandhase*, sand-hare. See article on 'Soldiers' Slang' in *The Quarterly Review*, April, 1931.

HAPPY VALLEY: There were several; one on the Somme front became famous in the summer and autumn of 1916.

HARD SKIN: A rough, wild-living man.

HARD TACK: Bully-beef and biscuits eaten uncooked and cold. Strictly *Hard tack* = biscuits; soft tack = bread: very old service expressions.

HARDENING SQUAD: Men undergoing physical training before returning to the front after convalescence.

HARNESS: The infantryman's equipment; belt, shoulder braces, ammunition pouches, etc., of khaki canvas-like webbing or, later in the war, of brown leather. The web did not cut into the shoulders so much as the leather, but when soaked with rain it became much heavier. (Cf. *Marching Order*.)

HARRY RANDLE: Properly *H. Randall*, the name of a comedian famous about 1900. A handle.

HARRY TATE: A plate. Also the *R.E.8*, a slow aircraft used for observation. From the name of a popular music hall comedian whose best sketch was 'Motoring'.

HARRY TATE'S CAVALRY: The Yeomanry.

HATE: A bombardment, e.g. 'The morning hate is due now.' An allusion to the German Lissauer's *Hymn of Hate*, composed in August, 1914, and directed against Britain. (Cf. *Strafe*.)

HAVERSACK: Canvas bag worn on the hip at the left; on the back in Battle Order (*q.v.*); discarded in Drill Order (*q.v.*). Literally = oat sack, being originally a 'trooper's bag for horse provender'.

HAZYBROOK: Hazebrouck, in the North of France; a rather gloomy railway town of some importance.

H.E.: High Explosive. Shells used more for destroying fortifications and trenches than for murder and maiming.

HEAD-WORKER: A shirker, probably *not* rhyming slang; cf. the equivalent *Nut Worker* and cf. page 233, the chant 'Swinging the lead'.

HEAVY: A cannon of large calibre, whether sixty pounder or howitzer or 'naval' gun; whether 'ours' or 'theirs'. Owing to the loud and violent noise of the explosions, heavies 'put the wind up the troops' more than 'whizz-bangs'. This was not rational for the smaller shells were far more numerous and arrived too quickly to be evaded. It was often possible to estimate correctly the incidence of a 5.9, for example, and move away fast.

HEDGE-HOPPING: Flying very low. R.A.F.

HEINE, HEINIE, HINEY: A German. Canadian and American term, mostly in *Heinie Up*, i.e. *Jerry Up*.

HELL-FIRE CORNER: On the Menin Road, near Ypres. So named in October, 1914; the name soon became official. There were numerous other, but less famous, Hell-Fire Corners on the Western Front.

HIGH JUMP: Used only in the phrase – *For the High Jump*, meaning, due to be tried by the Commanding Officer for some military misdemeanour. (Cf. *Cap off*, *For It* and *Orders*.)

HIGH STEPPER: Pepper.

HIGH VELOCITY: The shell from a high velocity gun moved not only fast but along a flat trajectory: it was the more dangerous because it arrived almost as soon as it was heard coming.

HILL 60, 63, 70, 145, etc.: So named from the height in metres on the contour maps. *Hill 60* was the best known.

HINDENBURG LINE: The formidable trench system in front of Cambrai and southward to which the Germans withdrew, secretly and successfully, in the spring of 1917.

HIPE: Rifle. Used in such expressions as, 'Where's my hipe?' or 'Get your hipes quick!' The word is derived from the parade-ground practice of malforming words in order to attain an effect of smartness and authority. One of the forms which 'Slope-arms!' took, coming from the mouth of some N.C.O.'s, warrant officers and officers, was 'Slope-Hipe!'.

HIS: The enemy's. Used especially of shell bursts and aero-planes. (Cf. *Ours.*)

HITCHY-KOO: Itchy from louse-bites. From the nonsense chorus of one of the earliest 'ragtime' songs, pre-1914, in which, however, the expression was in no way connected with lousiness.

HOLD-ALL: See Note on page 66.

HOM FORTY: A goods wagon on the French railway, in which troops were transported at an average speed of $1\frac{1}{2}$ miles an hour. From the inscription on the outer walls: *Hommes 40, Chevaux 8.*

HOO-HA: An argument, trouble, hubbub, an artillery 'demon-stration'. 'There's a hell of a hoo-ha going on over there.'

HOOKUM: A rule, a regulation; 'the correct thing'. From Hindustani.

HOOP: *Through the hoop*, up before the orderly room. Circus slang for dogs and other animals forced to perform 'tricks' at the word of command and for the amusement of the unthinking.

HOP OUT: Hopoutre, a suburb well-known to frequenters and 'residents' of Poperinghe.

HOP OVER: Facetious for attack; noun or verb. (Cf. *Over the Top.*)

HORSE LINES: The place where transport horses were stabled or tethered.

HOT: An adjective of intensity, especially of skill or amorous propensity. Used also of a sector of the front subjected to heavy shelling, raids and other enemy activities. (Cf. *Hot stuff.*)

HOT AIR: Loose talk with less significance than is intended by the talker; unfounded rumours; bumptiousness; official phraseology; the whiting on the sepulchre. (Cf. *Latrine Rumour.*)

HOT STUFF: A woman willing to forgo the usual sexual reticences in conversation and perhaps in behaviour. Not applied to a professional harlot. The expression was also used of a book, a picture or a theatrical entertainment not blatantly obscene but toying with impropriety. (The journalistic equivalent at the period was 'suggestive'). Also used of any special application of skill, e.g. 'He's hot stuff at the piano.'

HOT STUFF, To: To appropriate illicitly, to steal. Hence *Hot-Stuffer*, a thief, a man given to promiscuous borrowing and dubious removings.

HOTCHKISS: The Hotchkiss Machine-Gun. Apparently the British Army in 1914–18 used five different kinds of machine-gun at one time or another: Colt, Hotchkiss, Lewis, Maxim, Vickers.

HOUSE: A favourite gambling game in Army and Navy. Discs and cards marked with a variety of numbers; the numbers were called out, in order, by the banker, as he removed discs, one at a time, from a bag. The winner was the man who first collected a 'full house' of numbered cards. The usual exhortation to join in a game was:

> 'Now then, lay it down, thick and heavy;
> The more you put down, the more you pick up.'

or

> 'Housey, Housey, who'll have a card?
> You come here in wheelbarrows
> And go away in motor-cars.'

HOUSEWIFE, HUSSIF: See the Note on page 66.

HOW: An artilleryman's abbreviation for howitzer. A gun which lobbed heavy shells on a high trajectory so that they descended, it seemed, almost vertically.

HUMP: To lift, to carry. An Australianism. Cf. *hump it*, to carry, march with full pack (up).

HUN: German: singular and plural, adjective and noun. Little used by the other ranks, but occasionally applied – 'You Hun!' – to an unpopular comrade. From a newspaper application of the name of the invaders of the old Roman Empire to the invaders of Belgium and France (Cf. *Boche, Fritz, Jerry.*)

HUSH-HUSH: The Secret Service; Intelligence work, naval or military.

HUSH-HUSH ARMY OR PARTY: Early in January 1918 volunteers were called for a secret enterprise. The secrecy was maintained. Even those who began special training were not informed of either their task or their destination. The force was gathered from Egypt, Africa, India, and the Western Front, this last quota being sent to the Tower of London and kept under lock and key. The several parties eventually arrived at Baghdad and were later employed in the Caucasus and at Baku in the 'Dunster Force' commanded by General Dunsterville. Their friends spoke of them as having 'gone east' in much the same tone as if they were dead. (See *West.*)

HUSH-HUSH CROWD: The Tank Corps, inaugurated in mid-1916. The development of tanks, a new weapon of war and a British invention, was prepared with the utmost secrecy.

HUTCH: Guard-room; cells; prison.

HUTMENT: A camp formed of huts. Hutments could be pretty desolate in winter but they provided good shelter: some were only four to five miles behind the front line.

I: That section of the General Staff which obtained and handled 'Intelligence' information about the enemy. (Cf. *A*, and *G & Q.*)

IDDY-UMPTY: Dot and dash, from the Morse code; derivatively, a signaller.

IDENTITY (or IDENTIFICATION) DISC: Made of metal or composition (plastic) and stamped (incised) with name, regimental number, unit, religion. At first only one identity disc was worn, but in late 1916 or early 1917 ('The Somme did it') each soldier was issued with two, one green, one red. If and when he died on active service, the red disc was removed and sent to the base (to Records department) and finally to the next of kin; the green one remained on the corpse to ensure identification before burial. In many units, both discs were worn round the neck, No. 2, the red, depending from No. 1, the green; in others, one was worn round the neck, the other round the wrist. When men were blown to pieces identity discs recovered later might be the only evidence of death.

IGGRY: Hurry up! (from the Arabic *iggri*). The Australians appropriately named a crossing in Bullecourt: Iggry Corner.

IKEY: Clever. From *Isaac, Ikey*, generic for a Jew.

IMPROPERLY DRESSED: A military offence. Not indecently undressed, but dressed in a manner that was technically, i.e. officially, incorrect. To be without a hat on parade or to have a tunic button not fastened was to be improperly dressed.

135

Imshi: Go! Away with you. (Arabic, picked up in Egypt.)

In Bed or Out of Barracks: Exhortation on Sunday afternoons to men either to 'get down to it' (*q.v.*) or to leave the barrack-room. From the pre-1914 Regular Army. (Cf. *Blanket Drill.*)

Ips: Ypres (*q.v.*).

Irks: R.A.F. slang: 'air mechanics' concertina-ed into one syllable.

Iron Foundries: Heavy shelling.

Iron Hoop: Soup.

Iron Rations: Cf. *Emergency Rations.* Also sometimes used for shells, e.g. 'There goes Jerry's iron rations!'

Issue: Adjective applied to anything officially supplied to the troops, especially to cigarettes, tobacco, etc., which might also be bought in canteens and elsewhere. *The issue* was also used for 'the whole lot', e.g. 'There's no rum tonight. The sergeant's snaffled the issue.' Often, also, '*the whole issue*'.

I Salute the Brave Dead: A formula affected by some officers of high rank visiting troops at the Front. On one legendary occasion these ritualistic words were addressed to a man laid out by rum, who staggered to his feet and attempted a salute.

Jack or Johnny Horner: A corner.

Jacko: A Turk, generally a Turkish soldier. Gallipoli and Palestine.

Jacks: Military Police. (Cf. *Red Caps.*)

Jacks Alive: The number 5, especially at House.

Jag: A bout of drinking; an extended period of hard drinking. From dialect. In 1899, and probably much earlier, anyone rather drunk was in Westmorland said to 'have a fairish jag on'.

Jake: Good. Canadian and Australian. Often *jake-a-loo*; occasionally *jake-a-bon, tray jake*.

Jakes: Latrine. The word dates back to Elizabethan times.

Jam on It: Luxury, surplus. Used in the phrase, 'What do you want? – Jam on it?' as a rebuke to one grumbling at his lot or the scantiness of his blessings. Sometimes varied to *jam on both sides*.

Jam Tart: The heart.

Men of the Royal Fusiliers marching 'up the line' at St Pol. Some wear empty sandbags over their steel helmets, and the 'bite' of the heavy equipment on their shoulders can be felt. British troops had already lost hundreds of thousands killed and wounded on this, the Somme front, when the photograph was taken in November 1916

'Arf a Mo, Kaiser!' This drawing by Bert Thomas first appeared in the London *Evening News*, and was afterwards widely reproduced

An infantry private in full marching order. The two gold stripes on his sleeve show that he has already been wounded twice

So Obvious: 'Oo made that 'ole?' – 'MICE.' A typical cartoon by Bruce Bairnsfather exemplifying the 'spirit of the troops' in the middle years of the war

'Walking Wounded'. An infantry private, happily on his way out of the line at Beaumont Hamel in December, 1916. This is a canvas cover on his rifle to guard it against mud

Anzacs practising an assault, probably in Egypt in 1915

Near Ginchy, on the Somme, 1916. German prisoners, disarmed, bring back a British soldier who seems not displeased to have got a 'Blighty one'

The sergeant is cooking in the lid of a mess tin. Near Beaumont Hamel, 1916

The chalky ground suggests the Somme or the Arras front. Two men without steel helmets suggests reserve trenches

Flanders, 1917, men of the East Yorkshire Regiment on their way to the line

Time and place unknown: the troops (perhaps Canadians) are probably a raiding party – they wear no equipment, not even belts

JAM-TINS: Make-shift grenades made from jam-tins. Used in 1915 in France and Gallipoli, before the Mills bomb came into its own.

JAMMY: Lucky; e.g. 'he's a jammy bugger!'

JANE SHORE: Whore. In 1872 J. C. Hotten gave *sloop of war* and *Rory o' More* for the same.

JANKERS: C.B. (cf.), or confinement in a military prison. Perhaps from the jangling of fetters (in old-time prisons). Hence *Jankers King*, the provost sergeant; *Jankers Men*, defaulters.

JAPAN: Bread. From French *du pain*. Some correspondents have claimed that in 1918 *Japan* was more often heard than Rooty, the New-Army word displacing the Regular-Army word.

JEM or JIM MACE: A face. From the 19th century boxer.

JENNY LEE: Tea. Rhyming variants: *Rosy Lee* and *You and Me*.

JERK: 'Put a jerk into it' meant, Be quick, hurry! (Cf. *Stuck*.)

JERKS: Physical training: Swedish drill, exercises, gymnastics and games. Commonly shortened to P.T.

JERRY: German, singular or plural, noun and adjective. A familiar expression, almost of affection, derived from *German*. Used constantly by private soldiers in such phrases as 'Jerry's damn quiet, tonight'.

A somewhat more fanciful, though improbable, source for the origin of the word lay in the appearance of a group of German tin-hats: in outline they looked not unlike chamber-pots, vulgarly known as 'jerries'.

JERRY UP!: A word of warning meaning that German aircraft were overhead by night and might drop bombs. By daylight when fighter aircraft sometimes, in the later years of the War, made low-level attacks on infantry or artillery positions the warning might be much more urgent. *Jerry Over* (i.e. overhead) was an occasional variant.

JEWEL OF ASIA: A big Turkish gun at the Dardanelles.

JIG-A-JIG: Copulation, especially illicit or mercenary. Although known in the United States, it may be considered as French slang, used by touts, very often small boys. The favourite phrase was 'Jig-a-jig très bon,' with a price named. The word is onomatopoeic. (Cf. *Zig-zag*.) In an English street-ballad of the 1840s entitled *Jig-Jig to the Hirings* (fairs where labourers sought employment) *jig-jig* occurs as a verb, with the meaning to have sexual intercourse.

JILDI (often *Jeldi*): Quick, look sharp, hurry. Also used in the phrase 'on the jildi', e.g. 'Get those bags filled on the jildi'. (From Hindustani.)

JIMMY RIDDLE: To urinate: rhyming slang for 'piddle'.

JIPPO: Juice or gravy, especially of bacon. Greatly prized. Someone from the back of a queue was always to be heard adjuring the orderly men to 'steady on the jippo, chum'. Sometimes used also for stew, especially among Australians. Transferred use from an obsolete word meaning a scullion.

JOANNA: Piano.

JOCK: A Scottish soldier; or more precisely, a soldier in a Scottish regiment. *Jocks* meant Scottish troops in general. The phrase was sometimes *The hairy Jocks*.

JOHNNY: Short for *Johnny Turk*. Very rarely for a German. (Cf. *Abdul* and *Jerry*.)

JOHNSON: Synonymous with Coal-box (cf.). Name given from a negro pugilist, Jack Johnson, and in the early days of the War the phrase was always Jack Johnson. One of the 'advertisements' in *The Wipers Times* of February 12, 1916, has: 'The Johnsons. A Shout. A Scream. A Roar,' a most apt description of their advent and explosion.

JOLLY POLLY: Gallipoli.

JONNOCK: Less used variants in the Army were *jannick* and *jannock*; in English dialects, however, *jonnock* is the most frequent form. It means honest, straightforward, fair, whether of persons or of things. The War may be said to have made *jonnock* a slang word, for previously it was rarely heard outside dialect, except in Australia, where it appeared at least as early as 1890 (see Ferguson's *Bush Life*, 1891). Eric Partridge heard it in S.W. Queensland in 1913 and among Australian soldiers before they came in contact with English troops in Egypt and Gallipoli.

JOY-STICK: The pilot's controlling lever on an aeroplane. So named because of the thrills its operation could produce. Also for the penis.

JUG: Detention; either a regimental guard-room or a military prison, staffed by military police. (Cf. *Clink*.) Probably from thieves' slang: *stone(ware)jug*, meaning stone-walled prison.

JUGGED: Arrested, imprisoned; a variant, *juggo*, could mean in cells, or, alternatively, sick or disabled.

JUICE: Petrol, especially for a 'plane.

JUMP TO IT: Hurry! Carry out quickly the command given. Used chiefly by N.C.O.'s. (Cf. *Jerk.*)

JURY, CHUMMAGE, and CONTER: Knife, fork, and spoon. Regular Army, chiefly among those with Indian service.

KI (K ONE): The first 100,000 of the New (Kitchener's) Army of 1914 volunteers.

KAMERAD: Comrade. A German expression, used by prisoners requesting mercy. Often put to facetious uses by British soldiers among themselves, e.g. 'Kamerad!' when a story showed no signs of ending.

KAMERAD, TO: (facetious). To surrender; to yield in an argument.

KAPAI: Good; nice. Maori word common among New Zealand troops.

KATE KARNEY: The Army.

KEEP: A position in a trench system so fortified as to enable a small body of men to resist attack from any direction. Not easily distinguishable from *Redoubt*; one or other was favoured.

KELLY'S EYE: One, especially a solitary one. A term used in the gambling game of House (*q.v.*).

KHAKI: From the Hindustani for dust (-coloured). Khaki uniform: white uniforms of British troops in India were dyed khaki during the Mutiny. Khaki was first 'officially' worn by the British Army in the 1882 campaign in Egypt. Brought into general use in India about the same time: in 1884 the old 15th (now the East Yorkshire) Regiment sang at Poona *The Khaki Recruit*, a parody by a Private Burns of *The Kerry Recruit*. In 1885 *Life in the Ranks* referred to 'drab-coloured linen clothing called *kharkhi*'. From 1900 the term began to be applied to uniforms of heavier, woollen cloth worn in colder climates.

KHAKI BLANCO: Blanco was and is a white dressing for canvas and buckskin shoes. A similar dressing for webbing equipment was known anomalously as *khaki blanco*. It was put on wet and allowed to dry. See *Marching Order*.

KIBOSH: A sudden end or a severe punishment. A popular comic song early in the war ran 'Belgium put the kibosh on the Kaiser.' Also used as a verb. The word is pre-Victorian in origin. Dickens uses it.

KILOS: Short for *kilometres*, only very rarely for *kilogrammes*. Some men oddly put the accent on the second syllable of the full word.

KILTIE: A name for a Highland soldier, taken from popular journalism and used only mockingly, sometimes for the purpose of starting a row. (Cf. *Jock*.)

KIP: Noun: sleep or a place to sleep in, e.g. 'My kip's round the corner' or 'I'm going to have a kip now.' Verb: to sleep, e.g. 'I'm going to kip here, while the company's on parade.' *O.E.D.* gives 'a common lodging-house; also a lodging or bed in such a house; hence, a bed in general,' and states that the origin of the word is uncertain. The verb also has the form *kip down*. (Cf. *Get Down to It*.) Perhaps from Dutch *kippe*, an alehouse, a mean hut.

KIP-SHOP: A brothel. *Shop* loosely for any building or place, just as *merchant* loosely = chap, fellow, man.

KIRCHNER: A French artist, who drew coloured illustrations of young women in lacy coloured lingerie, exhibiting their thighs and breasts and striking alluring poses. Many a sulbaltern collected Kirchner pictures and pinned them on the walls of billets and dug-outs to cheer his lonely heart.

KISSER: The mouth. Used only in abuse or derision.

KIT: Already defined in 1785 as 'the whole of a soldier's necessaries, the contents of his knapsack.'

KIT INSPECTION: Held at irregular intervals and at short notice. The whole kit had to be laid out, on a groundsheet usually, in due order. Missing items were replaced at the owner's expense. Until quite late in the War 'issue' razors of the cut-throat type had to be kept and carried although the owner preferred to use a safety razor.

KITCHENER'S BLUE: Blue serge uniforms supplied to some recruits in 1914, khaki being scarce.

KITCHENER'S MOB: Those who enlisted in response to Kitchener's official appeal in August, 1914. (See *K.I.*)

KITE BALLOON: Called 'Kite' because it was secured and controlled by a cable attached to a winch on the ground. See *Ballon, Observation.*

KIWI: A ground-duty Air Force man, from the pedestrian New Zealand bird. Also a well-known dressing for leather: hence *Kiwi King*, any officer fussy about spit and polish.

KLAXON: See *Gas Alarm.* A Klaxon horn was sometimes used by pilots of observation or scouter aircraft, flying low, to signal in Morse code to the ground.

KNAPPER: The head. Grose gives 'knapper's poll: sheep's head.'

KNAPSACK: More formal name for the *Pack, q.v.* Literally a food-sack and, like so many military words, from the Dutch.

KNIFE-REST: A portable entanglement of barbed wire stretched on X-shaped frames. Used for stopping gaps in No-Man's Land and in trenches.

KNOBKERRY: Its military application was the wooden stick or helve of an entrenching tool to which might be fastened a small but substantial cog-wheel. Used by raiders. See *Cosh.*

KNOBS ON: Above the average; also an intensive conveying amicable insult, especially in the repartee, 'the same to you with knobs on.' Pre-1914.

KNOCK IT BACK: To drink beer, wine or spirits.

KNOCK OFF: To stop work or, used transitively, to steal. (Cf. *Scrounge.*)

KNOCKING ABOUT SPARE: [of soldiers] Idle, having nothing to do; [of things] suitable for stealing.

KNOCKING-SHOP: A brothel. Probably from eighteenth-century slang 'to knock' = to lie with a woman; or perhaps derived from establishments which endeavoured to conceal their true character and which admitted strangers only in response to a pre-arranged series of raps on the door. (Cf. *Red Lamp.*)

KNUT: See *Nut.*

KOSH: See *Cosh.*

K.R.: King's Regulations. The book of customs, orders of procedure and general routine and ceremonial. Designed rather to preserve tradition than to increase efficiency, which was catered for, fairly adequately, in various manuals such as *Infantry Training, Musketry Regulations*, etc.

141

LACHRYMATORY SHELLS: Those containing 'tear' gas.

LADY OF THE LIMP: Also the *Virgin of the Limp, the Hanging Madonna*, and, especially, *the Leaning Virgin*: high upon La Basilique de Notre-Dame de Brébières, at Albert. Damaged by shell-fire the figure was displaced till it leaned out almost parallel to the ground far below. It could be seen from a great distance.

LADY, OR LORD, OF THE MANOR: A 'tanner', a sixpence.

LAGGED: Arrested; under arrest. Originally thieves' cant; from ca. 1800.

LANCE-JACK: Familiar for Lance-Corporal, the lowest rank of N.C.O. – one stripe.

LANCE-PRIVATE: Lower than a private, i.e. on approbation. A facetious or a derisory term. Sometimes *rear-rank private* was preferred.

LANDOWNER: *To become a landowner* meant, to be killed, the grave being the estate.

LARRIGANS: Waterproof, leather knee-boots issued to Canadian troops in 1915.

LASH UP: A fiasco, a failure, a break-down, especially of raids and attacks.

LAST HOPE, THE: Iron rations (*q.v.*).

LATCH-OPENER: The 'price' of a drink. (Cf. *Entrance-Fee.*)

LATRINES: Built-in in barracks. Outdoors in camps, screened by corrugated iron or lath and plaster walls; in the line usually sited in a sap. Generally, though not always edifices distinct from *Urinals* (q.v.) Places where private soldiers could sit down.

LATRINE RUMOUR: Wild and insubstantial stories and prophecies. These usually took one of the following forms: (1) Rumours about German strategic and tactical plans, new weapons and traps; (2) Changes of High Command, new theatres of war, Napoleonic schemes for victory; (3) Secret doings by one or other of the Allies which would relieve the pressure on the British front; (4) Spy and treason stories; (5) Auguries of a life of comparative ease and luxury in the near future. Some battalions were always about to be moved to India, Egypt or even Samoa; others were to be employed sweeping the paths in the grounds of G.H.Q. chateaux. Such rumours became associated with latrines because these shanties were practically the only places in which a private soldier could be comparatively secure from the eye and voice of authority. Consequently men sat there for long periods, reading newspapers, gossiping and exercising their imagination and credulity. (Cf. the scene early in *All Quiet on the Western Front.* British latrines, however, were slightly less open to the public view and not so lugubrious.) Variants were *Cookhouse Rumour, Ration-dump Yarn, Transport Tale*, from three popular meeting places.

LAUGHING: Adjective: comfortable, safe, fortunate, especially in contrast with others or with normal circumstances. E.g. 'He's got a job at Brigade Headquarters, so he's laughing'; 'Once I get to the C.C.S., I'll be laughing.'

LAWYER: A man given to excessive argument or complaining, or one always talking about his rights. Pre-1914 Regular Army 'barrack-room lawyer': in the Navy 'sea-lawyer'.

LAZY ELIZA: A long-range heavy shell passing well overhead.

LEACH TRENCH-CATAPULTS: (Discontinued and recalled by an official order of July, 1916.) They were equipped with rubber springs, which were tautened with a winch. Where No-Man's Land was narrow, they were used for pitching Mills bombs at the enemy.

LEAD-SWINGER: An habitual malingerer. Often used with only the faintest suggestion of reproach. E.g. 'Lend a hand, you old lead-swinger.' (Cf. *Swinging the Lead.*)

LEAF: Leave. One of the oddities of speech peculiar to the pre-1914 Regular Army. (Cf. *Route March.*)

LEAP-FROGGING: Advance by successive 'assault waves', each 'wave' holding the trench or other objective that it captured, and allowing the following wave to pass through to continue the advance. Introduced by the British in 1917.

LEBEL MA'M'SELLE: The French rifle. This French slang term (a form of punned-rhyming slang: *la belle*: from the inventor, M. Lebel) was known to some British soldiers; a variant was *Ma'm'selle Lebel.*

LEG: Show a leg = begin to get up, waken. Bawled by the responsible N.C.O.'s in huts, tents or billets at reveillé. See 'Chants and Sayings', page 224.

LEG-SHOW: A vaudeville entertainment in England in which chorus girls exposed their silk-clad legs to considerably above the knee and brandished their feet at the audience in time with a popular melody. This was considered by the civilian populace to be an adequate compensation to any and all soldiers for the horrors of war; many men on leave or in hospital did not disagree as long as the show lasted. Probably no later generation will be able to understand the excitement and pleasurable atmosphere of naughtiness generated between 1914 and 1918 by the word *legs*.

LEGS ELEVEN: Seven; but also, especially in the game of House, eleven, this latter, as the numerals '11', giving rise to the application of the term to any tall, thin man.

LETTERS UP: A shout announcing the distribution of letters by the Battalion mail-corporal, sometimes by the Company Quartermaster-sergeant.

LEWIS: Short for Lewis machine-gun, a portable weapon. It was invented by Isaac Newton Lewis, American soldier-inventor, in 1913, and adopted by the British, French, and Belgian Governments after being rejected by the U.S.A.

LIAISON OFFICER: One who keeps formations of allied armies or the same army in touch with each other.

LID: Hat or steel helmet. (Cf. *Tin Hat* and *Battle Bowler*.)

LIFEBOAT PARTY: Same as *Cadre, Battle Surplus*, and *Skeleton Battalion*.

LIFT: To steal, to purloin. Now slang, but once cant; recorded since the sixteenth century.

LIGHT DUTY: When a man reported sick and was obviously ill, but not dying, the M.O. ordered him *Light Duty*. This consisted of fatigues, such as unloading lorries, shovelling coal or carrying heavy buckets of urine. The whole system of *M.D., Light Duty*, etc., broke down in the line. Men seriously ill there were evacuated as soon as possible; those with minor complaints made shift as best they could. A sick man in the line or on the march usually did his best to keep going and was helped through his duties by his friends. The irrationality, the pettiness and the maddening repetitions of military life helped to swell the sick parades out of the line, at the Base and in England. Men 'went sick' less to malinger than as a gamble against the odds for a break in the monotony. (Cf. *Sick*, *M.D.*, *M.O.*)

LIGHT HORSE: Mounted Infantry; they carried rifles, not swords or lances. In Gallipoli the Australian Light Horse served in the trenches. Light Horse were particularly effective in Palestine.

LIMBER: The detachable wheeled-front of a gun-carriage.

LIMBO: Bread. Origin obscure.

LINE: See *Up the Line*.

LINSEED LANCERS: The Royal Army Medical Corps.

LIP: Impertinence. Especially in 'None of your lip now'. (Cf. *Dumb Insolence*, also the civilian slang – 'cheek'.) Pre-1914 civilian.

LISTENING POST: A concealed or underground position in No-Man's Land where two or more men would keep vigil through the night with two or three reliefs. Also in mine galleries to detect enemy mining operations or counter-mining.

LITTLE GREY HOME IN THE WEST: Rhyming slang for under-vest. From the popular song of that name.

LITTLE WILLIE, BIG WILLIE: The Crown Prince and the Kaiser. Journalese. So used occasionally by the troops, who applied the terms to all manner of things: e.g. a long-range naval gun operating on the Western Front.

LIVE ONE: A live-fused-shell. Of rifle and other S.A. ammunition – as distinct from blank or dummy rounds.

LIVELINESS, A CERTAIN: Originated, like some other good things, by Mr Winston Churchill in 1914, this phrase came to be applied, by understatement, to shell-fire.

LOAD OF SLACK: The debris thrown up by a big shell, or the burst of that shell. From slack = small, dusty coal.

LOAF o' BREAD: Dead. Also head, in this sense, often abbreviated to *loaf*. A variant was *Strike me dead*.

LONE PINE: A famous position on Gallipoli; near Anzac Cove. It passed into Australian folklore. Originally from a pre-1914 music hall song 'The Trail of the Lonesome Pine'.

LONE STAR: A second-lieutenant, from his badge of rank.

LONG-EARED CHUM: A mule or a horse.

LONG-HAIRED CHUM: A girl. Dates from ca. 1890, and was originally tailors' cant.

LONG HORN: A Farman two-seater bi-plane.

LOOK-IN AT: A share of. 'The Tank Corps blokes gave me a look-in at a tin of milk, so the tea was bon.'

LOOK SEE: Verb and noun, meaning look. (Cf. *Butcher's, Dekko, See*.)

LOOK STICK: Trench periscope or a telescope.

LOOPY (or LOOBY): Silly; slightly insane; unwise; eccentric. According to Grose the eighteenth-century sense was merely 'awkward' or 'ignorant', and the word was used as a noun. Soldiers in 1914–18 generally made it an adjective. The word belongs to the North Country. (Cf. *Tap, Dekko, lally, Touched*.)

LOOS(E) WALLAH: From Hindustani *lus*, a thief. In India especially a rifle-thief. Became generic for a thief or a rascal.

LOOT: Lieutenant. E.g. 'He's a loot now'; but not 'Loot Robinson'. Also *Second Loot* or *One-pip Loot*. (Cf. *Pip*.) Officers below the rank of captain were always addressed and spoken of as 'Mr So-and-so'. *Mr* was also a privilege of the *R.S.M.* (cf.).

LORD LOVEL: A shovel.

LORD MAYOR: To swear.

LORRY JUMPING: The science or art by which small parties or individual soldiers, detached from their units, travelled about France without wearing out their legs. It was necessary to dodge the A.P.M. and his satellites and find a suitable road outside the town or village. Sooner or later a motor-lorry appeared, and was stopped with civil words, and the driver cajoled into giving 'an unofficial lift' – usually to a larger town with shops and cafés.

LOSE ONE'S NUMBER: To be up for orders, to be crimed. Contrast the Naval expression *lose the number of one's mess*, to be killed.

LOUSE-TRAP: Woollen body-belt, cf. *Belly-band*. Or a woolly sheepskin coat or jerkin worn in winter.

LOUSY WITH: See *Crawling with*.

LOUSY WOOD: Leuze Wood, the scene of some hard fighting in 1916.

LUCKY ONE: A lucky hit by, or a lucky wound from, bullet, bomb, or shell. Lucky = not too painful or too maiming but severe enough to ensure a spell in hospital. (Cf. *Blighty One.*)

LUMBERED: Found out. Exposed in an act of deceit. Arrested. Perhaps a corruption of *limbo'd,* an unrecorded verb from *limbo,* which dates from the late sixteenth century in the sense of confinement, prison.

LYDDITE: Explosive used in bombs and shells. Discovered at Lydd, in Kent.

M. and V.: A ration of tinned meat and vegetables.

MA'ALISH: Never mind! It doesn't matter. From Arabic.

MACARONI: An Italian soldier. (Cf. *Russki, Pork-and-Beans, Chink, Froggie, Gyppie, Aussie, Yank.*)

MACE: A club with a knobbed or a spiked head. See *Cosh* and *Knobkerry.* Used chiefly on raids.

MACONOCHIE: A tinned ration consisting of sliced vegetables, chiefly turnips and carrots, and a deal of thin soup or gravy. Warmed in the tin, *Maconochie* was edible; cold, it was a man-killer. By some soldiers it was regarded as a welcome change from bully-beef. Named after the inventor or manufacturer. *Maconochie Medal,* the Military Medal (M.M.); *Maconochie Cross,* the Military Cross (M.C.).

MAD MINUTE: A newspaper phrase for British rapid fire during the Retreat from Mons. On the rifle range every man was trained to put 15 aimed shots in one minute on to a 4-foot target at a range of 300 yards. The name was also applied to the frenzied minute spent charging down the assault course, bayoneting straw-filled dummies representing enemy soldiers.

MADELON: A dance, a tune, and a famous French marching song, not yet [1964] dead.

MAFEESH: There is none: nothing; dead; finished. An Arabic word used in Egypt, Gallipoli, Mesopotamia and Palestine, much as *napoo* (cf.) was used in France and Belgium.

MAGAZINE: A famous billet at Ypres.

MAGGIE ANN: Margarine.

MAGHNOON: Fool, dolt, idiot. Arabic.

MAIDAN: (Pronounced *Mydahn.*) A plain, a space, a parade ground. Regular-Army word from India.

MAIL UP: A shout of joy and expectation when letters and parcels arrived from Blighty.

MAJOR, THE: For Sergeant-Major; in vocative: 'Major'. By N.C.O.'s.

MAKE: To acquire illicitly, to borrow forgetfully, to steal. An actual C.S.M.'s report to his C.O. ran 'We made three shovels last night, Sir. That brings us up to correct.' Originally thieves' cant of the late seventeenth century.

MALE TANK: See *Tank*.

MALUM: To understand; transitive and intransitive. Hindustani.

MANDARIN: An oppressively pompous (especially War Office) official. Officers' slang.

MAP, OFF (or NOT ON), THE: Of uncertain locality, of doubted existence, incredible.

MARCHING ORDER, FULL: On the road the infantryman carried besides his rifle and webbing or leather equipment, 60 rounds of ammunition, haversack [full], waterbottle [full], valise or pack (containing overcoat) a spare pair of boots, his steel helmet, a blanket, a gas respirator, a rubber ground sheet, iron rations, bayonet, entrenching tool and handle and sundry other articles. Spare boots and blanket were often omitted. The rifle alone weighed nine pounds and the total weight at times was probably seventy or even eighty pounds. Full Marching Order was sometimes abbreviated to *F.M.O.* or more properly *F.S.M.O.*, i.e. Field Service Marching Order. In popular speech it was *Full Pack*. (Cf. *Battle Order, Pack.*)

MASSEY-HARRIS: Cheese. Canadian. From a *self-binder*, i.e. a machine that cuts growing corn and binds it in one operation. (Cf. *Bung.*)

MATE: Friend, comrade. (Cf. *Chum.*)

MATERNITY JACKET: The Royal Flying Corps (R.F.C.) double-breasted tunic, khaki, with no collar and tie showing, fastening down the right side of the body.

MATEY: Friendly, or helpful, especially in the phrase 'Be matey'.

MATLOW: A sailor. From French 'matelot'. This was an inheritance from the pre-1914 Regular Army and not acquired in Northern France.

M.D.: Medicine and Duty. A pill was given to a soldier who reported himself sick, without serious cause, together

148

with orders to report himself to his platoon sergeant for immediate duty. (Cf. *Sick, M.O.*, and *Light Duty*.)

MEDICINE AND DUTY: At the game of House, the number 9.

M.E.F.: Mediterranean Expeditionary Force, which landed at Gallipoli; commanded by General Sir Ian Hamilton.

MESOPOLONICA: Rumour had it in every battalion on the Western Front that the next move would be to the East and comparative ease and safety. In time this hypothetical and unknown destination came to be called *Mesopolonica* – a compound of Mesopotamia and Salonica.

MESPOT: Short for Mesopotamia.

MESS, OUT OF: Dead; *to be put out of mess*, to be killed.

MESS PRESIDENT: The ceremonial head of an officers' mess.

MESS-TIN: Popular name for a soldier's *Canteen*. (Cf.)

METHUSILIER: One of the Australian Remount Unit, consisting of men for the most part over the normal maximum age for active service.

MICKS: Any Irish unit.

MIKE: To dodge duty or to work half-heartedly.

MILITARY POLICE: See *Red Caps*.

MILLER'S DAUGHTER: Water.

MILLS BOMB: Named after the inventor. A bomb serrated on the outside, like a pineapple, to form shrapnel on explosion. The fuse to the detonator was ignited by first withdrawing a pin and then releasing a lever. (Cf. *Stick Bomb* and *Egg Bomb*.)

MINCE PIES: Eyes.

MINGLE, A: A social meeting of officers with nurses under an official aegis. Hospital term.

MINNIE: Minenwerfer. German for Mine (i.e. Bomb) Thrower. Also the bomb itself, which was sometimes called *football, rum jar, Christmas pudding*. (Cf. *Trench Mortar*.)

M.O.: Medical Officer attached to a battalion or battery. M.O.'s varied considerably in quality; some were brutes, some were born underlings, most were quite human. In the line all worked hard, many were notably brave. They were good to wounded men unless they suspected S.I. (*q.v.*) but towards some other ranks reporting sick, it is said that many *M.O.*'s exhibited neither intelligence nor courtesy. Malingerers could *get away with it* (cf.) again and again; men that their comrades knew to be ill would be ordered back to duty sometimes to die soon afterwards. As the war progressed and more and more men were conscripted to replace those killed, wounded or diseased, the medical profession appeared to lower its professional standards astoundingly. Old soldiers still weak from un-healed wounds were sent back up the line and among the conscripts making up drafts of 'reinforcements' were many incapacitated by age, by physique and by chronic ailments.

MOB: A battalion or other unit. E.g. 'What mob is he with?' The use of the word implied no disrespect; it was almost affectionate. (Cf. *Batt.*)

MOBILE, TO DO A: To march in the desert. Egyptian service.

MOIR'S PILL-BOX: A cylinder-shaped machine-gun turret made of pre-cast concrete slabs threaded on to steel rods. Named after the designer, Sir Ernest Moir. About 4 tons 18 cwt. of material were needed. This could be transported by three lorries and erected in about 21 working hours by one N.C.O., one fitter, one fitter's mate, a mason and six labourers. The components of these pill-boxes were manu-factured at Richborough, Kent; a large number were sent to France and erected during the summer of 1918. They became much better known during the 1939–45 (Hitler) War. See *Pill box.*

MONEY FOR JAM: An easy job; also = 'too easy!'

MONGEY: Food. From the French *manger*, to eat; *du manger*, colloquial for food.

MONGEY WALLAH: A cook or assistant cook.

MONS MAN: One of the original B.E.F. in France. Popu-larized by journalists, who, however, got it from the troops. *The* 1914 *Star*, unofficially the *Mons Medal*, was awarded to all who served in France in a B.E.F. unit between August 5 and midnight of November 22–23, 1914.

MOO-COW FARM: Moquet Farm. A scene of fierce Australian fighting on the Somme.

MOPPING UP: The capture or subjection of isolated machine-gun posts and other positions after the main body of the attack had passed on. A necessary operation if the assault-ing troops were not to be fired on from the rear, and reinforcements shot down. The domestic metaphor for a murderous business is typically English. (Cf. *Pudding-basin.*) *To mop up* was used in another sense for drinking in quantity, e.g. 'The new officer can fairly mop it up, he can.' Also varied to *mop it down* (cf. the song, 'Here's to the Good Old Beer,' page 41).

MORSE CODE: Much used by the Army. Even Brigade Observers who almost never used it, had to learn it. Devised in 1837 by Samuel Morse, American inventor (1791–1872), in collaboration with Alfred Vail.

MOTHER, GRANDMOTHER, GREAT GRANDMOTHER: Names given to big guns, 9-inch, 12-inch, 15-inch, used to destroy concrete emplacements near Festubert in 1915.

MUCKING-IN: A method of sharing rations, sleeping quarters and certain duties. Quite informal and arranged by the men themselves. A set of *mucking-in pals*, two, three or four, formed the true social unit of the army. Such a set would receive rations in a lump for all its members and divide them out; it would 'brew' its own tea and do its own cooking, when the company cooks provided nothing. *Mucking-in-pals* would defend each other's property against scroungers, receive letters and parcels for an absent member of the group and – out of the line – drink and feast together.

MUD-HOOK: See *Crown and Anchor*.

MUFTI: Civilian clothes. An officers' expression.

MULLIGAN: Camp stew. Pre-1914 Canadian and American.

MUNGAREE: Bread; food in general. From the Italian *mangiare*.

MUSH, THE: Sometimes spelt and pronounced *moosh*. Guardroom or cells. Derivation obscure.

MUSTARD GAS: Or *Yellow Cross Gas*. A poison gas which blistered the skin and eyes, and caused complete physical collapse. Named from the smell. Introduced by the Germans in July, 1917. Used in gas shells.

MUTT AND JEFF: The British War Medal and the Victory Medal of 1919. From comic paper characters.

MUZZY: Drunk. Dates from early eighteenth century.

NAB: To take quickly and sometimes illicitly; to steal. Also to arrest. Development from an old cant word.

NAIL: To accept or take without hesitation; to steal. In Chaucer as 'to take'; as 'to steal', from early nineteenth-century thieves' cant. See also *Coffin nails*.

151

NAME, TO LOSE ONE'S: To have one's name noted for a charge and so for punishment.

NAPOO: Finished; empty; gone; non-existent. Corrupted from the French *Il n' y en a plus* = there is no more, given in answer to enquiries for drink, when the estaminet keeper expected officers or highly paid troops – Australian, New Zealand, Canadian or A.S.C. men who could afford to pay higher prices. From this the word came to be used for many of the destructions, obliterations and disappointments of war, e.g. 'The bread's napoo'; 'The old dug-out's napoo'; 'Napoo rum'. (Cf. *Fini Kapout*.) Also sometimes as a verb.

NARK: A private currying favour with his superiors by doing odd jobs and especially by giving away things that private soldiers kept secret from N.C.O.'s and officers. A development from the ordinary-slang sense, a spoil-sport, and the thieves' slang (i.e. the cant) sense, a police spy or a common informer; the latter recorded for 1865. From Romany *nak*, the nose.

N.B.G.: No bloody good.

N.C.O.: Non-commissioned officer; e.g. a corporal or sergeant.

NEEDLE AND PIN: Gin.

NEXT OF KIN: Who had to be named by a soldier on enlistment. The next of kin's name and address was entered in his field service pay book, as the person to whom all effects and moneys due should be sent if and when the soldier died.

NICHEVO: No more; finished; gone, disappeared; dead. From the Russian. Used in prison camps in Germany and by the North Russian Expeditionary Force. So too the Russian *Niet Dobra*, meaning 'no good'.

NICK, THE: Guard-room, cells, prison. Probably from the late seventeenth-century colloquial *nick*, to arrest. Moreover the seventeenth-century sense of *nick*, to steal, has survived.

NICKNAMES: Certain nicknames inevitably accompanied certain surnames; *Darky* Smith, *Dolly* Gray, *Dusty* Miller, *Nobby* Clark, *Pedlar* Palmer, *Spud* Murphy, *Tug* Wilson are for various reasons listed separately. *Betsy* Gay; *Blanco* or *Chalky* or *Shiner* or *Knocker* White; *Bodger* or *Jigger* Lees; *Bogey* or *Chats* Harris; *Brigham* Young (from the Mormon leader); *Buck* Taylor; *Busky* or *Gunboat* or *Shoey* or

Smudger or *Darky* Smith; *Charley* Peace (from the nine-teenth-century burglar); *Chatty* Mather; *Chippy* Carpenter; *Dan* Coles; *Dinghy* or *Jesso* Read; *Dodger* or *Jimmy* or *Shiner* Green; *Doughy* Baker; *Dusty* Jordan or Rhodes or Smith as well as Miller; *Edna* (from the actress) or *Piggy* May; *Fanny* Fields (from the music hall actress, Happy Fanny Fields); *Flapper* Hughes; *Frog* or *Froggy* with any French name; *Ginger* Jones; *Granny* Henderson; *Happy* Day; *Hooky* or *Johnny* Walker (from the whisky); *Ikey* with any obviously Jewish name; *Jack* Shepherd, Shepperd, etc. (from the eighteenth-century highwayman); *Jock* with any very Scottish name; *Jumper* or *Lottie* Collins (from the music hall singer); *Kitty* Wells; *Knocker* Walker; *Knocky* Knight; *Timber* Wood; *Mouchy* Reeves; *Nobby* not only Clark but also Ewart, Hewart, Hewett; *Nutty* Cox; *Pincher* Martin; *Pills* Holloway; *Pony* Moore; *Rattler* Morgan; *Shiner* not only with White and Green but also with Bright, Black, Bryant, Wright; *Shorty* Wright; *Slinger* Woods; *Smoky* Holmes; *Snip* Parsons or Taylor; *Spiky* Sullivan; *Spokey* Wheeler or Wheelright; *Taffy* with any Welsh name; *Tod* Hunter or (after the jockey) *Sloan*; *Tom* King (after the highwayman); *Topper*, *Tupper* Brown; *Tottie* Bell; *Wheeler* Johnson; *Wiggy* Bennett. Any man with red hair might be called *Bluey*; any with white or flaxen hair, *Snowy*; tall men were called *Lofty*, short men *Bunty* or *Shorty*. In the Australian Forces anyone named Baker would be called *Snowy*, after a famous Australian boxer and swimmer.

NICKY: The end of a cigarette carefully extinguished and providently preserved – 'nicked off'.

NIGHT OPS: Night operations: a part of training that was half romantic and half burlesque, hardly ever realistic.

NINE-TWO, or *Nine-Point-Two*: A German heavy gun much feared for the noise and destructiveness of its shell-burst.

NISSEN: A small rectangular hut, of wood or corrugated iron, or both. Named presumably after the inventor. (Cf. *Elephant.*)

NIX: Nothing. From the German *nichts*. Used also by French soldiers, with a variant *nib*.

Nix Goot: No good. From the German and chiefly among prisoners of war.

Noah's Doves: Reinforcements still *en route* at the signing of the Armistice. (Cf. *Olive Branch.*)

Nobby: Applied to any man named Clark. See *Nicknames.*

No Bon: Cf. *Bon.*

No Goody-la: (Cf. *Goody-la.*)

No Man's Land: A strangely romantic name for the area between the front line trenches of either army, held by neither but patrolled, at night, by both. Originally used, according to Farmer and Henley, and Weekley, for waste ground, barren stretches between two provinces or kingdoms. Defoe in *Robinson Crusoe* uses it to signify 'a border'. The *O.E.D.* notes that an official Roll of A.D. 1320 (written of course in Latin) contains *nonesmanneslond.* Defoe spells it *no Man's Land,* T. Hughes in 1881 *noman's land,* and Dilke in 1890 *no-man's land.*

Non-stop: A shell that has passed high overhead.

Noper Force: The North Persian Force, operating in the latter half of 1918.

No Robin Hood: No bloody good.

North: North and South, i.e. mouth.

Nose and Chin: Gin.

Not Half: Pre-1914 cockney, but soon spread all over working-class England. Used in all kinds of connections to express emphasis. 'Not 'alf I didn't mop it up' — 'I drank as much as I could.' The answer 'Not 'alf!' given in response to 'Are you coming out tonight' means 'Yes, I am; certainly and gladly.' (Cf. *You bet. Too bloody Irish.*)

Number Nine: See *Sick.*

Number Nine King: The Medical Officer (Cf. *Sick.*)

Number On: A fatalistic but consolatory superstition insisted that no man need fear any bullet or shell, however close it came, unless it *had his regimental number* (or his name and number) engraved on it.

Number Up, To Have One's: Fatalistic for to be in trouble, or even to be doomed to die soon.

Numerals and Title: Worn on the shoulder straps, 1914–16 in brass, 1916–18 often in khaki cloth. The name of the regiment or corps was the title: the number of the battalion or company the numeral.

NUT: A man, especially a young man, paying great attention to his appearance and to dressing in the fashion of the moment. Pre-1914 civilian slang. Variant: *Knut*. A comic song ran: 'I'm Gilbert the Filbert, the Knut with a K.'

NUT, TO DO ONE'S: To desert. An extension of the same phrase in cockney slang meaning to get flurried, and go crazy.

NUT-WORKER: A shirker. Also, a malingerer. (Cf. *Head-worker*.)

N.Y.D.: A medical term, sometimes written on labels. Technically, 'Not yet diagnosed'. Interpreted by the patient as 'Not Yet Dead'.

OBSERVER: One who kept watch from a front trench, and through a telescope, on enemy positions on behalf of either the artillery or the infantry. After 1916 each battalion maintained a section of observers, ten or twelve men with a corporal in charge. There were also brigade and divisional observers under an Intelligence Officer. The fullest account of infantry-observing is probably in *Frank Honywood* by Eric Partridge (see *Three Personal Records of the War*).

OCEAN VILLAS: Auchonvillers, a town near Arras.

OCEAN PEARL: A girl.

O.C.: Officer Commanding. A more official variant of the more frequently used C.O. *(q.v.)*.

O.C. SWILLS: The officer in charge of the Salvage Corps or of any portion thereof or of any salvage work.

ODDS: *To shout the odds*, meant to brag or threaten in a loud voice. Anyone who has ever heard a hullaballoo of race-course bookmakers will understand the derivation of the phrase.

ODDS AND SODS: 'Details' attached to Battalion Headquarters for miscellaneous duties: batmen, sanitary men, professional footballers and boxers on nominal duties, etc.

OFF DUTY: Those periods, brief, uncertain and terminable at a moment's notice, when a private soldier was free to amuse himself as he pleased: with certain reservations, such as that he might not be seen with his hands in his pockets or with a tunic button unfastened or his hat off or without puttees; that he might not wander beyond certain strictly-defined limits or ask for a drink in 'Officers Only' establishments or omit to salute any and every officer within sight. In practice, of course, privates quickly grew used to these prohibitions and obeyed them without thinking or found ways and means of dodging them. So, probably, did slaves in Ancient Rome.

OFF IT: To die. (Cf. *Packet* and *West.*)

OFFENSIVE: An attack on a large scale. Also used by G.H.Q. in 1916–17 for a frame of mind it desired to encourage in front-line troops in order to weaken the enemy's confidence. Enquiries were sent to commanding officers: did they consider they had been 'sufficiently offensive' that day. The word became a joke and another grudge against brass hats.

OFFICE: The cockpit of a 'plane; Air Force term. In the Army, often the Orderly Room.

OFFICER BLOKE: A batman's term for his officer.

O'GRADY: A mythical personage who said things. *O'Grady* was a favourite game organized by Physical Training Instructors to relieve the monotony of exercises. Various orders were shouted, but only those preceded by the phrase *O'Grady says* were to be obeyed. Those men who failed to discriminate properly were made to run violently to a distant point and back. The game may sound too simple to deceive even a ploughboy, but when conditioned to an instantaneous and mindless response to drill orders bawled with authority, to stop and think first was not so easy.

O. i/c: Officer in charge of, used for specialist appointments such as Signals and Intelligence, in an infantry battalion; usually held by a subaltern.

OIL: *The oil* meant 'The truth,' i.e. the real thing. Probably from prospectors in the oil-fields. 'Is that the oil?' meaning 'Is it authentic?' Sometimes *the good oil*. Originally and largely Australian slang, and synonymous with another Australianism, *the straight wire*.

OIL-CANS: German Trench Mortar shells, from their shape. (Cf. *Trench Mortar, Minnie.*)

OLD BEAN: Pre-1914. A familiar form of address, indicating affection. No meaning. Almost certainly derived from the musical comedy dude, perhaps by extension of *old man*, 'old' indicating affection and respect. (Cf. French *mo nvieux* and *vieille branche.*)

OLD IRON AND BRASS: A pass.

OLD MAN: The Colonel in charge of a battalion; any other Commanding Officer. In rhyming slang, *Old Pot and Pan*, which, in civilian slang and like *Old Man*, also = father.

OLD ONE O'CLOCK: Von Kluck, commander of the German First Army in 1914.

OLD SOLDIER: One grown old in sin. A term of mingled admiration and criticism, implying cunning in the art of dodging work and trouble from authority, to the point of malingering. See also *Come the Old Soldier*.

OLD SWEAT: A soldier with considerable service and therefore an accumulation of cunning; especially a *time-serving* (cf.) man.

OLIVE BRANCH: A reinforcement who arrived at a unit H.Q. on or after November 11, 1918.

'OLLER, BOYS, 'OLLER!: A collar.

O MY: Short for 'Oh my Gawd', i.e. sword.

ON THE MAT: To be tried by the Commanding Officer for a minor offence. A mat was often laid before the table at which the C.O. sat, and on this the offender stood at attention. (Cf. *Cap off, For It, High Jump, Orders.*)

ON THE NEVER: To obtain anything *on the never* was to get it without proper payment, either by credit or by *wangling* (cf.). Perhaps a contraction from *on the never-never*, which may be derived from the Never Never Land in J. M. Barrie's *Peter Pan* [1904].

ON THE SQUARE: Drilling on the parade ground. Its general sense, 'on the level', 'honourable', originated as a Masonic term.

ON THE TAPES: Lying out, by night, at a line of assembly tapes laid down in No Man's Land, waiting for the signal to start a raid or a night assault. Hence, ready, alert, prepared, expectant. See *Taped*.

ONCE A WEEK: Cheek.

ONE AND T'OTHER: Brother.

ONE OF THE BOYS: *To be one of the boys* or *one of the lads* was to be accepted, popular, cheerful and debonair.

ONE'S NAME ON IT: Fatalistic. A supposed enemy missile destined to hit one particular person – who would not hear it until too late. (Cf. *Number on.*)

OOJAH: Or, in full, oojah-cum-pivvy. A military equivalent for 'thingamybob'; a word substituted when the proper name cannot be remembered; or, for the mere fun of using the fantastic syllables, when it is perfectly well known, e.g. 'I saw the S.M. going into the oojah-cum-pivvy down the road' – an estaminet being implied and understood. The Canadians said *hooza-me-kloo*; an English variant was *oojiboo*. In the 55th Division (West Lancashire), *oojah-kerpiv* meant any trench utensil, e.g. a jack knife or a mess-tin. Variant: *oojah-ka-piv*.

O. PIP: Signalese for O.P., i.e. Observation Post. (Cf. *Pip Emma*.)

OPERA HOUSE: Guard room; cells; prison.

ORCHESTRA, THE: Short for *Orchestra Stalls*, rhyming slang for balls, i.e. testicles.

ORDERLY: A soldier accompanying an officer during an inspection or otherwise detailed for special duties. A man-servant in a hospital, hospital-train or Casualty Clearing Station.

ORDERLY BUFF: Variation of *Orderly Man* (cf.); or the Orderly Sergeant. The Orderly Corporal was often called the *Orderly Dog*.

ORDERLY CORPORAL: A corporal selected for temporary duty, by rota. (Cf. *Orderly Sergeant*.)

ORDERLY MAN: Two men from each platoon were appointed each day, by rota or by caprice of the sergeant, to do the odd jobs of tidying and cleaning the platoon's quarters. Their most important function was to fetch the platoon's food at meal-times and distribute it fairly. (Cf. *Dixie, Mess-tin, Dish-out*.)

ORDERLY OFFICER: An officer selected by rota to perform certain inspections and other duties, relating to the whole battalion, for a period of twenty-four hours. Almost all that private soldiers knew about the *Orderly Officer* was that he inspected the guard for the day and visited all platoons during dinner. This was a barracks or camp routine, not kept up in the line. (Cf. *Complaints*.)

ORDERLY ROOM: The administrative office of a unit. Here also *Orders* (cf.) were held.

ORDERLY SERGEANT: Selected by rota for twenty-four-hour duties, roughly parallel to those of *Orderly Officer* (cf.)

ORDERS: The daily trial, by the Commanding Officer of a battalion or other unit, of minor offences. So-called because

158

the punishments were listed the next day in Battalion Orders, displayed outside the Orderly Room. The practice was rarely, if ever, kept up in the line. (Cf. *Cap Off*, *For It* and *High Jump*.)

ORIGINALS: Those who survived from the personnel of a unit or a contingent when it first saw active service. The First Canadian Contingent, e.g., was known as either *Originals* or *Firsts*.

O.T.C.: Officers' Training Corps.

OTHER RANKS: N.C.O.s and privates.

OURS: British or allied. (Cf. *His*.)

OUTFIT: A battalion or other unit. (Cf. *Mob*.)

OVER THE BAGS: *Bags* here is *sandbags*. (Cf. *Over the Top* and *Hop Over*.)

OVER THE LID, OVER THE PLONK (The latter a 1916 phrase): The same as *Over the Top*.

OVER THE TOP: To leave the shelter of a fire trench in order to make an assault, troops had to hoist themselves over the front wall of sandbags (the parapet). Many were struck down by bullet or shell explosion before they had time to take a stride forward. The phrase was originally *over the top and the best of luck*, but as casualties increased and so many attacks ended in disaster, 'and the best of luck' was either omitted or spoken in bitter irony.

OWL: A painted figure of an owl; a warning-device, with or without a verse inscription, put up to enjoin discreet speech on all occasions. The French equivalent was the placard, *Méfiez-vous, les oreilles ennemies vous écoutent:* Be on your guard, hostile ears listen to you. The Germans used: *Vorsicht bei Sprechen. Spionengefahr:* Mind your words; spy-danger! The verse that went with the owl sign was pre-1914. It ran:

'A wise old owl lived in an oak,
The more he heard the less he spoke;
The less he spoke the more he heard;
Why aren't we all like that wise old bird!'

PACK: Used in two senses, to mean either the entire equipment which the infantryman carried on his back, i.e. belt, braces, pouches, haversack, valise, water-bottle, with their contents, as well as steel helmet, entrenching tool, bayonet, rifle, gas-mask, etc.; alternatively, the valise (or knapsack) with its contents. The men of the New Army carried an average weight of sixty six pounds each when they went over the top on July 1st, 1916 for the opening assault of the Battle of the Somme. The rifle alone weighed nine pounds and in winter there was the additional weight of heavy underclothing and a leather or leather-and-wool jerkin. Entering the trenches, extra ammunition, extra rations, grenades, sandbags and often picks and shovels, wire and picquets had to be carried, and each man took his share. One basic fact about the War on the Western Front is that it was fought by men who were almost always tired, because they got little and disturbed sleep in the line, and because they were, day in and day out, weighed down by appalling physical burdens. Officers, generally speaking, were exempt from carrying burdens, though some formed the prudent habit of disguising themselves as private soldiers in action by carrying a rifle and a 'skeleton' equipment. Many junior officers, however, on the march helped men in distress by relieving them of part of their load. This was a strictly unofficial practice. See *Harness, Marching Order, Pack.*

PACK-DRILL: Drill in full marching order performed continuously at high speed under the direction of a Provost Sergeant. This was carried out only as a punishment – an exceptionally severe one. (Cf. *F.P. No. 1.*)

PACKET: *To cop a packet* meant sometimes to be fatally wounded, sometimes simply to be wounded. *Blighty* or *Blighty one* (*q.v*) was more for a non-fatal wound. *Cop*, of course, is cockney for 'to catch'. (Cf. copper = a policeman.) The literal reference of *packet* was perhaps the missile, perhaps the gauze and lint of the First Field Dressing which the wounded man or his friends would apply to the wound. Sometimes abbreviated to *cop it*. (Cf. *West.*)

PACKET OF FAGS: A well-remembered Russian cruiser that in 1914 helped to escort British troops from the East. From the four thin upright funnels.

PACK UP: To finish, to yield; to die.

PADDY DOYLE, To Do: To be imprisoned, to be in cells.

PADRE: Chaplain. An accredited priest or minister wearing military uniform. From the Portuguese and Spanish *Padre* – Father, priest. This word was adopted by the Army from the Portuguese in India during the eighteenth century. A chaplain had few definite duties: he could make himself useful or he could slack. In general, it may be said that all Roman Catholic *padres* were respected, because they came into the line and because they lacked the haw-haw voice. Church of England and Nonconformist *padres* were popularly divided into three classes: (1) The man-of-the-world who swore and over-drank – he was despised and disliked; (2) the earnest but ineffectual; despised but tolerated; (3) the spiritual but determined, who made himself useful as a first-aid man and distributor of cigarettes. Chaplains were respected when they showed courage under fire and some for their moral and spiritual qualities.

PAHNY: Water (Hindustani).

PAKARU: Damaged, broken, smashed. New Zealand troops: a Maori word.

PAL: Friend, comrade. From Romany *pal*, a brother (especially in villainy); in eighteenth century often spelt *pell*. See Grose's Dictionary, edition of 1931. Rarely used in vocative unless with *old*. (Cf. *Chum*.) In Liverpool and Manchester in 1914 several thousand men volunteered almost *en masse* for the Army, forming two brigades, each of four 'Pals' Battalions.

PARACHUTE FLARE (or LIGHT): Originally of French design. Fired like a rocket and, thanks to its parachute-attachment, taking a long time to land. Later adapted so that it could be fired from a long-butted $1\frac{1}{4}$-inch Very pistol.

PARAPET: The side (topped by sandbags) of a fire bay which faced towards the enemy. The *parados* was the rearward side. Both words are taken from early French works on fortification; they have changed somewhat from their first significations.

PARK: Usually Artillery Park. Any enclosure or piece of ground where guns or vehicles were kept.

PART-WORN: Clothing which had been worn previously by another soldier, deceased, sick or otherwise having no use for it. *Part-worn* clothing could often be exchanged for something better by discreet bribery.

PASS: A form signed by a commanding officer stating that the soldier who held it had permission to travel to such and such a place from this date to that. Without a *pass*, a soldier 'out of bounds' was liable to be arrested by military police.

PAT AND MIKE: A 'bike'.

PATROL: Generally the nocturnal exploration and 'policing' of No-man's Land – a nervy job.

PAVÉ: The stone-block roads of northern France and Belgium.

PAY BOOK: The Field Service pay book covered in brown cloth also acted as a kind of identity document: see *Next of kin*.

PAYING OUT: The use, generally by an officer, of very forcible language, especially when fault-finding.

P.B.I., THE: Poor Bloody Infantry.

PECKHAM RYE: Tie.

PEDLAR: Nickname applied to any man named Palmer. Perhaps from a pugilist. Possibly from the late Middle Ages when palmer was a name for pilgrims who, returning from the Holy Land, carried a palm-branch. (Cf. *Nicknames*.)

PEG: *To be on the peg*, alternative to *on the mat* (cf.).

PERISHER: Periscope. A mirror device enabling a man in a trench to see over the parapet without exposing his head.

P.H. HELMET: see *Gas Mask*.

PHOSGENE: The most lethal kind of Poison Gas.

PIACHE: Mad; on analogy of *stone mad*, sometimes *stone piache*. Used by men with Indian service.

PICKELHAUBE: The German ceremonial and full-dress helmet made with patent leather and adorned with large metal badges and spikes. Protected by a cloth cover on the march. Much sought after as a souvenir in early days of the war on the Western Front.

PICQUETS (or *Piquets*): Wooden stakes or spirals of iron to support barbed wire entanglements.

PIECE: A girl; a wench. Used in this sense as far back as the eighteenth century, when the phrase was often *piece of furniture*, i.e. a kept woman in furnished rooms.

PIGGY-STICK: The wooden helve for the entrenching tool which the infantryman carried at his hip next his bayonet; it could be useful in a *rough house* (cf.). From a child's game, tip-cat, in which a chip of wood is tipped into the air, and then hit with a stick.

PIG'S EAR: Beer.

PILL-BOX: A small fortification of reinforced concrete used especially for machine-guns. A German invention. The English name is from the cylindrical shape. (See also *Moir's Pill-box*.)

PIMPLE: Name given to various small hills on the Western and other fronts.

PINCH: To steal. Pre-1914 civilian slang. Probably from the action of the thief's fingers closing on his prize. (Cf. *Snaffle, Half-inch, Scrounge*.) Also, to arrest.

PINEAPPLE: A German mortar-bomb with a wind-vane.

PIONEERS: There was a battalion of pioneers to each infantry division. Each battalion also had, in theory, a section of Pioneers with a Pioneer Sergeant. Grose, in 1786, writes: 'Pioneers were not formerly taken from the troops, as has been the practice of late years, but were sturdy labourers, pressed and equipped for the service they were to perform ... About the time of Queen Elizabeth, soldiers guilty of certain offences were degraded to pioneers.'

PIP: The star, in cloth or gilt, worn on the sleeve and on the shoulder-strap by a second-lieutenant. A lieutenant wore two, a captain three. Above that rank, a crown was worn until, with generals, there were various gilt devices of crossed batons and swords, all looking much the same to a private soldier who saw a general once in a blue-moon and that was often enough. Officers' slang referred to *one-pippers* or *two-pip merchants, artists* or *wallahs*. Junior officers became casualties in an attack in such numbers that a popular saying was – 'one star, one stunt' (i.e. attack).

PIP EMMA: Signalese for p.m. It was often difficult to pass messages accurately over a field telephone, and in order to differentiate similar sounds a system was devised by which A became ack, B – beer, D – don, M – emma, P – pip, S – esses, T – toc, V – vic. This pronunciation was often taken into the general Army vocabulary. A Trench Mortar Battery would be referred to, for example, as a Toc Emma Beer.

It may be noted the common phonetic alphabet was

changed by the War Office in February, 1921, as follows:

A. – Ac	N. – Nuts
B. – Beer	O. – Orange
C. – Charlie	P. – Pip
D. – Don	Q. – Queen
E. – Edward	R. – Robert
F. – Freddie	S. – Sugar
G. – George	T. – Toc
H. – Harry	U. – Uncle
I. – Ink	V. – Vic
J. – Johnnie	W. – William
K. – King	X. – X-ray
L. – London	Y. – Yellow
M. – Monkey	Z. – Zebra

Thus the Ac Emma; O. Pip; Emma Gee; Toc Emma Beer of 1914–18 soon receded into history.

PIPE-LINE: A ditch for telephone wires, 'permanent' lines being nearly always protected thus. The wire laid, the ditch was filled up again and roughly 'disguised'. (Cf. *Cable-Trench*.)

PIPPED: *To be pipped* meant to be hit, especially by a bullet.

PIP-SQUEAK: Sometimes, gas-shell. Loosely, whizz-bang. Properly, shell from small trench gun (German).

PLAIN CLOTHES: Cavalry, Guards and Naval equivalent to *Mufti*.

PLASTER: To shell; especially to shell heavily.

PLATES OF MEAT: Feet.

PLATOON: The sub-unit of an infantry company. It consisted of four sections, each of sixteen (later nine) men. It had a platoon commander (a lieutenant or second-lieutenant), a platoon sergeant, and at least four corporals, one to each section. See *Roll Call*.

PLINK-PLONK: Facetious for *vin blanc* (cf.). Variants were *plinkety-plonk, blink-blonk*.

PLONK: To shell. Echoic.

PLUG: To shoot and hit. Used only transitively. Occasionally, 'hit, strike with fist'. Abbreviated metaphor – to plug with lead.

PLUGSTREET: English approximation to Ploegsteert, a wood in Belgium. (Cf. *Etaples* and *Ypres*.)

PLUM AND APPLE: see *Pozzy*.

PLUM PUDDINGS: Trench Mortar Bombs. (Cf. *Trench Mortar*.)

PNEUMATIC CAVALRY: Cyclish battalions.

POILU: French for an infantryman – hairy. Déchelette defines: 'Soldat [français] de la Grande Guerre, c'est à dire gars à poil.' D. says that the word became popular almost from the beginning of the War, that it had been used for 'a soldier' by Rabelais and Balzac, and that 'hair has always been accepted as a mark of courage, of manly strength'; he adds that this is the real origin – not the fact that in the first months of the War French soldiers, of necessity, let the hair grow on their faces. He notes that during the War the word was more used behind the lines than at the front, and at the front only by officers and N.C.O.s. Dauzat in *L'Argot de la Guerre*, 1918, 2nd ed. 1919, has several pages on this word.

French soldiers seem to have liked 'poilu' as little as British soldiers liked 'Tommy'. The French preferred to call themselves 'les hommes' or 'les bonhommes'.

POINT BLANK: White wine: for French *vin blanc*.

POISON GAS: The Germans first used poison gas from cylinders on April 22, 1915, at Ypres. See *Der Chemische Krieg*, by Rudolph Hanslian, translated by Lieut. C. Stanford, R.C.C.S.

The British first adopted retaliatory measures on September 25, 1915, at Loos. See *Gas Mask, Mustard Gas, Phosgene, Respirator*.

POLICEMAN'S TRUNCHEON: A German hand-grenade: see *Stick Bomb*.

POMFRITZ: Chips (potato): French *pommes de terres frites*.

PONTIUS PILATE: A provost sergeant. In the eighteenth century, a pawnbroker.

PONTOON: A bridge built on water-tight metal cylinders floating in the water.

PONTOON: A card game, rather like vingt-et-un; in the Army as popular as brag and banker, but less popular than Crown and Anchor or House.

POODLEFAKER: An officer always ready, or indeed over-ready, to take part in the social side of military life. Pre-1914. Common also in the Navy.

POOP OFF: To fire a big gun (*not* a rifle).

POP: Short for *Poperinghe*, a town behind the line in Belgium, offering many amenities to troops on rest.

PORK AND BEANS: Facetious approximation to Portuguese, who maintained two divisions in France. *Pork and Beans*, with very little pork, was a staple part of Army rations. (Cf. *Antonio, Macaroni, Russki, Chink, Aussie, Froggie, Yank.*)

POSH: Bright; neat; smart; best in quality and appearance. Adjective: probably abbreviated from 'polish'. Used chiefly of clothes, but also of persons, e.g. 'That's a posh new tunic you've got,' or 'Proper posh you are tonight.' Farmer and Henley give *posh*: a dandy. (Cf. *Square-pushing.*)

POSH UP: Verb: To smarten one's appearance. (Cf. *Posh.*)

POTATO-MASHER: A type of German hand-grenade, see *Stick-Bomb.*

POULTICE WALLAH or WALLOPER: An R.A.M.C. orderly.

POW-WOW: A conference of senior officers.

POZZY: Jam. Derivation untraced. Sometimes pronounced *possy*. This word, of obscure origin, dates apparently from about 1884. Perhaps from Swazi, Basuto, or Zulu. Negroes in South Africa used the word, before 1900 at least, to designate any sort of sweetmeat or preserve. The word may possibly have owed its revival during the Great War partly, at any rate, to the fact that in 1914 and early 1915 English troops had (? from canteens) condensed milk in small tins bearing a carnation on the label and the legend 'Posy Brand'; when jam was 'napoo', this condensed milk was spread as a substitute on bread and biscuits, later, when jam became more plentiful, *possy* (or *pozzy*) may have continued to do service as a generic name.

In the first years of the War only one form of jam was available – plum and apple. Later other kinds were supplied, chiefly doubtful mixtures such as gooseberry and rhubarb. Tins also were replaced by cardboard cylinders. To the end an issue of strawberry or raspberry jam was an historic occasion.

POZZY-WALLAH: A man inordinately fond of jam.

PROMENADE: A stroll. A favourite opening to a conversation with a young French woman was, 'Mademoiselle, promenade avec moi ce soir?' This was rarely a serious invitation: mere raillery.

PROPAGANDA: Any exaggeration or baseless rumour. Officers' slang.

PROPER: Very, or very good. Taken from cultured English into the vernacular without any precise sense of its meaning and used as a vague intensive. (Cf. *Chronic.*)

PROVOST SERGEANT: Usually pronounced 'Provo'. An N.C.O. attached to Battalion Headquarters and responsible for the care of offenders and accused men in the guard-room. In charge of the *Regimental Police* (cf.). (Also cf. *Pack Drill.*)

P'S AND Q'S: Shoes.

P.T.: Physical Training. (Cf. *Jerks.*)

P.T.I.: Physical Training Instructor. An N.C.O. with this specialist full-time job.

PUDDING-BASIN: Steel-helmet. (Cf. *Tin Hat* and *Battle Bowler.*)

PUGGLED: Eccentric; odd, insane; mad-drunk; rattled. Sometimes *poggle(d)*.

PUKKA: Regular Army, pre-1914, for real, genuine, correct, smart, soldierly. (From Hindustani *pakkha.*)

PULL OUT, TO: When a battery of field guns was to leave a position, the horses were brought up by night to haul the guns out of the gun pits and on the road.

PULL-THROUGH: Facetious name for a very tall and thin soldier. Literally, a cord for cleaning the barrel of a rifle. See Note on page 66.

PULPIT: A ladder leading to an *O.-Pip.*

PUMP SHIP: To urinate. Metaphor from sailor's slang.

PUNG: A sly sleep at telephone duty. Signalese.

PUP: The fast though small Sopwith single-seater 80-h.p. 'plane.

PURGE: To grumble; to swear. Especially of an officer.

PUSH: An attack in force, by several infantry divisions working in co-operation. The word first became popular, perhaps through journalism, in 1916, and *The Big Push* was the general name at that time for the British assaults on the Somme in July and August. The word indicates the desired ideal rather than the actuality. (Cf. *Stunt, Show.*) Also an Army unit (Cf. *crowd, mob,* etc.)

PUSH A BIT OF BOW BACK: To have a sleep.

PUSHING UP DAISIES: Dead – and buried. A civilian phrase. 'To turn up one's toes to the daisies', dates as far back as Barham's *Ingoldsby Legends*, 1837.

167

PUT IT ACROSS: Cf. *Slip it Across.*

PUT SOME JILDI INTO IT: Same as *Jump to it.*

PUT UP: To charge with a military crime or misdemeanour, i.e. to put a man up before the C.O.

PUT WISE: To show a new officer over the trenches. An adopted Americanism.

PUTTEE: The cloth band wound round the leg from the upper of the boot to near the knee; to give support when walking. 'A whole pamphlet might be written on the artistic spiralling of putties, their helical cometry. The salvation of one's soul and the health of the sergeant's liver depend on that.' There were two accepted ways of winding the puttee for active service, and several dressy ways for social service. The word comes from the Hindustani for bandage. *Puttee* became accepted in English late in the nineteenth century.

PUTTY MEDAL: One earned easily.

Q.: See *G. and Q.*

QUAKERS: Slang for Conscientious Objectors.

QUARTER BLOKE: The Quartermaster, an officer usually commissioned from the ranks of the Regular Army and approaching (or ensconced in) middle age. Occasionally used loosely for the Regimental Quartermaster-Sergeant. Both men were responsible for providing supplies of food, clothing, etc., for the entire unit and distributing them to the Company Quartermaster-Sergeants. It is possible there were some honest men among Q.Ms.

QUARTER-BLOKE'S ENGLISH: The businesslike, itemized English affected by Quartermasters and their assistants. *Gum Boots* and *Thigh Boots* were in Quarterese described as *Boots, gum and Boots, Thigh, Soldiers, for the use of.*

QUEER: Unwell; the Australian equivalent was *crook.*

QUICK DICK: One of our guns, Western Front.

QUAIES KATEAH: Very good. Arabic. Very common with troops in Egypt or with Regulars that had been there. (Cf. *Trez beans.*

QUIFF: Carefully brushed and oiled hair, especially that part of it swept across or back from the temples. From Middle English and French *coif*: head-dress.

RACE CARD: The Sick Report, furnished after morning Sick Parade.

Rag Fair: Kit inspection. Recorded in its military sense by Captain Grose in 1785, *Rag Fair* was earlier applied to a district in Whitechapel, London, where old clothes and similar goods were sold. See *Kit Inspection*.

Ragtime: Music written in syncopated time. Now superseded by *jazz*. The troops used *ragtime* as an adjective for any manifestation of inefficiency or absurdity. See the song 'He's a Ragtime Soldier', page 58.

Raid: See *Trench raid*.

Rainbow: A new recruit arriving with reinforcements just after a battle. A 1917–18 word.

Ramassage Train: A train made up of sundry passenger coaches, horse-boxes, and goods trucks or wagons, collected apparently anywhere and going up near 'the line' with no fixed time-table.

R.A.M.C.: Royal Army Medical Corps, responsible for the transport of wounded behind the lines and the organization of hospitals. Often called the *Rob All My Comrades*, because the private effects and souvenirs of an unconscious or sleeping man might sometimes disappear on the way to hospital, never to be recovered. (Cf. *Ally Sloper's Cavalry*.)

Ramparts, The: At Ypres; famous for the billets they afforded.

Rapid Fire: See *Mad Minute*.

Raspberry: Civilian pre-1914 slang. A pseudo-fart, a method of expressing theatrical disapproval phonetically represented by Shakespeare as *buz, buz;* this the editors, so well brought up, fail to perceive or hesitate to recognise in Prince Hamlet:

> *Polonius.* The actors are come hither, my lord
> *Hamlet.* Buz, buz [i.e. giving him a raspberry].
> *Polonius [pained].* Upon mine honour.
> *Hamlet [always fond of puns].* Then came each
>   actor on his ass.

Showing contempt by blowing through the closed fist was and is known as giving (someone) a raspberry.

Raspberry Tart: Rhyming slang for 'fart'.

Rat and Mouse: A house.

RATION DUMP: Generic for a company, battalion, or brigade dump for stores, ammunition, and other supplies. (Cf. *Refilling Point.*)

RATIONS: *Dry Rations:* bread, biscuits, cheese, butter, jam, uncooked food. *Wet Rations:* porridge, tea, any cooked food. Before 1914, *rations* rhymed with *nations*.

RATS AFTER MOULDY CHEESE: The R.A.M.C.

R.A.V.C.: Royal Army Veterinary Corps.

RAZZLE: To be or go on the razzle = to make an expedition in search of entertainment and pleasure, to spend money. Not necessarily to get drunk. (Cf. *Binge.*)

R.E.: The Royal Engineers; the designers, constructors, and superintenders of military works.

READ A SHIRT: Examine the seams of a shirt for lice. The phrase, belonging to 1917–18, became generic for *chatt* (cf.).

RECONNOITRE: To scrounge (*q.v.*).

RED CAPS: Military Police. So called because they wore a lid-like cover of red flannel over the top of their khaki caps. Employed sometimes for the regulation of traffic, but chiefly to walk about the streets, examine passes, watch private soldiers, arrest absentees and generally enforce military law. They were also employed to staff military prisons and by all accounts fully exploited the opportunities for cruelty which the job gave them. Red Caps were not usually drawn from the civil police; the job was voluntary and few decent men would undertake it if they realized what it implied. (See *Battle Police* and *Etaples.*)

RED CROSS: The ambulance service in war; its emblem.

RED HAT: A staff officer.

RED LAMP: A brothel, licensed and under police surveillance. A red bracket lamp outside was the recognized sign. (Cf. *Knocking Shop.*)

RED LAMP CORNER: A very dangerous 'corner' near Festubert.

RED TABS: The gorget patches of a staff officer, who was therefore occasionally called a *Red Tab.*

REDOUBT: A position (usually in a fire trench) fortified to resist attack from any direction. (Cf. *Keep.*)

REFILLING POINT: The technical name for the divisional dump; a notorious source of scandal and gossip.

REGIMENT: Generally speaking, rather a popular than a technical name for an infantry battalion. Properly, a permanent unit of the Army consisting of several battalions. Also used of artillery and cavalry. The Engineers, the Signals, the Medicals were Corps.

REGIMENTAL: Proper noun; short for *Regimental Sergeant-Major* (*q.v.*) Used as an adjective, *regimental* meant excessively disciplinarian, enforcing every regulation in every detail. E.g. 'Up the line you don't hear a word from him, but when we come out he's too bloody regimental for words.'

REGIMENTAL NUMBER: A number given to a man on enlistment, and kept in the records throughout his service. When two men of the same name served in the same platoon or battery, they were distinguished by the two final digits of their regimental numbers: e.g. 03 Williams and 72 Williams.

REGIMENTAL POLICE: Not *Red Caps* (cf.), but a few men appointed chiefly to watch bounds and escort prisoners. Sometimes amenable to quite small bribes. There were also Brigade Police, who performed similar duties.

REGISTERING: Experimental shots by the artillery, of which a record was kept, so that concentrated fire could be directed on the target when necessary with some hope of hitting it. (Cf. *Bracketing*.)

RELIEF: The man who replaced a sentry on duty, allowing him to retire for a short rest: or the process of replacement. In this sense, an old military term, used in the opening scene of Hamlet ('For this relief, much thanks'). Also used for the process whereby a battalion or company filed into front line trenches and took over the duty of holding them.

RENDER: To work or 'go' properly, of any instrument or other mechanical contrivance. Officers' slang.

RESPIRATOR: Short for Box Respirator, which replaced the earlier *Gas Mask* (*q.v.*). From 1917 it was carried by all troops in forward areas and proved an efficient safeguard against poison gas. The principle was that air was breathed in through a metal box containing chemicals. See also *Gas Bag*.

REST. A temporary withdrawal from the forward trench-system. All troops were kept very busy when 'out at rest'.

REST CAMPS: Camps behind the lines where troops returning

weary from the line were harried with incessant parades and brass-polishing. Also used ironically for cemeteries.

REVEILLE: The rousing, the first bugle call of the day. From French, but not military French, which has long used *Diane* and *Reveil*. (Cf. *Last Post.*)

REVET: Originally to face an embankment or wall with masonry. In 1914–18, to strengthen a trench by facing it not with masonry but with stakes, or faggots, angle irons, wooden frames, or even (by extension) with sand-bags.

R.F.A.: Royal Field Artillery.

RHYMING SLANG: Some private soldiers of the pre-War Regular Army had a most intricate system of slang in which one word was referred to obliquely by means of another word or phrase rhyming with it. Rhyming slang is also found among cockneys, and probably originated as a device of thieves and other petty criminals for talking secretly in front of other people. The rhymes chosen, oddly enough, often indicate a religious upbringing or the memory of innocent nursery rhymes, e.g. 'Buckle-my-shoe' for 'Jew', 'Cain and Abel' for 'table', etc. (Cf. *Half-inch*, *Tit-for*, etc.)

Writing in 1858, J. C. Hotten (lexicographer of slang, and publisher) said that rhyming slang was introduced about 1843 by chaunters (street singers of low or very topical ballads) and patterers (cheapjacks relying on their eloquence) as distinct from costermongers. But probably, as in effect he admitted in a later edition, this very simple type of 'disguise' slang, which was considerably more obvious than the back-slang so general in the nineteenth century, was probably known to, and spoken by, coster-mongers as early as 1850, while nearly all cockneys were more or less acquainted with it by 1860. Neither rhyming slang nor back-slang was half so baffling as the cant (i.e. the lingo of thieves and other criminals, of gipsies and vagabonds) prevailing from about 1500 to about 1800, and persisting, Eric Partridge believes, to this day. Rhyming slang, though less interesting than cant, is more amusing. There exists a delightful specimen of rhyming-slang verse, entitled *The Dream*, of which we can, unfortunately, quote only the first two of the five stanzas:

I was sittin' alone by the fireside one night
A-warmin' me plates of meat;
When wot should I 'ear but a knock on the door
Which caused me old raspberry to beat.

So I puts down me glass and old cherry ripe
Which I 'olds in me German band,
And I goes to the top of the apples and pears *(stairs)*
Wiv me dooks all ready to land.

RICHARD or RANDY RICHARD: A common though not the general name for an observation balloon.

RICHARD THE THIRD: A bird.

RICKO: Ricochet.

RIGHTO: Yes; Yes, I'll do it; or, Quite correct.

RISE AND SHINE: See 'Chants and Sayings', page 225.

RIVER OUSE: Booze.

R.N.A.S.: Royal Naval Air Service.

ROCKER, OFF ONE'S: Mad. Civilian. Pre-1914.

ROCKS: See *Army Rocks*.

ROCKS AND BOULDERS: Shoulders.

ROLL CALL: At least once a day, usually in the morning, the roll was called and every man 'on the strength' had to be accounted for. In the infantry each section commander (corporal) would read out the names of all the men in his section. When this check was complete the platoon sergeant would report to the platoon commander (lieutenant or second-lieutenant). "All present and correct sir," or alternatively state the number of absentees.. Platoon statistics were reported to company commanders (captains) and so to the battalion commander, second in command or adjutant.

ROLL ON, DEMOBILIZATION: The nickname given to the engines of the Railway Operating Department plying between 'Pop' and 'Wypers'; because of the huge *R.O.D.* painted in white letters on their sides.

ROODY BOYS: Rue du Bois, near Neuve Chapelle.

ROOKY: A recruit. Corruption of *recruit*. Regular Army. Pre-1914.

ROOTY: Bread. Urdu, *roti*. Sala in 1883 records that he heard it used by a private about 1875. The word caught on in India among the rank and file *ca.* 1800; it did not become common in England until the Army-reorganization of 1881 led to frequent interchanges between battalions at home and abroad.

ROOTY MEDAL: Long Service medal, i.e. earned by eating army rations for a number of years. An old Regular Army variant: *Rooty Gong:* 'Eighteen years of undetected crime.'

RORY O'MORE. Door. In 1872 it seems to have stood for floor.

ROSEBUDS: Spuds.

ROSS RIFLE: Often *the Ross.* This .303 was used by the Canadians until May, 1915.

ROSY LEE: Tea.

ROUGH HOUSE: A general fight or disorder, arising from an argument, boasting or liquor. So called from public-houses in which such rows were frequent. Occasionally used as a verb. Civilian. Pre-1914.

ROUND THE HOUSES: Trousers, owing to slovenly pronunciation as *trouse's.*

ROUTE, COLUMN OF: A column of infantry four abreast for drill purposes or road marching. Corporals and lance-corporals were in the fours alongside privates. Senior N.C.O.s, warrant officers and officers marched separately. Their places in the column and the spacing between platoons and companies were formalised but varied with the occasion.

ROUTE MARCH: In the Army 'route' always rhymed with 'scout'. A march over a pre-determined route and along roads undertaken as physical training. Day-long route marches covered 12–16, sometimes 20 miles. The distances may not seem great but for men so heavily burdened [see *Marching Order*] route marching was a severe test of physical and moral endurance, especially to men 'resting' after a long spell in the line where conditions were not only dangerous but in many ways unhealthy.

R.S.M.: Regimental Sergeant-Major, the top-most authority among warrant officers of a battalion. Almost always a big man with a big voice and a fearsome manner.

R.T.O.: Railway Transport Officer. Very often an officer recovering from wounds or sickness. On the Western Front there was an *R.T.O.s* office in almost every station of any importance behind the lines, and it was his business to facilitate (a word of delightful vagueness) the transport of troop trains, and to assist soldiers rejoining their units from leave, hospital or a *course* (cf.). When a battalion was on the move, it was often very difficult for such men to rejoin it, and returning soldiers might easily and deliberately spend a week or more in making several short railway trips, a delightful holiday rich with new scenes and an air of personal freedom otherwise unknown in the Army. The principle was to board the wrong train, or at least to miss the right one, and then persuade the *R.T.O.* to date-stamp the pass, so that the *Town Major* (cf.) would provide a night's billet and a day's rations. Most *R.T.O.s* were ignorant of the location of any troops at all, and did not care where transients went so long as they moved on next day.

RUB-A-DUB-DUB: The club in Crown and Anchor.

RUBBER GUN: A big gun firing at extremely long range.

RUBY RED: Head.

RUIN: Rouen.

RUM JAR: A species of German trench-mortar bomb, from its shape.

RUMBLE: To detect. Pre-1914. As used by the troops, almost always in the passive: to have one's secret intentions – especially if illicit – dragged to the light. 'You'll be rumbled.'

RUN: To bring a soldier up before his commanding officer and charge him with some offence. E.g. 'Let them spades alone or I'll run you.' A variant was *run-in*.

RUN: To have the enemy *on the run* meant to force him to retreat continually, so that his sense of stability was lost. A very old phrase. It hardly ever happened.

RUNNER: A private soldier employed chiefly for bearing written messages between a platoon and Company Headquarters (*platoon runner*), between C.H.Q. and Battalion Headquarters (*company runner*), or between B.H.Q. and Brigade Headquarters (*battalion runner*). Runners were especially in demand when telephone or telegraphic communication broke down, i.e. when shelling and machine-gun fire were heavy. Consequently the job, though it offered reliefs from routine tasks, was a dangerous one.

Rush: *How much did they rush you?* meant 'How much did you have to pay?' Anyone who studies the method of certain salespeople will appreciate the force of the word *rush* in this connection.

Russian Sap: Dug as an ordinary sap but with the top left covered over with earth: like a small mine-gallery, the top being arched for safety. Not for permanency: mainly used to enable raiders to make a surprise entry into a nearby trench or post.

Russki: A Russian soldier. (Cf. *Macaroni, Pork-and-Beans, Chink, Froggie, Aussie, Yank.*)

S.A.A.: Small arms ammunition: *i.e.* for rifle and revolver.

Saïda: Good day! greeting! Arabic, from Egypt.

Salamander: The first type of Sopwith 'plane with an armoured fuselage.

Salient, The: The Ypres Salient, formed in October, 1914, and held until left behind by the final advance of 1918. There the British lost 160,000 dead and had 410,000 wounded. In general, a *salient* was any part of a trench-system jutting out towards the enemy's line.

Sally Booze: Sailly la Bourse, a small but famous village on the Western Front.

Salmon and Trout: Snout, i.e. nose. Can also mean gout, and stout (the beverage).

Salvation Corner: A famous spot near Ypres.

Sam Browne: Officers' (field-service) belt with shoulder strap. Introduced about 1850 by General Sir Sam Browne who won a V.C. in the Indian Mutiny; a cavalry officer, he died in 1901 at the age of seventy-seven.

San Fairy Ann: An extremely popular phrase, approximated into English from the French *ça ne fait rien* – It doesn't matter, it makes no difference, why worry? Fatalistic, cynical, applicable to all kinds of situations. 1916 and later. Variants were *San Fairy* and *San Fairy Anna*.

Sandbag: Sandbags, filled with earth, were the constructional unit of fortified trenches. To sandbag a person was to hit him over the head or neck with a sandbag filled about one quarter full with sand or earth. A quiet way of stunning a man. Deserters lurking and living in the woods near Etaples practised this method of obtaining money.

SANITARY FATIGUE: One of the most unpopular duties in the Army, except with a few who wangled it permanently as a cushy job. It included the digging of latrine-trenches and the emptying of the buckets; the burial of dung and urine; and the disinfection, in the line, with chloride of lime of places where old corpses were unearthed. (Cf. *Fatigue*).

SANKEY: A five-franc note, from *cinq*.

SAP: See *Trench and sap. Russian Sap.*

SAPPER: A private soldier in the Royal Engineers who were often called, as a Corps, the Sappers.

SARNT: A smart and soldierly pronunciation of sergeant. Used only before the N.C.O.s surname, e.g. 'Sarnt Smith', but 'Here's the Sergeant.' Also in *Sarnt-Major*, but here it could be used without the surname being added.

SAUSAGE: An observation balloon *(q.v.)*. Usually applied only to German balloons.

SAWMILL: A hospital operating theatre.

SCARLET RUNNERS: Battalion runners, from their red brassards.

SCATTY: A little mad.

SCENE SHIFTER: A famous English heavy gun near Arras in 1917.

SCHWARZ BROT: German black bread; chiefly among prisoners of war.

SCOFF or SKOFF: To eat: also, as a noun, any sort of food. Dates from *ca.* 1790.

SCOTCH PEGS: Legs.

SCRAN: Food in general, a meal in particular: both senses date back, in the Regular Army, to about 1870. Also, occasionally, bread and butter. In the eighteenth century the word meant: refuse; broken victuals; hence, food. *Scran-Bag*, haversack. Perhaps Irish in origin.

SCREW-PICKET, -PIQUET: See *Corkscrew Picket.*

SCRIM: See *Camouflage.*

SCROUNGE: To steal, not personal belongings, but from a department or some other embodiment of authority. More Army property changed hands in France by *scrounging* than by legitimate means. A soldier *scrounged* food, clothing, firewood and replacements for items missing from his kit. The unfortunate loser cursed but then promptly set out to replace his loss by *scrounging* from someone else. A certain

177

platoon once removed a whole elephant hut from a number of engineers sleeping in it. This feat in time became legendary. Also used intransitively *to scrounge about*, i.e. to go seeking an opportunity of stealing, either a particular article or whatever fortune offered. From North Country dialect. Joseph Wright's *Dialect Dictionary* gives as a secondary meaning – 'to wander about idly,' and, for the noun, 'a thorough search.' (Cf. *Half-inch, Pinch, Snaffle, Win.*)

SCROUNGER: An adept at the art. Used both insultingly and admiringly.

SCUPPERED: Killed; dead. Originally nautical.

SECTION: In 1914 a section of an infantry platoon consisted of sixteen men, one being a corporal or lance-corporal. Later the number was almost halved.

SECTOR: French *secteur*. A well-defined district, including a section of the front line. The extent of the front line held by a company, a battalion, etc., was called the *company front, battalion front*, etc.

SEMAPHORE: Visual signalling with arms or flags held at different angles. Taught and practised but of little use up the line.

SEPARATE PEACE: Soldiers often talked, with wistful humour, of *making a separate*, or *a private, peace*.

SERGEANT-MAJOR'S: Better-than-usual tea was known as *sergeant-major's* on the assumption that the S.M. would always get the best of everything.

SERVICE: *To sling one's service about*. To boast about past martial experiences.

SEVEN: *It's all in the seven*, a philosophic exclamation used by Regular soldiers who had enlisted for seven years with the colours (i.e. on continuous day-to-day service). It meant, 'I was a fool to enlist and now I've got to stick it out.'

SEXTON BLAKE: The provost sergeant. (From popular fiction, pre-1914: a detective with a bloodhound.)

SHAVE: A rumour. From a barber's shop, the home of gossip. It dates from the Crimean War.

SHEET, ON THE: Charged with a military offence. Any conviction would be entered on the man's 'crime sheet' (*q.v.*).

SHELL SHOCK: Acute and persistent nervous fear. The term became official only in 1916.

178

SHELTER, TRENCH: See *Dug-out*.

SHIRTY: Angry, malicious, fighting-mad. Civilian pre-1914. From the habit of certain sorts of men who would, on small provocation, begin to remove their jackets as an indication that they would fight.

SHIT: Very widely used for mud, and (cf. *dirt*) for shells or shelling. Also, a term of opprobrium for a person disliked. See *Four Letter Man*.

SHOCK TROOPS: Battalions, brigades or divisions selected to lead an attack and be the first to enter the enemy trenches. The same as Storm Troops.

SHOCKS: Choques, a town near Bethune, France.

SHOOTING GALLERY: The front line.

SHOOTING IRON: Any fire-arm, but specifically either rifle or revolver as the occasion demands. The term dates back about a century and does not seem to be American in origin.

'SHORT ARM' INSPECTION: Conducted periodically by the M.O., to detect symptoms of venereal disease. A platoon of men would be lined up, without privacy, in a hut. The name is derived, by obvious analogy, from the inspection of rifles on parade.

SHORT HAIRS: 'To have a man by the short hairs' meant to possess an advantage over him or to be in a position to prevent his punishing you if he were your superior, e.g. 'He daren't bring me up for orders because he's trying to dodge the Colonel just now. So I've got him by the short hairs.' Presumably from the hairs at the back of the neck, very painful if plucked, but *by the testimonials* (i.e. testicles), a gloss on *by the balls*, seems to carry the same meaning.

SHOT, THE: Aldershot. Regular Army.

SHOT UP THE BACK: To be detected; disabled.

SHOW: A theatrical entertainment of the lighter sort. Hence, also, an attack, promoted (it often seemed) for the amusement of the Staff and newspaper magnates. A similar use of the word occurs in the phrase – *to put up a good show*: to fight a losing battle well; to acquit oneself honourably. (Cf. *Stunt, Push.*)

SHRAP: Shrapnel. Invented *ca* 1803 by General Henry Shrapnel, Inspector of Artillery. The body of the shell was filled with pellets, about the size of marbles; H.E. shrapnel contained larger pellets. These shells explode by a time fuse and produce a 'hail-storm' of lead. (A famous spot on the Western Front was named Shrapnel Corner.) 'The H.E. German shrapnel shells – 'air burst – have a double explosion, as if a giant shook a wet sail for two flaps; first a dark green burst of smoke; then a lighter yellow burst goes out from the centre forwards.' – Lieut.-Col. John McCrae, May 17, 1915, in a letter.

SICK: When a soldier was, in his own opinion, so ill that he was unable to perform his duties, he *went sick* by giving his name to the orderly corporal and reported the next morning very early for *sick parade*. The regimental Medical Officer saw him, asked him a question or two, usually gave him a standardized purgative pill, known as Number 9, and marked him down as *M.D.*, i.e. medicine and duty, *Light Duty* or *Excused Duty*. Malingerers were reported for punishment, if the M.O. were sufficiently sure of his diagnosis; those who were unable to hold themselves upright were – in time – removed to an ambulance. The Number Nine pill was said to counteract the constipating nature of much of the only food available up the line. (Cf. *M.O.* and *M.D.*)

SIDE KICK: A chum. Canadian.

SIGARNEO, SIGARNO: All correct; O.K. A corruption of *Sir Garnet*, as in 'It's all Sir Garnet' or 'I give you my Sir Garnet', my word. From old Regulars, who thought the world of General Sir Garnet Wolseley.

SIGNALESE: The use of *Ack* for A, *Beer* for B, etc.

SILENT DEATHS: Night patrols armed with daggers.

SILENT PERCY: A frequent synonym for *rubber gun* (*q.v.*).

SILENT SUSAN: A German high-velocity shell.

S.I.W.: Self-Inflicted Wound. A most serious crime committed by men temperamentally or physically unfitted for the line, or men so over-strained by service that they were no longer responsible for their actions. Many cases of S.I.W. were hushed up by sympathetic authorities, but there were several special *S.I.W.* hospitals at the Base, where conditions were said to be severe to the pitch of persecution.

SIX BY FOUR: Bumf – toilet paper – these being the dimensions in inches of the Army article. Naval bumf was 5 inches × 5 inches.

Six-o-Six: Salvarsan, a compound (containing arsenic) discovered by Paul Ehrlich (1854–1915) as a remedy for syphilis, a disease frequently euphemised as *Phyllis*.

Skeleton Battalion: Same as *Cadre*.

Skilly: Thin stew. Civilian. Pre-1914 – from workhouses, i.e. for paupers.

Skin, Next of: Next of kin (*q.v.*). Facetious.

Skindles: A restaurant at Poperinghe frequented by officers, from the hotel at Maidenhead, Berks.

Skint: Skinned, meaning: having lost or spent all one's money.

Skipper: Officer's slang for a captain commanding a company; never used as a prefix.

Skirt: A young woman. An obvious example of metonymy. (Cf. *Tart, Piece, Square-pusher.*)

Skite: Blatherumskite (as noun). Irish.

Skive: To dodge duty, especially a fatigue.

Skrimshanker: Malingerer, shirker. (Cf. *Malinger* and *Sick.*) An old Army word.

Sky Pilot: An Army chaplain. Originally nautical slang. Became general for a padre as early as the 'nineties; see E. J. Hardy: *Mr Thomas Atkins*, 1900.

Slack: 'Cheek', impertinence, insolence. Pre-1914, but until the War rare except in dialect and American colloquial speech. See *Lip*.

Slacks: Trousers, especially without puttees. Chiefly an officers' term. (Cf. *Fatigue Dress.*)

Slip it Across: *To slip it across a man* meant to hit him, to take advantage of him, or to reprimand him severely.

S.M.: Sergeant-Major. Always introduced by 'the', without the surname. Otherwise, the rank was given in full. Used only of Company Sergeant-Majors. (Cf. *Regimental.*)

Smoke: Any sort of cigarette. (Cf. *Fag, Gasper* and *Woodbine.*)

Smoke, The, or The Big Smoke: London. Originally a nineteenth-century tramps' slang word.

Smoke Bomb, Shell: Those which emitted a volume of dense smoke, usually employed to make a *Smoke Screen*.

Smudger: See *Nicknames*.

Snaffle: To steal. In eighteenth-century slang a 'snaffler' was a highwayman. (Cf. *Pinch, Half-Inch, Scrounge.*)

Snip: A soldier regimentally employed as a tailor. Also, an easy job or a good bargain.

Snipers: Riflemen who were specially detailed to fire at any enemy soldiers who showed themselves at certain places in the enemy lines. After 1916, a section of snipers was attached to brigade and divisional headquarters but no longer to battalion H.Q.; each section had several telescopically-sighted rifles. Occasionally snipers worked in conjunction with observers.

Sniperscope: A complicated contraption fastened to a rifle so that it could be fired over the parapet without the rifleman exposing himself. To enable him to take aim along the sights, a periscope was also attached. These contrivances attracted much attention from enemy snipers.

Snob: A soldier employed, in the Army, in cobbling. Civilian pre-1914.

Snuff It: To die, not specially to be killed. From the old method of putting out candles. Pre-1914. Civilian.

Soak: Let in for or compel. Usually in the passive, as 'I was soaked for a fatigue'.

Soap and Water: Daughter.

Sock: 'Put a sock in it!' (i.e. the mouth) was a vivid and peremptory method of telling a man that he had talked too long, especially if he were complaining. (Cf. the phrase 'put the wood in the hole' used when when a man left a door open.'

Soft Number: A pleasant or an easy job. In the 1940s–50s it became soft option.

Soldier's Friend: A well-known brand of brass polish – a pink tablet on which the soldier spat to produce a paste. Used for cleaning buttons, badges, etc. The manufacturer's name misinterprets the soldier's attitude to the commodity.

So Long: Corresponds to *au revoir, a reverderci*, etc.

Some Hopes!: It is *most* unlikely! (Cf. *What Hopes!*)

Something to Hang Things On: An infantry soldier self-described.

Somewhere in France: Journalese. Troops on active service did not put any address on their (censored) letters except name, regimental number, and unit.

Sopwith Pup: An aeroplane.

Sorry: Mate, pal, chum. Usually in vocative and chiefly among Yorkshire and Lancashire troops. Perhaps from *sirrah*.

S.O.S.: The extreme appeal for help. Used by ships at sea since before 1914, the three letters being very distinctive in the Morse code. The same combination would be used over the field telegraph by troops in great danger, but in such emergencies wires were often cut and the signal was given by rockets in a previously-arranged combination of colours. On perceiving an *S.O.S.* rocket group from the front line the artillery would know that the enemy was attacking or raiding, or about to do so, and would begin to concentrate heavy fire on his front trench. Sentry-work being nervy work, especially for tired men, *S.O.S.* rockets were usually entrusted only to officers and Company Sergeant-Majors. (Cf. *Very Light* and *Three Blue Lights*.)

Souvenir: Keepsake: which old English word it completely displaced, partly because *souvenir* could be used without sentimental associations, partly because it was *à la mode* to be French in France. All sorts of things were collected as *souvenirs*, especially pickelhaube helmets, revolvers, badges, knives, watches, German razors (though these were prized for use, their edge being famous), nose-caps, bullets, etc. *Souvenirs* were picked up, taken from the dead, or prisoners, either forcibly, or more often, as a free gift or by barter or purchase. So many were collected that ex-R.A.M.C. men must have started many shops after the Armistice. *Souvenirs* were also sold by French touts and in French shops. The word was also applied, in jest, to the baby with which some soldiers offered to supply any young French woman who would bother to listen to them. The jocularity was made every night in estaminets behind the lines and became quite meaningless. Finally a verb was formed, e.g. 'I'm going souveniring tonight' or 'Harry's gone to souvenir [i.e. find or steal] a brazier.'

Spanish Knight Trick: A barrier designed to cut off enemy raiders after they had entered a trench. An officers' expression.

Spare Part: An incompetent or unsuitable man.

Sparks, To Get the: To obtain the range of the enemy's trench by firing into *the wire* (i.e. the wire-entanglements just in front of the trench) and observing how the sparks flew off – their 'angle', their brightness, etc.

SPECIALISTS: Those, whether officers or other ranks, engaged on special work – bombers, snipers, observers, Lewis-gunners, etc. Also, though less frequently, men claiming to be already detailed for duty when they had not been so detailed.

SPENT BULLET: One that had reached its extreme range; if it hit a man it might do very little harm.

SPIT-AND-POLISH PARADE: An inspection of a whole battalion by its commanding officer or a General: an occasion for much application of *soldier's friend* (*q.v.*), *khaki blanco* (*q.v.*), and leather polish.

SPITTING BUTTON-STICKS: Same as *Paying Out* (*q.v.*).

SPLIT-ARSE CAP. The old R.F.C. cap, rather like a Glengarry bonnet.

SPLIT-ARSING: An R.A.F. term: Stunting low and flying near the roofs of billets or huts.

SPOKEY: An Army wheelwright.

SPOUT: 'One up the spout', a standard jocularity for a round of ammunition raised, by the action of the bolt, out of the magazine and into the breech of the rifle, ready for firing.

SPUD: Nickname for any man named Murphy; potatoes, like pigs, being eternally associated in the English mind with the Irish, and an association being, to an Englishman, half-way to a joke. (Cf. *Nicknames.*)

SPUD ADJUTANT: An orderly corporal; from one of his cook-house duties.

SQUAD: A small number of men, perhaps haphazardly assembled, on a parade ground to be drilled or required for other duties.

SQUAD, HALT: Salt.

SQUARE: To bribe or in other ways to secure the favour or neutrality of a superior. Civilian. Pre-1914.

SQUARE DINKUM: Correct; true; honest. An Australianism. (Cf. *Dinkum.*)

SQUAREHEAD: A German. (Cf. *Jerry, Boche.*)

SQUARE-PUSHER: A young woman, especially a young woman being courted with a view to marriage or otherwise. The term probably arose from the practice of some pre-1914 soldiers who would escort a nursemaid as she pushed a perambulator around the central gardens of a city square. Frequently abbreviated to *pusher*. (Cf. *Piece, Tart, Skirt.*) Farmer and Henley state that in American slang (1895) *square-push* meant *pudendum muliebre*, and this may indicate an origin of the phrase in physical sexuality.

SQUARE-PUSHING: *To go square-pushing* meant either to go out to court a particular girl or to go out in the hope of clicking (*q.v.*). This involved a general smartening of appearance, hence the derived adjective *square-pushing*, meaning neat, brilliant or of good quality, e.g. 'I'm putting on my square-pushing tunic tonight.' The verb *square-push* existed as early as the 1880s, among Garrison Artillery men. As early as 1900 a *square-pusher* was a slang name for a sexually-promiscuous woman. In 1914–18, in Britain, *square-pushers* was used, sometimes, for civilian boots or shoes worn illicitly on leave or in the evenings off duty.

SQUIFFY: Drunk. *Squiff* appears to be connected with *askew* and *squint* and *squiffy* probably refers to the deranging effect of liquor on eyesight. (Cf. *Binge, Blind, Blotto, Tight, Zig Zag.*)

S.R.D.: Service Rum Diluted. The initials stamped on the body of a rum jar. The dilution must have been infinitesimal. Popular amplifications of the initials were Soon Run Dry and Seldom Reaches Destination.

STAFF: Staff Sergeant – in the vocative only.

STAFF CRAWL: A tour of inspection of trenches by a general and some of his Staff.

STAND AT EASE: Cheese. Like *Army Rocks* and *Squad, Halt!*, this rhyming slang is genuinely and wholly military.

STAND BY or STAND BY FOR ORDERS: An intimation, to men not actually on duty, that they would shortly be wanted: to move away after that would have been a military offence.

STAND-DOWN: The order given (and the action ensuing) at the conclusion of *Stand-to*; when darkness or daylight has become definite. All but sentries stood down from the *fire step* (*q.v.*).

STAND-TO: The vigilance kept in all trenches, especially before dawn and nightfall, when everybody stood to arms to repel any attack which might be launched by the enemy.

STAR OF THE MOVIES: The No. 9 pill: see *Sick*.

STEALTH RAID: On a small scale, short and sharp. Carried out by the infantry without assistance from trench-mortar, machine-gun, or artillery. Often these raids were the most successful because the enemy was taken off guard.

STEEL JUG: The British steel helmet, basin-shaped, invented by Alfred Bates (who died in 1930), was first used on August 12, 1915. (Cf. *Tin Hat.*)

STELLENBOSCHED, TO BE: To be superseded, to be sent home, more or less in disgrace, but not cashiered. Officers' slang. Pre-1914. From the name of a camp during the South African War.

STICK BOMB: A German hand grenade, cylindrical, with a rounded wooden handle and a string which had to be pulled sharply before the bomb was thrown.

STIFF: A corpse. Also varied to *stiffie*. Used in friendly invective with the prefix 'big', e.g. 'You big stiff!' meaning, 'You are clumsy, stupid or incompetent.' Rarely used of dead bodies on the battlefield or at hospitals.

STING THE QUARTER FOR: To wangle an issue from the Quartermaster: quite a feat.

STINKER: A goat-skin jerkin, maladorous when wet.

STINKS or O.C. STINKS: An officer or N.C.O. instructor at an anti-gas course where men went through 'chambers' filled with different gases to give them confidence in the Box Respirator. See *Gas Mask.*

STOCKING-FOOT or -FOOTER: Any missile approaching fast but quietly.

STOKES GUN: Sir Frederick Stokes, K.B.E. (1927), invented both the mortar and the grenade. (Cf. *Trench Mortar.*)

STONKERED: Put out of action or use, whether man or weapon or conveyance! From the Italian stanco – exhausted.

STOP: *To stop one* was vivid for 'to be hit by a bullet' or shell fragment. (Cf. *Packet.*)

STOP A BLAST: To be blamed, rebuked or censured by a superior. Chiefly among officers.

STOP AND STARE: A chair.

STORM TROOPS: Synonymous with *Shock Troops* (cf.).

STOUT FELLOW: Officers' term of commendation, meaning a worthy man, a good comrade, a reliable friend, a brave soldier.

STRAFE: Noun and verb: a punishment or admonition, e.g. 'I just heard the C.O. strafing the cooks like hell.' Also used for a bombardment by shells, 'There's a bit of a strafe going on in the supports.' From the German phrase and song – 'Gott strafe England.' See *Hate*.

STRAIGHT WIRE: See *Oil*.

STRAY BULLET: The missile blamed when men were hit at some distance from the front line, especially by night or in any circumstances that seemed to preclude deliberate aim by the enemy. There were soldiers who would occasionally fire a chance shot, at a high angle ('into the blue', as it were) hoping that it might strike an unlucky German somewhere. Presumably there were men on the German side with a similar mentality.

STRETCHER-BEARERS: Those who carried wounded or very sick men. Two bearers to a stretcher. An arduous task and a dangerous one for regimental stretcher-bearers, who went over the top either at the same time as the main attack or immediately after. *Stretcher-bearers up!* = a cry heard immediately after a shell burst in a trench and on similar occasions.

STRIKE ME DEAD: Head.

STRIPES: The one, two, three V-shaped chevrons in khaki embroidery worn by Lance-Corporals, Corporals and Sergeants respectively on the upper arm of each sleeve. (Cf. *Chevron*.)

STRIPPED: Reduced in rank; as a punishment an N.C.O. might have some or all of his stripes taken away.

STRUGGLE AND STRAIN: A train.

STUCK: 'Get stuck into it!' meant 'Work hard, don't dally!'

STUFF: Shellfire. *Heavy Stuff*: big shells.

STUMER: A blind or 'dud' shell. An incompetent person. A failure or a defeat. From civilian pre-1914 slang for a worthless cheque.

STUNT: Any performance of outstanding skill or effectiveness, e.g. an acrobatic performance or a clever ruse at football; a trick or other means of benefiting oneself, e.g. 'It's a good stunt to fall out before they pick the fatigue party.' In time the quality of cleverness became inessential: all that was needed was the unusual element, the break in routine, and 'stunt' was applied especially to a battle, e.g. 'The Somme stunt,' 'The March 1918 stunt', or to a smaller, localized raid, e.g. 'a bombing stunt at night'. Also as a verb, especially of airmen. (Cf. *Show, Push.*)

SUB: A subaltern, i.e. a first- or a second-lieutenant.

SUICIDE CLUB: A bombing squad in the infantry.

SUICIDE CORNER: An exceptionally dangerous point in the Salient. There were other places so named, but none so well known.

SUMP: One method of draining a trench was by digging an adjacent sump – a hole or pit – especially for the removal of liquid mud.

SUN CURTAIN: The official term for the khaki drill flap worn in hot climates attached at the back to the service cap to protect the neck from the sun.

SUN, IN THE: Drunk. – A Regular-Army term from hot countries, especially Egypt and India. First recorded, 1770.

SUNKEN ROAD: A road with banks varying from three to thirty feet in height; it ran below ground level without perceptible mounds on either side; a regular feature of the French countryside. Often used as a temporary trench or assembly place on the Western Front in 1917–18.

SWADDY: A private soldier. In the eighteenth century the form was *swad, swadkin* or *swad-gill.* Originally dialect, not slang, meaning 'a country lout' or 'an awkward fellow'. From this in the early nineteenth century was derived the slang *swaddy,* used chiefly by sailors of soldiers, but by the B.E.F. freely in 1914–18.

SWAGGER-STICK: A short, thin cane, with a metal head, often flexible, carried ornamentally in England by soldiers going out of camp.

S.W.A.K.: Sealed with a kiss. Often written on the flap at the back of the envelope enclosing a letter home. Actually it was the censoring officer who did the sealing.

SWEATING ON: To be 'sweating on' something meant to be in a state of hopeful anticipation that something favourable would occur, e.g. 'I'm sweating on leave next week.' *Sweating on the top line,* from the gambling game *House* (cf.): when the top line was nearly filled, success was in sight. (Cf. Also *Bobbing on.*)

SWEET FANNY ADAMS: Nothing at all, with emphasis. Originally a naval term for tinned meat. From the notorious murder at Portsmouth of a girl so named in 1812. Variants were *Sweet Fanny* and *Miss Adams*. (Cf. *F.A.*)

SWIG: Drink, noun or verb. Also as *take a swig*. Used especially of a hurried or illicit drink. Perhaps from the gulping noise in the throat. Pre-1914.

SWING IT: An abbreviated form of *Swing the Lead* (*q.v.*).

SWING IT DOWN THE LINE: To wangle a job at the Base or somewhere else well away from the line.

SWINGING THE LEAD: Malingering: or otherwise evading duty. A great source of pride with some soldiers and – in certain circumstances – with all soldiers. A *lead-swinger* who let other men do work he was able to do, or who practised his craft when danger was threatened, was beloved of no one. But the man who *swung it* skilfully on experts, such as doctors, in England or behind the line, received genuine admiration and kept up no pretence before his comrades. The phrase is said to have come from the sea: a sailor would be set to taking the depth from a ship's bows as she approached inshore, but instead of letting the plummet sink he would swing the lead idly through the air and call out fictitious depths. The phrase entered the Army probably through seaport-cum-garrison towns such as Portsmouth, and perhaps through troopships. It also took the preposition *on* in two senses – *to swing the lead on* a superior officer, i.e. to deceive him, and *to swing it on* a sore foot, or an imaginary pain, i.e. making these the instrument of deceit. (Cf. *Leadswinger, Cushy, Scrounge, Wangle.*)

SWIPE: To take illicitly; to steal. Civilian. Pre-1914.

SYNCHRONIZATION OF WATCHES: A runner would carry a specially set time-piece to the various commanding officers in order that adjustment of their watches, if necessary, might be made prior to an attack.

TAB: A staff officer. Also a cigarette.

TACK WALLAH: A total abstainer; *on the tack*, temporarily abstinent. From *soft tack*, in the sense of soft drinks.

TAILS UP: Happy, cheerful, confident. E.g. 'The gunners have got their tails up now the old guns are replaced.' An officer's usage, perhaps from terriers or fighting cocks. Pre-1914. Civilian.

189

TAKE!: All right, all correct, jake-a-loo, O.K. – Canadian Forces. (Cf. the British soldier's *Take eight!* = you've won; I give you best.)

TAKE HIS NAME!: A superior officer's command to an N.C.O., meaning that the offender was to be brought up at Orderly Room next day and charged.

TALK WET: To talk nonsense. It was always the other person who *talked wet* and was told not to with considerable emphasis. The phrase is perhaps derived from the habit of some excitable people of projecting a spray of saliva out of their mouths as they talk. Civilian. Pre-1914.

TAMASHA: A display, show, entertainment; an exciting incident. From Hindustani.

TANK: Wet canteen. Regular Army. Pre-1914. (Cf. *tanked*, drunk, and *tank up*, to drink hard.)

TANKS: Armoured fighting vehicles moving on a caterpillar track and able to cross rough ground. The name was used as camouflage, so that the enemy should not, through spies, anticipate their appearance in September 1916. *Male Tanks* had two six-pounder and four machine guns; *Female Tanks* six machine guns. Other types were used for transport. They worked with and just in front of the infantry in attack.

TAP: A wound. 'A nice little tap on the shoulder.'

TAPED: Tapes were sometimes laid, in No Man's Land, to indicate the 'jump-off' of an attack. 'Jerry has us taped,' i.e. has the range; 'The S.M.'s got you taped,' i.e. weighed-up. (Cf. *On the Tapes.*)

TAPPED: Slightly mad, below the normal in sanity; of eccentric behaviour. Metaphor perhaps from a barrel from which part of the contents have been drawn or from Hindustani for a fever. (Cf. *Doolally*, *Touched* and *Dippy*.)

TART: A prostitute, or a promiscuous woman. Also often used, familiarly but without sexual insult, of any young woman. Grose gives the word only as an adjective, meaning 'pert'. This suggests a possible origin. Pre-1914. Civilian.

TASSIE: Soldier from Tasmania. Confined in use to Australians and New Zealanders. Formed by analogy with *Aussie* (cf.).

TAUBE: A German aeroplane of the early days of the War; the standard monoplane. Literally 'dove' from its bird-like appearance.

Tovarish: Comrade. Russian.

Taxi-Driver: A pilot in the Air Force.

Tear Gas: The official name was *Lachrymatory Gas*.

Tear Up for Arse-Paper: 'The Colonel tore him up for'—, i.e. ticked him off, reprimanded him, very severely. A New Zealanders' phrase, but not unknown among British troops.

Teddy Bear: A shaggy fur or goatskin coat issued for trench-wear in 1915.

Teddy's Hat: The crown in Crown and Anchor: a survival from the days of King Edward VII (d. 1910).

Telling the Tale: Explaining away military offences, deficiencies, delinquencies – the offender doing the explanation. Or wheedling.

Temporary Gentleman: A civilian become an officer for the duration. Snob journalese.

Terps: An interpreter.

Terriers: The Territorial Force (later Territorial Army). Part-time volunteers. They provided the first reinforcements organised in battalions and other units for the Western Front from October 1914 on. Pre-1914.

There First: Thirst.

Thick: Friendly, intimate, as in 'thick as thieves'. At least as old as eighteenth century.

Thigh Boots: Longer than *Gum boots* (cf.).

Third Man: A powerful and universal superstition on the Western Front was the belief that the *third man* to light a cigarette from the same match would inevitably be killed then and there or very soon afterwards. It was so strongly established that anyone inadvertently attempting *to go third man* would have his hand or his face pushed violently away. See C. E. Montague's story, 'The First Blood Sweep' in *Fiery Particles* (Chatto and Windus, 1923).

Three Blue Lights: It was a standard joke among soldiers who despaired of the War ever ending that the coming of Peace would be announced by rocket: *three dark-blue lights*, quite undetectable against a night sky. (Cf. *Flare Pistol, S.O.S., and Very Light.*)

Three-o-Three: .303-inch was the standard calibre of the British army-rifle, the beautifully balanced Short Lee Enfield.

THROW ONE'S WEIGHT ABOUT: To bluster, to assert one's authority or to attempt to intimidate or impress one's equals.

THUMBS UP: An expression denoting intense joy or gratification. Perhaps from the Roman arena gesture when the spectators decided to let a gladiator live. E.g. 'Thumbs up, lads. There's buckshee rum tonight.' Also as an adjective, 'It's thumbs up in this company now the S.M.'s gone on leave.' Often accompanied by a gesture, both thumbs vertical above clenched fingers. Occasionally used with a sexual meaning.

TICKET: Official discharge from the Army, especially a discharge given for medical reasons before the full period of service (in the pre-1914 Regular Army seven years with the colours) had expired. (Cf. *Ticket-of-leave:* given to discharged convicts.) To *work one's ticket* was to scheme, by bribery, malingering or any other means, to get out of the Army. It would be noticed that a certain man kept complaining of chronic pains or began to behave peculiarly. Comments would be turned aside by old soldiers with the remark, 'He's only trying to work his ticket.' Thus the phrase in time became a facetious suggestion that a man was slightly insane.

TICKLER'S: The prevalent brand of issue jam in the early war years. *Tickler's* became generic for jam. Also an early, roughly-made hand-grenade, contrived from a jam tin.

TICKLER'S ARTILLERY: The grenade just mentioned. In a Tickler's jam tin were placed a 1-oz. dry cotton primer and twelve rounds of S.A.A. well packed with clay; to these were added a short length of fuse and a detonator. In January, 1915, there was at Nieppe a school for bombers unofficially called *Tickler's Artillery H.Q.* It was organised by the Royal Engineers.

TIC-TACS, TIC-TOCS: Signallers.

TICKY: Verminous.

TIGHT: Drunk. (Cf. *Zig-zag, Blotto, Squiffy, Binge, Blind.*)

TI-IB: Excellent. Very good! Arabic: used on the Near Eastern Fronts.

TIME-SERVING MAN: A Regular Army soldier who had enlisted not for the vague and elastic *duration of the War* (cf.) but for a definite period, usually seven years. Needless to say, such men were not in time of war discharged when the period of their contract expired, but often easier and safer employment was found for them if they re-enlisted.

TIN HAT: Typical British facetiousness for a steel helmet. See the note at *Steel Jug.*

TIN-OPENER: Facetious for a bayonet.

TIN TOWN: A hutment of corrugated iron huts: there were many.

TIT-FOR: Tit-for-tat, i.e. hat.

T.M.B.: A trench-mortar battery.

TOAD: A German hand-grenade from its shape.

TOASTING FORK: A bayonet, which was in fact often used for toasting bread or sausages.

TOC H: Talbot House, Poperinghe.

TOFFEE APPLES: Trench mortar bombs, so-called from the haft, like the skewer in a toffee-apple. (Cf. *Minnie, Trench Mortar.*)

TOM TIT: Rhyming slang for 'shit'. *Pony and trap* was rhyming slang for 'crap'.

TOMMY: Short for *Thomas Atkins,* a journalistic name for a private soldier from one T.A. who mythically distinguished himself at Waterloo; or perhaps a formal name on documents like 'John' and 'Richard Doe'. Never used by English troops except derisively or when imitating the style of a newspaper or a charitable old lady. Used by Australians and New Zealanders; also as an adjective, e.g. *Tommy Officer,* or *a Tommy N.C.O.,* but never 'Tommy Private'. Picked up by the French and Germans from newspapers. See article on Soldiers' Slang in *The Quarterly Review* of April, 1931.

TOMMY: Bread. A very old Service term.

TOMMY BAR: A bent-wire spanner used to unscrew the bases of Mills bombs.

'TOMMY' (or TOMMY's) COOKER: Tiny solidified-alcohol stove, producing very little heat very slowly. Officially distributed at periods when the normal cooking arrangements could not be continued. (Cf. *Canteen, Dixie, Orderly Man, Dish Out.*)

TOO BLOODY IRISH!: Of course: I entirely agree with you. Analogous to *Not Half* (cf.). Variant: *too bloody right.*

Toot Sweet: Quick, as an adverb or an admonition. Widely used. From the French *tout de suite*. A popular variation was, '*Toot Sweet – and the Tooter the Sweeter.*' (Cf. *Jildi*, *Jerk*.)

Tooth Pick: Facetious for bayonet, entrenching tool.

Top of the House or Shop: 99 in House.

Topee: The Wolseley type of sun helmet used in Egypt and other hot climates.

Torture Truck: A hospital term for the trolly bearing lances, probes, hot fomentations and similar unpleasantnesses.

Tot: The issue of rum: $\frac{1}{2}$ gill; 64 tots to the gallon.

Tot Sack: A bag for carrying rations, usually a sandbag.

Touch: *To touch* a superior for some personal advantage meant, to ask for it ingratiatingly at a suitable moment. 'Wait till the canteen's open, and I'll touch the S.M. for a pass.' From pre-1914 civilian slang in the sense of cadging a loan.

Touch Out: To meet with a stroke of good fortune. Used absolutely or with a subordinate clause, e.g. 'He touched out for a week-end pass.'

Touched: A little mad. Temporarily insane, especially on one particular subject, e.g. 'He's touched about that estaminet – can't keep away from it.' Probably from 'touched by the heat of the sun.' (Cf. *Doolally* and *Tapped*.)

Tour of Trench Duty: The period of duty for infantry in the front line or the supports varied. In normal conditions (they rarely were normal), reliefs were made after a four- or six-day tour. On a very quiet sector, it might be better to be in the line than out, because there were fewer fatigues and inspections.

Town Major: An officer, usually of a rank considerably below that of Major, permanently stationed in a town or large village, with the task to find billeting accommodation as requested by the *Area Commandant* (cf.) for large or small parties of troops passing through. At one period Arras possessed a *Town Major* of eccentric character who used to stroll through the streets under shell-fire, serenely confident, holding an umbrella over his head.

Towse: To punish, to thrash, to defeat. This civilian variant of *tousle* was adapted to Army uses. (Cf. *Towser*, pre-1914 civilian name for a bulldog or rough terrier.)

TRACER BULLETS: Machine-gun bullets first used by airmen; phosphorescent so that they could be seen by day or night and their effect estimated. Also incendiary.

TRACTOR: An aircraft with the propeller in front. (Cf. *Pusher*.)

TRANSPORT LINES: The 'base' from which Transport went forward as near to the trenches as possible.

TRAVELLING CIRCUS: A detachment of machine-guns operating at no fixed point: very unpopular with the troops who after the visit were left to endure the enemy's retaliation. An inspection of the trenches by the staff: also unpopular.

TRAVERSES: 'Thick sandbag partitions built in trenches, to prevent enfilading, and to confine the effects of shell-fire.' (Mottram).

TRAVERSING: 'Sweeping fire by pivoted machine-guns' (Mottram).

TRAVERSOR MAT: An expanded-metal carpet to enable attacking troops to clamber over wire entanglements. As the nails on the soles of his boots usually caught in the mesh and threw the soldier down practice did not live up to theory.

TRAY BON FOR THE TROOPS: Good; very good; (of a girl) attractive.

TREK: A march; to march. A survival from the South African War.

TRENCH AND SAP: The former represents a line of defence: *front trench, support trench, reserve trench*, for the most part running approximately parallel to the line held by the enemy. A sap was a line of communication, whether from the rear to the front or from a trench to an emplacement, kitchen, latrine, store, etc. The main links between the front line and the supports and reserves were called communication trenches. Technically and correctly, a trench was made by digging downwards, a sap by digging outwards from an existing trench. Almost always it was the infantry who dug both saps and trenches.

TRENCH BOOTS: Boots and leggings combined. See *Gum Boots*.

TRENCH FOOT: Feet frost-bitten in the trenches. A common winter ailment; at one period it was a crime to get trench foot, but no humane commander enforced the penalty. He might wake up next day to find that he himself had trench foot.

Trench Fever: A mysterious, perhaps rheumatic fever induced by the conditions of trench life. Many suffered from it.

Trench Mortar: A small gun, fired from a front trench into the enemy's line. There were various forms of trench mortars, all hurling over, and quite slowly and visibly, large bombs which spun unevenly in flight. Popular names for trench mortar bombs were *Footballs*, *Flying Pigs* and *Toffee Apples*. Later, a more efficient weapon, the *Stokes Gun*, was invented, which fired cylindrical-shaped bombs instead of spherical. Trench mortars caused as much trouble to their own infantry as the enemy's, and were everywhere unpopular. When a T.M. battery had fired a few shots it departed with speed, while infantry remained to await the inevitable retaliation from the enemy. (Cf. *Minnie.*)

Trench Mouth: Infectious Stomatitis was little known before the War. In 1914–15 many men caught it.

Trench Raid: Infantry raids were frequently carried out with a view to decreasing the morale of the enemy; to test the strength of the garrison and to obtain identification of the troops holding the position. The first trench raid is said to have been launched on the Ploegsteert-Messines front on the night of November 16–17, 1914; twelve prisoners were brought in without any loss being sustained by the raiders.

Trench Ring: A (finger) ring made from any suitable war material – shell case, nose cap of shell, etc.

Trench Waders: Gum thigh-boots; a post-1914 issue for winter use in the trenches.

Trez Beans: A facetious and deliberate corruption of 'très bien', used as a general exclamation of pleasure, e.g. 'My word, it's trez beans here.' (Cf *Fray Bentos.*)

Trip Wire: Wire laid close to the ground to catch the ankles; usually further away than the ordinary entanglements from the trench defended. A frequent cause of strong language.

Trooper: Officially, a private in the cavalry; slangily, a troop-ship.

Troops, The: A semi-jocular form of referring to oneself; used instead of *I*, *me*; e.g. 'the troops could do with some leave.'

Trumpet-Cleaning, Gone: Deceased; dead.

Truce: A temporary armistice for the burial of the dead. Not unknown on the Western Front.

Tube-Train: A heavy shell passing well above with a rumble.

Tug: All men named Wilson were 'Tug' Wilsons. (Cf. *Nicknames*.)

Tumble Down the Sink: Drink, noun and verb.

Tumpline: The Red-Indian method of carrying; by the aid of a strap attached to the load, the whole weight was borne on the shoulders.

Tunic: Correctly the full-dress jacket of pre-1914. In 1914–18 invariably used for the khaki jacket of service-dress.

Turd-Walloper: Sanitary-fatigue man. From civilian slang.

Turkish Medal: A button undone or showing on one's fly. Common slang in Egypt, Syria, etc.

Tutoring: Trench-instruction to new troops.

Two by Three: A kind of canteen cake.

Two Five Two: The *crime sheet* (*q.v.*).

Uckeye: All right, O.K. From Hindustani.

U Frame: Used in trench-improvement. (Cf. *A Frame*.)

Umpteen: A large number, many, lots. E.g. 'There's umpteen parcels down at H.Q.'

Umpty Iddy, To Feel: To be unwell.

Umpty Poo: A little bit more (please). French *un petit peu*.

Uncle Charlie: Slang name for Marching Order (*q.v.*).

Uncle Ned: Bed.

Undertaker's Squad: The stretcher-bearers.

Unhealthy: Dangerous (of a locality).

Unknown Warrior: From places near Ypres, Arras, Cambrai, on the Marne and 'in two other salients', six shell-torn and unrecognizable British corpses were disinterred by an impartial commission; placed in six coffins, all exactly alike. The unknown remains were placed in a hut, each draped with the Union Jack. All concerned then retired to a distance. Lastly 'a British officer of very high rank' was blindfolded, led into the hut, which he had not previously entered. Groping about, he finally touched one of the coffins and so selected the Unknown Warrior who was buried in Westminster Abbey on Armistice Day (November 11), 1920, with simple and solemn funeral rites. The inscription on the tomb runs as follows:

'Beneath this stone rests the body of a British warrior unknown by name or rank, brought from France to lie among the most illustrious of the land and buried here on Armistice Day, in November, 1920, in the presence of His Majesty King George V, his Ministers of State, and the Chiefs of his Forces, and a vast concourse of the nation. Thus are commemorated the many multitudes who during the Great War of 1914–1918 gave the most that man can give, life itself, for God, for King and country, for loved ones, home and Empire, for the sacred cause of justice and the freedom of the world. They buried him among the Kings because he had done good toward God and toward His house.'

Great Britain set the example by making the remains of an Unknown Warrior represent the great host of the Empire's dead, and giving those remains burial honours such as are usually reserved for royalty. Britain's allies were prompt to follow her example. France's *Soldat Inconnu* sleeps beneath the Arc de Triomphe in Paris. Italy's Unknown Soldier is interred in front of the massive Vittorio Emanuele monument in Rome. The Belgian Unknown Warrior is buried in the principal beauty spot of Brussels. The American Unknown lies in the national military cemetery at Arlington, within sight of the Lincoln memorial and the dome of the Capitol at Washington. Germany chose differently – the most famous German combatant slain in the war, the airman Baron Manfred von Richthofen. Richthofen's body was disinterred from the graveyard at Amiens, France, where it had been buried by his enemies with full military honours, and reinterred in the Invaliden cemetery, Berlin.

Britain's 'Unknown' is always referred to as 'Warrior'. It is understood that among the several bodies originally collected, although the remains were unrecognizable, the uniforms included those of members of the Royal Naval Division, R.F.C. (R.A.F.), as well as the Army.

UP FOR OFFICE: Up before the orderly room; to be due to go there.

UP THE LINE: *To go up the line* from the Base camps at Etaples,

Le Havre, Rouen, meant to travel twenty or thirty miles to within marching distance of the trenches. *To go up the line* from billets in 'back areas' meant to move into front, support, or reserve trenches. The expression probably originated with the Regular Army on campaigns where 'line' meant 'line of communications' and was often in fact a railway line.

UP THERE: 'It's up there you want it' ('want' meaning 'lack'): a boastful expression accompanied by a significant tap on the forehead, to indicate intellectual superiority after a soldier had 'wangled' extra leave or a cushy job or some such privilege.

URINAL: Pronounced in the Army with the accent on the second syllable to rhyme with 'final'.

V.A.D.: Voluntary Aid Detachment. More usually any trained but not professional nurse who volunteered for hospital service abroad or in England. Navy blue outdoor uniform. (Cf. *W.A.A.C.*, *Women's Legion*, and *W.R.A.F.*)

VALISE (Private Soldier): The khaki canvas knapsack carried on the back in which were stored spare underclothing, overcoat, ground sheet, emergency rations, etc. (Cf. *Marching Order*, *Pack*.) (Officer): a canvas kitbag, carried on a messcart.

VALOOSE: Money. The soldier's usual reply to beggars and touts in Egypt was *Mafeesh valoose* or *feloose*.

VAMOOSE (or VAMOSS): To go quickly, to make off, to escape. From the Spanish *vamos* = let us go. Perhaps preserved in the Regular Army by oral tradition from the Peninsular War, from garrison duties at Gibraltar, or brought from Spanish and South American ports by sailors. Current first in London; *ca.* 1840. Kingsley in *Two Years Ago* has the variant *vampoose*.

VAN BLANK, BLONK: French white wine. Variant *van blonk anglais*.

V.C. MIXTURE: Rum. A winter issue – occasional. Rarely issued before an attack.

VELVET: To be on velvet = to be in exceptionally fortunate and comfortable circumstances. (Cf. *Cushy*.)

VERMOREL SPRAYER: The Vermorel Sprayer was a device for spraying rose trees to keep down the Green Fly. They were used on the Western Front for dispersing low-lying gas. During the summer months, in quiet sectors of the line, Vermorel Sprayers were sometimes filled with diluted insecticide (instead of the Hypo Soda mixture for Gas defence) and were used to spray trenches and dugouts to keep down flies.

VERTICAL: *To suffer from a vertical gust or breeze, or to have the breeze vertical*, to be nervous, apprehensive. See *Wind Up*.

VERY LIGHT: A rocket fired from a brass pistol. Used in the front line to illuminate *No Man's Land* (cf.) at night, so that sentries could be sure the enemy was not approaching. Also for signalling that a position had been captured, or for help in emergency. One form of rocket floated slowly down attached to a small parachute, illuminating the earth beneath for what seemed a geological age, during which no one in the open dared move. The spelling of the British rocket used to be uncertain; variations of the form used here are *Verey*, *Véry* and *Vérey*; but *Very* is now given as the correct form by the *O.E.D.*, after Samuel W. Very, the inventor. (Cf. *Flare Pistol S.O.S.* and *Three Blue Lights*.)

VET: The Medical Officer.

VETTED: Medically examined.

VICKERS: The Vickers Machine Gun. Like the Maxim it required a firm emplacement and could maintain continuous fire. Confined to Brigade and Divisional troops. Both guns were more accurate than the Lewis, but more cumbersome.

VICTORIA CROSS: The Victoria Cross was created by Queen Victoria and was instituted by Royal Warrant dated January 29, 1856. The bronze Maltese crosses are made from a cannon captured at Sebastopol (Crimea). 632 V.C.s were awarded during 1914. Two men were twice awarded the Victoria Cross: both were members of the Royal Army Medical Corps: Lieut. (later Lieut.-Col.) Arthur Martin-Leake, who won the V.C. in South Africa, and Captain Noel Godfrey Chavasse who won both the V.C. and bar during 1914–18. One V.C. was earned in or over England when a German airship was brought down at Cuffley, near Enfield (September 3, 1916) by Lieutenant William Leefe Robinson, Worcestershire Regiment and R.F.C.

VIGILANCE: A crude periscope consisting of a mirror fitted to the top of a stick.

VIN BLANC: White *vin ordinaire*. Rarely good in Northern France, but in great demand because the beer was even worse, and spirits – except expensive cognac – not available. *Vin rouge* was not so popular, perhaps because its name was not so amusing to English ears unaccustomed to French. (Cf. *Estaminet.*)

VLAM: Vlamertinghe, a well-known town in Flanders.

W.A.A.C.: Women's Army Auxiliary Corps, members of which were known as Waacs (pronounced 'wacks'). They wore khaki uniform and performed clerical, cooking, and waiting jobs at the Base Camps. Civilians were always ready to spread scandal about *Waacs*; to the French it was inconceivable that decent women could live in close proximity to so many men and remain virtuous; and most soldiers were ready to invent and pass on ribald stories, just as boys do about girls' schools. The *Waacs* and the *V.A.D.s* roughly correspond to the 1914–15 volunteers: there were no conscripts among them. (Cf. *V.A.D.*, *W.R.A.F.* and *W.R.E.N.*)

WADS: Cakes or buns sold in a dry canteen. Hence *Wad-Scoffer*, a teetotaller.

WAKEY WAKEY: See 'Chants and Sayings', page 224.

WALKING WOUNDED: The others were Stretcher Cases.

WALLAH: Chap, fellow. Used especially of an officer with special duties, e.g. 'He's the new Lewis-gun wallah.' (From Hindustani).

WANGLE: Verb: to procure goods or an advantage of some kind illicitly but without punishment, by the exercise of cunning, moral pressure, blackmail or bribery. Almost everything could be *wangled* in the Army by certain people, from a 'sleeping-out' pass in barracks to promotion. In fact, *wangling* became semi-official. A man who had lost say an entrenching tool or a blanket would not be punished, but would be told openly by his platoon commander to *wangle* or *scrounge* (*qv.*) another. Noun: a successful piece of jobbery or unwarranted privilege.

WANGLER: One who was expert and habitual at *wangling* (*q.v.*).

WANTS HIS LIVER SCRAPING: Used of an officer or N.C.O. in a bad temper.

WAR AND STRIFE: Wife; more frequently *Trouble and Strife.*

WAR BABIES: The illegitimate children with which, on the outbreak of war, sensational newspapers predicted England would be crowded. Also, in the singular, any young soldier in general or any youthful subaltern in particular.

WAR HOUSE: The War Office. This term was rarely used except by the General Staff and officers of some rank.

WAR ON: *Remember there's a war on* meant 'Don't waste time; don't be frivolous; let's get back to our real job.'

WARWICKS: The 6 on cards. From the old Sixth Foot Regiment, now the Warwickshire Regiment.

WASH-OUT: Verb: to cancel, to disregard, to supersede, e.g. 'Wash out that order for early parade.' Noun: a failure, a disaster or an incompetent person, e.g. 'This raid's going to be another wash-out.' From target-practice in the old days, when, on the iron targets, the marks of previous shots were washed out with a fresh coat of whitewash. In musketry the term still signifies a miss, no shot on the target. (Cf. *Dud.*)

WATERLOO DAY: Pay-day. A nineteenth-century Regular-Army term.

WATERPROOF SHEET: A sheet just big enough for a soldier to spread blankets on, whether in a funk-hole, a dugout, a billet, or out in the open (i.e. in bivouac). It had, at the edges, perforations so that it could be used as a cape, sometimes over the greatcoat. The waterproof sheet was also used to prevent the entry of gas into dug-out or pill-box, and as an awning against either sun or rain. Considered indispensable, it formed part of 'battle-order' (*q.v.*) (as well as Marching Order) (*q.v.*) when it was carried, folded, on the back.

WAZZA: A low native quarter of Cairo. The Battles of the Wazza were two Australian brushes with the police in 1915.

WEAR: To brook, to put up with. Usually in negative. E.g. 'He won't wear that.'

WEARY WILLIE: A long-range shell passing well overhead with apparent slowness. From a tramp in 'Comic Cuts', pre-1914 childrens' magazine.

WEBBING: Khaki equipment of woven, canvas-like cloth, as distinct from brown leather equipment.

WEEPING WILLOW: A pillow.

WEIGH UP: To *weigh up* a man or a situation meant to estimate at the proper value and to be in a position to master the man or the situation. Frequently used in the passive, e.g. 'The S.M.'s got you weighed up, my lad.'

WELL OILED: Very drunk. This sense of *oiled* was very general in the Army.

WEST: *To go west* was the most popular euphemism in the Army for 'to be killed'. Used in such phrases, as 'Bill went west at Ginchy.' One of the few expressions which revealed the suppressed emotions of the soldier, and his secret sense of the tragedy in which he was caught. The origin of the phrase is obscure; Weekley suggests it is a natural analogy from the setting sun. It may possibly be a survival from the pioneering days in America, when to go further west into unexplored country often meant death at the hands of Indians. Another suggestion is that it is a survival from thieves' slang, meaning to go to Tyburn, to be hanged. The phrase was also used trivially of things lost, stolen or strayed, e.g. 'My razor's gone west again.'

WEST SPRING GUN: A mechanical catapult.

WET BEHIND THE EARS: A term of reproach imputing ignorance or youth.

WHACK: Share, especially an equal share. E.g. 'I've not had my fair whack of the fags.' Probably from the noise made in shaking out a spoonful of sticky porridge or rice.

WHACK OUT: Variation of *Dish-out* (cf.).

WHACKED or WHACKED TO THE WIDE: Completely exhausted.

WHALE OIL: For the feet, to prevent frostbite.

WHAT ABOUT: A peculiar idiom capable, according to the inflexion of the voice, of conveying many meanings, e.g. 'What about a rest, corporal?' meant, 'Will you consider our proposal for a rest.' 'What about the poor bleedin' sentries?' meant, 'Don't forget those who are absent when you share out rations.' And 'What about it, now, what about it!' bawled by an N.C.O., meant, 'Hurry up,' or, at reveille, 'Get out of bed!'

WHAT HOPES!: A retort expressing strong disbelief in some promise or prophecy of a future good (or not so bad as at present) time. A variation, addressed to a man confident of securing an advantage for himself, was *What a hope you've got!*

WHIPPET: A lighter and more mobile form of *tank* (*qv.*) armed with four machine-guns.

WHISTLE AND FLUTE: A suit (of clothes).

WHISTLING PERCY, WALTER, WILLIE: Enemy high-trajectory guns and their shells. *Whistling Percy* was also specifically applied to a German 9-inch naval gun of a flat trajectory which was captured late in 1917 at Cambrai. To the same kind of shell and gun the name *Pissing Jenny* was given.

WHITE FEATHER: It was in 1914–15 the practice of some women to present white feathers to young men in civilian clothes but apparently fit enough to join one of the Services. Never very common, better known through the press than at first hand.

WHITE SHEET: Wytschaete, a town in Flanders.

WHIZZ-BANG: A light shell fired from one of the smaller field-artillery guns – the British 18-pounder, the French 75 (millimetres), the German 77 (millimetres). The term is onomatopoeic, and was applied to the explosion. Owing to the short range and low trajectory, whizz-bangs arrived as soon, if not sooner, than anyone heard them. See *Pip Squeak*.

WIDOW'S MITE: A light.

WILKIE BARD: A (playing) card. Usually in the plural. From the name of a music-hall comedian.

WIN: To acquire unlawfully. E.g. 'Where did you get that fountain-pen?' – 'Won it from an Aussie when he wasn't looking.' From thieves' slang of the seventeenth–eighteenth centuries. Although obsolete it may have survived, like other pieces of 1914–18, by direct descent in families from a reprobate grandfather. In such semi-isolated survivals the meaning may be slightly amended. As recently as July 1964 a seven-year-old girl, carefully brought up, when questioned about her possession of a woolly animal toy, explained 'I won it.' It turned out that she had not stolen it but obtained it by cajolery and careful planning. A 1914–18 soldier would have used the word 'wangle'.

Wind-Jammer: An inspecting officer, or one prone to veto the men's leave. Hence any unpopular officer.

Wind-up: Fear. Used with *have*, not *feel*. *To have the wind-up* implied no disgrace, and could be mentioned casually in conversation, though usually in the past tense. The term appears to be a 1914–18 creation, although it is just possible it harks back to the days when felons were transported. *Wind-up* then would mean the end of their last hope, for the ship could sail. Perhaps the gulping and other sensations in the throat which are extreme symptoms of 'wind-up' reminded some father of a baby's 'wind' troubles. A later variation was *wind vertical*. Another development was 'to put the wind up', meaning 'to make afraid', e.g. 'Those minnies fairly put the wind up me.' (Cf. *Windy*.)

Windy: Adjective = apprehensive of personal danger or trouble. Derived from *wind-up* (cf.), but unlike that term it could be used of others in a derogatory sense, e.g. 'He's too windy to stir out of his dug-out.' It was also more freely transferred to the uses of ordinary routine, apart from shelling and other dangers, than 'wind-up', e.g. 'He's windy of going out without a pass.'

Windy Corner: Any place dangerous because of shell-fire or machine-gun fire, the most famous being that near the Menin Gate (Ypres).

Winick: *To be* or *to go winick* meant to be mad or foolish. From a lunatic asylum in the Lancashire town of Winwick. (Cf. *Doolally*.)

Winkle Out: To force or bluff a small number of German soldiers, during a raid or an attack, to come up out of a dug-out.

Wipers: See *Ypres*.

Winkle-Pin: A bayonet. (Cf. *Tooth-Pick*.)

Wipers Express: The German 42-centimetre shell (a calibre roughly equivalent to our 16-inch) first used, or first notably used, at the Second Battle of Ypres.

Wire, Give the: To give warning surreptitiously.

Wire-Cutters: Carried by some of the assailants in an attack involving the capture of a trench guarded by wire-entanglements. Also used at night to get through entanglements. In one form it was fitted to the muzzle of a rifle.

WIRING PARTY: A 'squad' detailed to erect wire-entanglements.

W.O.: The War Office, or, Warrant Officer, e.g. Regimental Sergeant-Major: a rank and status between non-commissioned and commissioned officer.

WOMEN'S LEGION: A corps of women volunteers, employed chiefly in driving motor-cars and lorries. Khaki uniform. (Cf. *W.A.A.C.*, *W.R.A.F.* and *V.A.D.*)

WONKY: Adjective = defective, not working properly. E.g. 'The Lewis gun's wonky again.' Origin obscure.

WOODBINE: A cheap cigarette popular with some soldiers from the urban working classes. Kind-hearted civilians believed (from Kipling and the magazines, no doubt) that all soldiers delighted in Woodbines. Also, derivatively, an Australian's term for a Tommy. Those who smoked them sometimes called them *Woods*.

WOODEN OVERCOAT: A coffin. Like the synonymous though obsolete *wooden surtout*, an eighteenth–nineteenth-century term. Dialect has such synonyms as *wooden breeks* and *sark*, *wooden cloak* and *dress*.

WOODEN TRACK: A rough road over boggy country, made by laying wooden planks transversely. Unsheltered and extremely visible, most wooden tracks were heavily shelled and needed constant repair.

WOOLLY BEAR: The burst, especially the resulting smoke, of any big German H.E. shell, particularly of 5.9 shrapnel. Also, confusingly, for a *small* German H.E. shell bursting with black smoke.

WORKING ONE'S TICKET: See *Ticket*.

WORKING PARTY: A party detailed to dig a trench, build a road or a dug-out, etc. A *carrying party*: a party detailed to carry rations (though this was more properly called a *ration party*), picks and shovels, gas-cylinders, 'A' frames, etc.

W.R.A.F.: Women's Royal Air Force. Women volunteers employed chiefly as chauffeurs and clerks. Sky blue uniform. Known as *Wrafs*. (Cf. *W.A.A.C.*, *V.A.D.* and *Women's Legion*.)

WRISTWATCH: Noun and adjective: (in) the best style. An actual example: 'He was talking pukka wristwatch,' i.e. he was talking in a blasé (or in a 'la-di-da') way. In 1914–18 a watch worn on the wrist instead of in a pocket was still comparatively a novelty.

WRITE OFF, A: The irreparable crash of a 'plane. Air Force.

W.R.N.S.: Women's Royal Naval Service. Women volunteers for clerical and motor-driving work. Occasionally seen at the Base in France. Navy blue uniform. Known as *Wrens*.

WYPERS: See *Ypres*.

XAROSHIE: Generally pronounced *sharoshie*. Very good! O.K.! From the Russian.

YALLAH: Arabic. Be off with you!

YANK: Short for *Yankee*: A New Englander, but applied by the British to all Americans, not always politely. (Cf. *Russki, Macaroni, Pork-and-Beans, Chink, Aussie, Froggie*.)

YELLOW CROSS SHELL: A mustard gas-shell; from the marking.

YELLOW PERIL: A cheap cigarette. From Journalese, early nineteenth century. Yellow Peril – political or military danger from China.

Y'IBN: Scoundrel, sometimes affectionately for scamp. Often *Y'Ibn Elkalb*, literally, son of a dog. Arabic; among natives a deadly insult.

Y.M.: Young Men's Christian Association hut for recreation and the sale of tea, cocoa and biscuits. Often *Y. Emma*.

YOU BET!: In full *You (can) bet your life*. A popular expression of certitude or emphasis. E.g. 'Would you like to get your own back on the Q.M.?' Answer: 'You bet I would!' Almost a form of oath. (Cf. *Not Half*.)

YOURS AND OURS: Flowers.

YPRES: According to the press of the time, the British soldier pronounced this word *Wypers*. He may have done so in 1914 or early 1915. After that, the majority of the troops seemed to harbour a suspicion that French was not properly pronounced by the same rules as English. They never attained a French pronunciation, but they avoided a straightforward anglicization. The commonest methods of tackling Ypres were 'Eepray' and 'Eeps'. (Cf. *Etaples*.) The Scottish surname *Wiper, Wypers*, is from *Ypres*, and the medieval Ypre Tower of Rye, one of the Cinque Ports, was long known as the *Wypers* Tower.

Z.: Short for *Zero (Hour)* or *(Day)*.

ZEPPELIN IN A CLOUD: Sausage and mash[-ed potatoes].

Zero Day: That fixed for any important military operation, especially an attack.

Zero Hour or Zero: The time fixed for an attack or other operation to start.

Zero, To: To study, experimentally, the peculiarities of a rifle. Marksman's and sniper's term.

Zig-Zag!: Drunk. Heard in France, among French civilians. Picked up probably from England, but it is hardly common English slang. Onomatopoeic. (Cf. *Jig-a-jig*; also *Binge, Blind, Blotto, Squiffy, Tight*.) The following is a piece of badinage overheard in a shop: 'Marie, ally promenade ce soir?' – 'Non, pas ce soir.' After an interlude of unsuccessful blandishments: 'Moi ally au estaminet, revenir zig-zag, si vous no promenade.'

NOTE TO THE GLOSSARY

AN experience so wide-spread and so deep-sunk as the War of 1914–18 was bound to modify the language considerably. The surface, at least, of all emotions must late or soon be expressed in words, for our own comfort, and the English language – it is its great glory, its mark of superiority over, for example, French – is infinitely susceptible to modification and to individual use. Probably the most imaginative and sensuously exact language of all, it is continually unfolding springs of metaphor within itself. An English word is never content to do as it is told. Its marriages are not often arranged. It prefers romantic elopements with some other word for which the purists never intended it. *Push up* will couple with the ineligible *daisies*, and so form a new phrase, a new metaphor, and enrich the English consciousness by an illuminating flash of sardonic humour.

This faculty of creation and variation, the genius of the language, was enormously stimulated by the Great War. New recruits reached out eagerly for the traditional vocabulary of the old Army, and rolled it over on appreciative palates. *Dodging the Column, Rooty, Swinging the Lead, On the Jildi:* these were all quickly-adopted and mouthed with an air, just as a new boy at school is all ears for the niceties of its special slang. A new occupation, a new vocabulary, but presently the occupation changed, grew to vast proportions and assumed horrible aspects beyond the knowledge and capacity of the old Army. Another vocabulary was needed, and day by day it was supplied by inventive spirits responding to the onslaughts of circumstance. Physical fear became a commonplace of routine, but a commonplace that had to be conquered by private resolution and outward derision. It was made a guy, and *Wind-up* was the placard pinned upon it.

Only a small portion of the words and phrases forming this Glossary are pure creations out of nothing. *Wind-up, Oojah-*

cum-pivvy, *Stunt*, *Napoo*, *Posh* and their kindred are necessarily rare. The majority are common words adapted or extended in meaning. Thus *Eye-wash*, *Landowner* and *Packet* each became charged with new content far removed from the original reference.

The definitions and occasional 'dissertations' given in the Glossary under each word render any detailed examination here superfluous; but one or two main characteristics may be noted. First, the extremely wide range of sources. Dialect and urban (especially Cockney) slang is resuscitated: and the Old Army slang draws upon Hindustani, Persian and Arabic. The downright English habit of anglicising French, that prevailed before everyone had a smattering, does not persist: The phrases of the country are transformed into something neither English nor French, as in *Cumsah* and *Etapps*. By contrast, out of the forgotten depositories of eighteenth-century slang, an odd word or two turns up refurbished, like *Binge* and *Clink*.

Second, irony is frequent, almost prevalent. It is the typically British irony of understatement and ridicule. Some of the terror disappeared, together with the pomp, from war and military glory, when the soldier decided to call his steel-helmet a *Tin-hat*, his bayonet a *Tooth-pick*, his entrenching-tool handle a *Piggy-stick*, and a murderous bombardment a *Strafe* or *Hate*.

Third, the exhilaration which most men felt in the hardening of their bodies and the sharpening of their physical faculties is clearly to be traced in the imagery, the onomatopoeia and the sensuous fidelity of many of these words. *Brass-hat* conveys so vivid an image of a general's resplendent cap that the mind easily sketches in a petulant wine-dark face beneath it. *Blimp* by its sound suggests the resilient flabbiness of the airship it signifies, and anyone who has ever emptied a scuttle of coal knows a good deal of what that shell-burst called a *Coal-box* looked like – in the distance. Even in the two short syllables of *Dug-out* is suggested all the impetus of the spade-edge and the stiff resistance of the clay. It is a word you can feel in the palms of your hands and the sinews of your arms: the smell of broken soil lingers in it under the warm fuggy aromas of its later associations.   J. B.

OTHER KINDS OF WORDS AND MUSIC

JOHN BROPHY

I. From the Music-Hall

In the British music-hall of 1914 'ragtime' or syncopated music had just established itself, and had not yet developed or degenerated into 'jazz'. It flourished chiefly through a kind of entertainment known as *revue*, more spectacular and less satirical than the French original, and only slightly influenced by American 'hustle'. The music-hall then, with no rivalry from television or even radio and merely stimulating competition from the silent cinema, was a firm institution in every town of any size. Its variety shows and revues (usually twice-nightly) made popular throughout the land comic and sentimental songs both in the old tradition and in the new fashion of 'ragtime'.

Tipperary, the best-known of the songs taken up by the New Armies in 1914, owed nothing to syncopation. It was in the late Victorian and Edwardian style, a style beloved of pierrots upon sea-shores decked with straw boaters and donkeys and lemonade-sellers and parasols. In fact, *Tipperary* had enjoyed a limited vogue the previous summer without ever really 'catching on', but a war-correspondent heard some troops of the original Expeditionary Force singing it as they disembarked in France. In a few days every newspaper had printed the words of the chorus, and music-hall, café and cinema orchestras, as well as recruiting bands, speedily made the tune known everywhere. To sing, to hum, or to whistle *It's a Long Way to Tipperary* was the patriotic and cheerful thing to do. It symbolized the bland, confident and sentimental ignorance with which England entered the War. *Tipperary*, good tune though it was, received too hearty a welcome. Before the end of 1914, although civilians retained their affection for it, the New Armies were nauseated. Attempts to start it were often howled and whistled down.

In the early months of the War there seemed to be a strange pause in the supply of popular melodies. Men subsisted on the favourites of yesteryear, *Hitchy Koo* and *When the Midnight Choo-Choo Leaves for Alabam*, and in softer moods whistled *In the Shadows* and *Nights of Gladness, Nights of Joy*. Few songs arrived to offer any serious rivalry to *Tipperary*, except *Sister Susie's Sewing Shirts for Soldiers* and

> Here we are, here we are,
> Here we are again!
> There's Pat and Mac and Tommy and Jack and Joe.
> When there's trouble brewing, when there's something doing,
> Are we down-hearted? No, let 'em all come!
> Here we are, here we are,
> Here we are again!
> Fit and well and feeling as right as rain.
> Never mind the weather,
> Now then, all together,
> Hullo! Hullo!
> Here we are again!

Secondary to this, was:

> Who were you with last night,
> Out in the pale moonlight?
> It wasn't your sister,
> And it wasn't your ma,

and so on, very archly. And in a similar strain *Hold Your Hand Out, You Naughty Boy*, and:

> Hello, hello, who's your lady friend,
> Who's the little girlie by your side?
> I've seen you, with a girl or two,
> Oh my word, I *am* surprised at you.
> Hello, hello, what's your little game?
> Don't you think your ways you ought to mend?
> It wasn't the girl I saw you with at Brighton,
> So who, who, who's your lady friend?

The words were sung loud and with gusto. For men newly in the Army, the autumn of 1914 was a gay time of ill-fitting puttees and tunics flapping at the waist, when the War was expected to end at Christmas or soon after, and meanwhile it was pleasant to grow hard and brown in the open air, and after duty stroll through the dusk with some girl who wore long skirts and had bound her hair into a 'bun'. Off duty at least the feeling of the time was romantic, glamorous and uplifted.

1915 began *piano* with *My Little Grey Home in the West* and *Because I Love You*. Dates are difficult to fix because a song might be published and achieve an almost immediate success or it might gain ground slowly. Men returning to their units from leave were expected to produce 'glimpses of notes' from the newest tunes; battalion and divisional concert parties, and (to a lesser degree) gramophone records, made known the authorized versions and the complete texts. The flourishing period of songs varied; usually the more intense the 'rage', the briefer the popularity. However, some of the best never fell wholly out of favour. Two which came in about the end of 1915 persisted in full blast through the following year, and were heard from time to time till after the Armistice. These were the American *The Long Trail* and the British *Keep the Home Fires Burning*. They were frowned upon later by more experienced soldiers, because the plaintive tunes carried such melancholy associations of 1915–16. They epitomized the character of the stern middle years of the War, and to these two songs the New Armies marched to make the acquaintance of trench warfare and, a little later, into the shambles of the Somme. The first lightsome, unembittered emotions of homesickness are inlaid in:

> Keep the home fires burning,
> Though your hearts are yearning,
> Though the boys are far away
> They dream of home.
> There's a silver lining
> Through the dark clouds shining.
> Turn the dark clouds inside out
> Till the boys come home.

The Long Long Trail moves more slowly: it has the rhythm of the daily routine of war, the huge, complicated task of which no end was yet in sight. It is a lovesick song, too, and was sung appropriately by men conscious of their separation from those they most loved, and secretly wondering whether the separation might not be for ever.

> All night long I hear them calling,
> Calling sweet and low,
> Calling till it seems
> The world is full of dreams,
> Just to call you back to me:
> There's a long, long trail a-winding
> Into the land of my dreams,
> Where the nightingales are singing
> And a white moon beams.
> There's a long, long night of waiting,
> Until my dreams all come true,
> Till the day when I'll be going
> Down that long, long trail with you.

1916 was a vintage year for charming tunes, not all of them melancholy. One—*Pack Up your Troubles in Your Old Kit Bag*—was so old fashioned in phrasing and philosophy – with its reference to long out of date 'lucifer' matches – that it seems now almost Victorian: *The Bing Boys* sent out that merry catch:

> Oh, another little drink,
> Another little drink,
> Another little drink wouldn't do us any harm.

From the same revue came the lilting loveliness of *If You Were the Only Girl in the World*, a tune which enchanted almost everyone.

> If you were the only girl in the world,
> And I was the only boy,
> Nothing else would matter in the world today,
> We would go on loving in the same old way.
> A Garden of Eden just made for two,
> With nothing to mar our joy,

> There would be such wonderful things to do,
> I would say such wonderful things to you,
> If you were the only girl in the world,
> And I was the only boy.

Among other anomalies and chronological confusions of that 1963 musical melange, from Miss Joan Littlewood's Theatre Workshop, called *Oh What a Lovely War*, the tune of *Waltzing Matilda* was played. It may be as well to record that the song was unknown, at least to British troops, during 1914–18. It belongs to the 1939–45 (Hitler) War. The 1914–18 Australian song, which for all its period naïvety, will always be affectionately remembered, was this:

> Rally round the banner of your country,
> Rally round the banner of the free.
> Sing Long Live the King wherever you may be
> And to hell with Germany!
> Should auld acquaintance be forgot,
> Sing No, no, no, no!
> Australia will be there,
> Australia will be there!

This middle period of the War, extending well into 1917, was rich in songs of absence and longing for home. It is easy to see where the soldier's heart lay, and how little militarism and posturing-heroics possessed it. He dramatized his wife, his girl or his mother at home, and sang with intense feeling *God Send You Back to Me* and *When You Come Home, Dear*. More robust and direct was:

> Carry me back to dear old Blighty,
> Put me on the train to London Town.
> Take me over there,
> Drop me anywhere,
> Liverpool, Leeds or Manchester,
> I don't care.
> I should like to see my best girl,
> Cuddling up again we soon shall be.
> Hi-ti-iddley-hi-tee,
> Carry me home to Blighty,
> Blighty is the place for me.

Hereabouts the United States of America, in the intervals of supplying munitions and food at a profit (thus playing the part England had so often taken in European wars), provided two good marching songs, dealing with her own provinces, Texas and Tennessee. To the British soldier (who then had very little idea where those places might be) any name sung with feeling was synonymous with 'home'.

Way down in Tennessee,
That's where I long to be.
Right at my mother's knee,
She thinks the world of me.
All I can think of tonight
Is the fields of snowy white.
Banjos ringing,
Darkies singing,
All the world seems bright.
The roses round the door
Make me love mother more.
I'll see my sweetheart Flo,
And friends I used to know.
They'll be right there to meet me,
Just imagine how they'll greet me,
When I get back,
When I get back,
To my home in Tennessee.

The frequent parenthetical comments, 'Without a shirt!', were, of course, a purely British gloss. *Down Where That Swanee River Flows* (also with a 'Flo', but this time a sister) and *Texas Way* were even more popular.

Down Texas way,
'Mid the clover and the new-mown hay,
Where they'll be so glad,
Yes, so glad,
To see-ee me-ee.
Night and day
I can see their happy faces gay,
And hear a sweet voice say
Come along there,

To a beauty little, cuty little
Spot down yonder.
Let me play
'Mid the clover and the new-mown hay,
And once again at dear old mother's knee,
I long to kneel and pray,
God bless mother,
God bless dad,
Make them happy,
Make them glad,
I'm in heaven
Down old Texas way.

Roses of Picardy, addressed to 'Colinette with the sea-blue eyes', had an elusive text which few were able to sing in full. It was more often whistled mellifluously, and went very well on a mouth-organ or a concertina. No soldier, of course, ever dreamed that Picardy was a real place where he himself had swinked and sweated. *Oh, Oh, Oh, It's a Lovely War* counter-balanced this Arcadian nonsense with its broad sarcasm.

Oh, oh, oh, it's a lovely war!
Who wouldn't be a soldier, eh?
It's a shame to take the pay.
Form fours, right turn,
What do you do with the money you earn?
Oh my word it's a lovely war!

Sergeant Brown, Keep Your Eye on Tommy for Me was boisterous and light-hearted, invoking imaginary amours in Paris. The British soldier was prepared to sing anything at all that went with a swing. Words were pleasant noises to be rung in the throat, and few acknowledged any necessity to bother with their meaning.

Good-bye-ee!, arriving early in 1918, was a quaint half-breed. Ostensibly it was a skit, a parody, a satire on home-sick and leave-taking songs, but often the melancholy it was intended to whip out of existence would creep quietly back into the singing voices.

Good-bye-ee! Don't sigh-ee!
Wipe the tear, baby dear,
From your eye-ee.
Though it's hard to part I know,
(Still) I'll be tickled to death to go.
Don't sigh-ee! Don't cry-ee!
There's a silver lining in the sky-ee.
Bon soir, old thing! Cheerio, chin-chin!
Napoo! toodle-oo! Good-bye-ee!

Through a hot summer and a mellow autumn of belated, wearied victory 1918 moved to new songs, still celebrating the attractions of home, peace and domesticity, but set to brisker tunes. *Give Me a Little Cosy Corner* was one, and another:

Give me a Blighty girl,
A Blighty girl for me.
I've been across the sea,
I know what's good for me.
French girls are very nice
For Frenchmen I can see,
But when I get back to Blighty,
A Blighty girl for me.

The Armistice, arriving incredibly and, at first, unbelieved, found the troops fortunate enough to be still alive and very conscious of their luck taking up this apposite prothalamion:

The bells are ringing
For me and my girl.
The birds are singing
For me and my girl.
Everybody is knowing,
Everybody is going,
Every Susie and Sal.

The parson's waiting
For me and my girl.
They're congregating
For me and my girl.
And some day we'll build a little home
For two or three or four or more,
In Love Land
For me and my girl.

In the minds of some people the music-hall songs of 1914–18
will always be apart, superior, more emotionally potent than
any others. Compared with their predecessors of the 'eighties,
the 'nineties and the Edwardian age, they may be technically
poor. For those who sang them all those years ago a critical
judgment would be impossible.

II. Chants and Sayings

It is probable that catch phrases have always been popular, because wit, however much desired or striven for, does not rise to everyone's lips pat to the occasion. Even Whistler and Wilde were said to rehearse their effects and to bend and urge the conversation till a suitable moment for intervention arrived. Many people are thankful to adopt their wit ready-made, and an important function of the Victorian and Edwardian music-hall was to furnish phrases suitable for use in all the emergencies of life and recognizable at once as humour. A year or two before 1914, if your hat blew off, or a dog chased a cat, or an old gentleman slipped on a banana-skin, or a baby swallowed a plum-stone, a laugh could always be raised among certain people if the would-be wit ejaculated, 'Keep your hair on!' At other periods the phrase was, 'Chase me, girls!'; 'Does your mother want a rabbit?'; 'Get your hair cut!'; 'Ginger, your barmy!' (barmy = less than sane); 'Have a banana!' and so on. The requisites for such phrases were homeliness and directness, for ready-made wit always tends to become repartee.

When the War began the new armies subsisted for a time on what catch phrases the music-halls produced. 'How's your father?' was one of the most popular, turned to all sorts of ribald, ridiculous and heroic uses. This was the last utterance of at least one dandified but efficient subaltern, dying of stomach wounds.

As time went on the soldier began to produce his own sayings, even as he produced his own songs, to help him through his cataclysmic days. In his first disillusionment, he turned and picked up some of the fine phrases which had stirred his heart into the patriotic desire to enlist.

Kitchener Wants You!

became a method of telling a man he had been selected for some especially disgusting, arduous or dangerous duty.

Remember Belgium!

was heard with ironic and bitter intonations in the muddy
wastes of the Ypres Salient. Another 'slogan' from recruiting
posters repeated scathingly in times of distress and misery was:

What Did You Do in the Great War, Daddy?

A phrase called into use whenever the incompetence of authority
became more manifest than usual was:

Thank Gawd, we've got a Navy!

It was always 'Gawd', even with north-country troops, to
indicate the burlesque of the original sentiment.

Are we downhearted? – No!

was, in the later years of the war, always produced ironically
or varied to:

Are we downhearted? – Yes!

Sometimes it would be expanded, and declaimed by alternate
voices, thus:

Are we downhearted?
No!
Then you damn soon will be!

Among invented sayings there were two especially directed
against the private soldier's superiors. One was general and
typified concisely the implied and the often explicit arrogance
of some senior officers towards the ranks. In its original form
– 'I'm in the boat, so push off!' – it may date back to some
evacuation of regular troops, in the Peninsular War perhaps,
or have been borrowed from the Royal Navy. It was best
known on the Western Front as:

—— you Jack, I'm all right!*

* A bowdlerised version of this is current everywhere, through the title of the
film, in the 1960s – *I'm All Right, Jack.*

This was – to the marching troops – a convincing reading of the expression to be seen on the sleek faces of staff officers perched on their sleek horses or reclining in their sleek motor-cars. To the private soldier the Staff were much what the capricious gods must have been to the Greek and Trojan infantrymen. They were known only by occasional glimpses. The platoon-sergeant, whatever his defects, was visible and human. He might be fussy, 'windy' or ill-tempered, but when he had taken too big a share of the rations and the next best dug-out to the officers', he had almost reached the limit of his power for evil. Many N.C.O.s were in fact liked and respected. On the individual's conduct and character it depended whether the privates shouted with rancour or with quite affectionate jocularity:

> Some say 'Good old sergeant!'
> Others say '—— the old sergeant!'

A common piece of facetiousness, uttered after a sergeant had been more than usually officious, and often in camps, to the orderly sergeant after he had commanded 'Lights out!' was:

> Kiss me, sergeant!

The Biblical David, for some unknown reason, was held responsible for rainfall, and drenched, shivering troops would apostrophize the dripping skies:

> Send it down, David, send it down!

To express general fed-upedness and exasperation, the most popular phrase was:

> Roll on, Duration!

The volunteers of 1914–15 enlisted for 'four years or the duration of the war, whichever shall be longer'. *Roll on, Duration!* thus meant, May the end of the War come quickly and deliver us from these miseries! In a similar mood all rumours of good times to come and promises from authority would be met by the singing of the first line of a Nonconformist hymn –

Tell me the old, old story.

For chronic grousers the favourite reprimand was –

What do you want? – Jam on it?

This was also used, bitterly and ironically, when extra fatigues or working parties took the place of a promised rest, or anything fell short of the normal standard.

Soldiers? I've shit 'em!

was an expression of contempt for another man or another platoon, company or battalion.

Who pulled your chain?

was a snub for anyone talking too much or too loudly.

After the Lord Mayor's Show comes the shit-cart,

a comment used to describe any anti-climax, was clearly of Cockney origin and originally pre-1914 civilian.

More genuinely sympathetic than these was the frequently-heard saying:

Soldier on, chum!

The next, also very common, is probably Regular Army, pre - 1914.

Dear Mother, the Army's a bugger: sell the pig and buy me out.
Your loving son John.
– Dear John, pig's gone: soldier on.

On parade, on parade; off parade, off parade

was taken from the Regular Army and used as a reminder that what was permissible on certain occasions might be a military crime on others.

No names, no pack drill!

was a way of boasting that the speaker was too clever to make specific accusations against superior officers.

Carry on, Sergeant-Major,

a legitimate order from a Company Commander, was often spoken, in a genteel voice, by the 'other ranks' as a satire on the privileges of the officer class.

You'd be far better off in a home

was sympathetic in a derisively jocular manner.

Share that among you

sounds like a reminiscence of the indigent civilian's resentment against 'charity' at soup-kitchens and by the well-to-do on slumming expeditions. It belongs to that part of soldier's lore which was maintained to keep up a pretence of callousness. The phrase was often alleged to have been shouted by a bomber as he tossed a grenade into an enemy dug-out.

Where did that one go?

is short for a phrase from a popular (war-time) music-hall song – 'Where did that one go to, Herbert. Where did that one go?' The reference was to a shell that had dropped near by.

The orderly-corporal's conventional early-morning call in camp, billet or barracks was:

Show a leg! show a leg!

It dates from the early nineteenth-century Navy and was often facetiously burlesqued. Variants were:

Wakey, wakey!*

* This phrase has since been widely publicised through its use by Mr Billy Cotton in his Band Show on the music-halls, radio and television.

Rise and shine,

and, no matter if the sun were not due to appear for some time,

The sun's scorching your eyes out (*or* burning a hole in your blanket).

Besides these catch phrases, used chiefly in dialectic or invective, there were certain sayings and chants which were shouted aloud on the march or in any place where soldiers congregated 'off parade', in the hope of causing amusement. There were mother jokes, like this reminiscence of childhood:

Remember I'm your mother and get up those stairs!

There was a legendary opening to a letter home:

Dear Mother, I am sending you ten shillings – but not this week.

Heard practically every day, this retained to the end of the War its power of amusing simple men.

You may have broke your mother's heart: you won't break mine!

was originally a stock phrase of drill-sergeants taking recruits in hand. It was intended both to intimidate and to reassure the new soldiers that the tyrant of the barrack-square was human underneath.

A Soldier's Farewell

was invective – the farewell being in full, 'Good-bye and ——— you!' At a guess the phrase originated as a low-life burlesque of a popular picture at the time of the South African War. It is not, and never was, funny, and it reveals a good deal about the drearier side of Army conversation.

That's the stuff to give the troops!

was heard whenever rations or billets, rum or any other creature comfort turned out better or more plentiful than might

227

have been expected. It was varied into *That's the Stuff to give 'em!* and even *That's the giv to stuff 'em!* and in this form might by some men be shouted approvingly to artillery in action.

A crushing retort to a superior officer was always the private soldier's dream and delight. One very popular snatch dramatized the officer or N.C.O. inspecting the appearance of the men and growing facetious as he found an offender who, however, was more than a match for him. It ran –

> Ah, ah! no bloody shave this morning?
> Ah, ah! no bloody razor!

The bathetic descent from the heroic strain was another form of stock humour. Imitating a reciter's announcement of the title of his 'piece', someone would shout:

> Napoleon's Greeting to his Troops –
> 'Good morning, troops.'

To the same category belong the next two:

> They came to the Red Sea
> And Moses said unto the Israelites:
> 'In two ranks – Fall In!'

And he said: 'I will arise and go to my father, and will say unto him, "Father – *Stand at ease!*" '

The two longest were also the best. Both were dramatic. The first actually rhymed and was metrical:

> Today is my daughter's wedding day,
> Ten thousand pounds I'll give away. (*Three cheers!*)
> On second thoughts I think it best
> To put it away in the old oak chest.
>
> You mingy bastard! Chuck him out! etc, etc.

The second was declaimed like a scene from a pantomime or a melodrama, and sometimes two men would take alternate lines:

> Help, help, there's a woman overboard!
> Who will save her?
> I will!
> Who are you?
> Ballocky Bill the sailor, just returned from sea!

Always chanted very loud and with pseudo-refined enunciation was:

> Oh do not drive those sparrows away,
> You may be a sparrow yourself some day.
>
> Who is the man with the big red nose?
> (*staccato*) Who? Ah! Who – ah – ah!

Very often this chant was taken up as soon as the command 'March at ease!' was given: it served as a prelude to a spell of singing. The same purpose was fulfilled by:

> *First Voice:* Let's have a song, lads!
> *Second Voice:* What shall we sing?
> *First Voice:* 'Hands across the Sea.'
> *Every man within earshot, fortissimo:*
> Hands across my bloody arse!

The next was intoned with mock respectfulness:

> Halt the Buffs, and steady the Buffs, and let the Guards go by.

This must have originated with the pre-1914 Regular Army. It was sometimes varied, in estaminets where Guardsmen were present, in order to start a fight:

> Halt the Buffs, and steady the Buffs, and let the Guards withdraw
> to a position of safety in the rear!

Sergeants, especially drill sergeants, had anecdotal addresses so well rehearsed that they amounted to chants. The best-known is that of the sergeant who, giving his squad of recruits the 'stand easy', says:

While you're resting, I'll tell you a little tale. When I was a kid I had a box of wooden soldiers, and I thought the world of them soldiers. Well, somehow or other I lost 'em, and it nearly broke my little heart. Well, my old mother, she says to me, 'Never mind, lad, you'll find your wooden soldiers again some day – and by the hokey I have too!

Another was:

Strong men! You couldn't knock the skin off a rice-pudding!

Pre-war, but made much more generally known during the War, was a lengthy recitation, *The Showman*, which many learned by ear or by heart. Several versions are known. This is one of the best:

First of all, ladies and gentlemen, and I trust that you ladies will forgive my French, we have the chamois. Well, the shameless chamois jumps from precipice to precipice and back to piss again . . .

Ah, now the rhinoceros, the richest animal in the world. To those familiar with the Classics, the derivation of its name is interesting; *rhino*, meaning money, *soreass*, meaning piles. There you have it, ladies and gentlemen: piles of money.

And next the leopard, one spot for every day of the year. 'What about Leap Year?' Bill, just lift his tail.

This is the laughing hyena. The animal drinks once a week, eats once a month, and never has any sexual intercourse, so what he's got to laugh at *I* don't know!

Here is the Wild Man of Borneo. He has no cock. 'How does he ——, guv'nor?' He can't; that's what makes him so bloody wild.

I will now show you the camel. This peculiar animal eats mud, shits bricks, and has a triangular arse-hole. Hence the Pyramids.

We now come to the whoo-hoo bird. He eats red pepper and flies backwards . . . Hence the trade winds.

Here we have the wagga-wagga bird, which scours the local villages in search of his prey. On finding the finest specimen of the female of his species he carries her off to his mountain lair, where he proceeds to —— her, uttering the while his plaintive cry of 'wagga-wagga'. This, being interpreted from the language of birds, signifies 'Gawd, how lovely!'

230

The armoured armadillo! This is an extraordinary beast. When pursued by his foes, does he run away? No! Does he climb trees? No!! He retreats and farts defiance at his nonplussed foes.

And finally we have the oozolem foozlem bird. This bird, ladies and gentlemen, once a year descends from his mountain fastnesses into the valleys below. He then stalks through the villages till he finds the fairest and most virtuous of the opposite sex. Then he —— her, and finally eats her, thus avoiding for his unfortunate victim the shame and disgrace which would otherwise be her lot.

Now then, you small boys, get into the boats: the elephant's about to piss.

III. Songs Related to Bugle Calls

In the line, bugle calls, together with ceremonies and 'compliments', were dispensed with, but in billets and rest-camps, at the Base and in England they were in daily use. Some calls, proper to the more leisurely routine of peace-time, were never heard from 1914 to 1918, and by the majority of war-time soldiers would not be recognized. The cavalry and artillery had trumpet calls, some of them exceedingly beautiful but too long and elaborate to be fitted with unofficial words as many of the infantry calls were. The cavalry *Reveillé* (pronounced always 'revally' or 'revelly') for example, was a sustained composition, but the infantry call went very well to:

> Get out of bed!
> Get out of bed!
> You lazy bastards.
> I feel sorry for you I do.

Scarcely a hut or a tent that had not a light sleeper sufficiently awake to murmur the chant in time with the bugler's brazen modulations, before the Corporal found a boot and threw it at some blanket-covered head.

Fifteen minutes before parade was due the *Quarter Dress* was sounded, slow, brief, pregnant:

> A quarter of an hour to do it in!

Parade itself was brisk and cheerful:

> Fall in A!
> Fall in B!
> Fall in every Companee!

232

The *No Parades* call was even more cheerful, but one seldom heard in war-time; to it was sung:

> There'll be no parades today,
> No parades today.

Meal-times were signalled encouragingly:

> Come to the Cookhouse door, boys,
> Come to the Cookhouse door.
> When you see the Sergeant-Cook smile,
> Come to the Cookhouse door.

When 'dry' rations (bread, butter, sugar, etc.) were to be issued for the day, the Orderly Men were warned by a deliciously plaintive melody to which was sung:

> How can I draw rations
> When I'm not the orderly man?

Officers' Mess (meal-time, especially dinner) had its own call, to which went a very gross chant indeed. Slightly amended, it runs:

> Officers' wives
> Get puddens and pies,
> A sergeant's wife gets skilly,
> But a private's wife gets nothing at all
> To fill her empty belly.

All these ditties are the invention of the pre-1914 Regular Army, as this reference to wives 'on the strength' (i.e. lodged and fed in barracks at the Army's expense) clearly shows. Another daily call was *Post*:

> Letters from Lousy Lou,
> Letters from Lousy Lou,
> Letters for you
> And letters for me,
> And letters from Lousy Lou.

Men who were confined to barracks as a punishment were *Defaulters*. A bugle was blown every half-hour at times when they were 'off-parade'; on hearing the call they had to report immediately to the Guard Room.

> You can be a defaulter
> As long as you like
> As long as you answer your name.

Pickets was thus accompanied:

> Come and do a picket, boys, come and do a guard;
> 'Tisn't very easy, boys, 'tisn't very hard.

The Dinner Call, generally known to the ranks as *Hot Potatoes*, had these words:

> Pick 'em up, pick 'em up, hot potatoes, hot potatoes, hot potatoes;
> Pick 'em up, pick 'em up, hot potatoes, hot potatoes, oh!

One of the most famous of all bugle-calls – part of it was used by R. H. Mottram in one of his *Spanish Farm* Trilogy stories – is *Sick Parade*:

> Sixty-four, ninety-four!
> He'll never go sick no more:
> The poor bugger's dead.

Once a week in England, and at irregular intervals of anything from four to ten weeks in France, soldiers were paid their wages, a whole company parading at a time, each man stepping forward as his name was called. To the *Pay Parade* call was fitted these words:

> Fall in for pay, boys,
> Fall in for pay.
> You've bloody-well earned, boys.
> Your shilling a day.

Occasionally varied to:

Swinging the lead, boys,
Swinging the lead.
Always remember
To work your head.

At sunset *Retreat* was sounded, a ceremonious and lovely call
without any utilitarian significance attached:

You won't go to Heaven
When you die, Mary Ann.
No, you won't,
No, you won't,
No, you won't, Mary Ann.

Final call of the day, and the loveliest, was *Last Post*. Of this
C. E. Montague wrote in *Disenchantment*:

'That most lovely and melancholy of calls, the noble death of each
day's life, a sound moving about hither and thither, like a veiled
figure making gestures both stately and tender, among the dim
thoughts that we have about death the approaching extinguisher.'

BIBLIOGRAPHICAL NOTE

This remarkable book, which by now can surely be claimed as a classic work relating to the First World War, has gone through numerous editions under various titles. It was first published as *Songs and Slang of the British Soldier 1914–1918* in 1930, with Eric Partridge and John Brophy named as joint editors-cum-authors. The Preface to that first edition, setting the tone for the whole subsequent enterprise, suggested that the task of creating it was undertaken with an acute awareness of the passage of time:

> If one left such a book any longer, it would be very difficult to remember and collect the slang, and still more difficult to remember and select the songs. It may be in place to say that both the editors served actively during the greater part of the War.
>
> It is not possible to declare that this collection is complete, depending as it does on memory and oral tradition. Moreover, propriety has suppressed one or two of the songs and amended a few others. But every effort has been made by consulting men of different ranks and widely varying experience to include all the soldiers' songs which were in use throughout the Army during 1914–1918, and not restricted to particular foundations.
>
> In the glossary, the editors have aimed to give not a mere dictionary-list, but a record-by-glimpse of the British soldiers' spirit and life in the years 1914–1918. Some of the comments are far from 'official' in tone and in matter, but the editors believe there will be no confusion between what is recorded as fact and what is opinion. They do not claim that these wartime 'grouses' and post-war reflections mirror the attitude of *everyone* who served (one of the editors is now a convinced pacifist). But they believe that substantially these are the views of the majority of

wartime soldiers, and that they have not portrayed their former comrades either as supermen or as whiners, as sots or as saints.

In 1965 a revised re-formatted edition was published by Messrs André Deutsch under the title of *The Long Trail*. An Explanatory Preface by John Brophy retold the history of the book's development to that point, with the specific intention of putting on record how the editorship had varied from time to time:

Songs and Slang, 1st edition. We both worked, by frequent consultation, on establishing the songs and the Glossary . . .

Songs and Slang 2nd edition. This edition was Eric Partridge's work throughout. Twenty pages were added at the end of the previous text, of additional songs, chants, sayings, slang and non-slang terms suggested by various correspondents.

Songs and Slang 3rd edition. This almost doubled the length of the book, with 157 pages added at the end, compiled from extra items and variant readings suggested by correspondents. Again all the editing was done by Eric Partridge. I contributed an essay on 'Music Hall Songs' (which survives in this book) but otherwise saw neither 'copy' nor proofs.

In reference to the forthcoming Andre Deutsch edition, John Brophy stated:

In 1964 circumstances seem to have been reversed. Eric Partridge has been unable to spare time from other commitments and, unwillingly, muttering under my breath like a soldier on parade, I have undertaken first a part, then another part, and finally the whole of the job of reorganisation, revision, rewriting, and supplying new passages and new entries. Except for the songs, or most of them, there is not one page that has not been heavily revised. I am grateful to Mr Oliver Stonor for some useful preliminary